America's Traditional
CRAFTS

AMERICA'S TRADITIONAL CRAFTS

CRAFTS

by Robert Shaw

KÖNEMANN

Copyright © 1993, Hugh Lauter Levin Associates, Inc.

Design by Kathleen Herlihy-Paoli
Photo research by Ellin Yassky Silberblatt
Editorial production by Deborah Zindell

Copyright © 1999 for this edition
Könemann Verlagsgesellschaft mbH
Bonner Straße 126, D-50968 Cologne

Production: Ursula Schümer
Printing and binding: Sing Cheong Printing Co. Ltd., Hong Kong
Printed in Hong Kong, China

ISBN 3-8290-2216-6

10 9 8 7 6 5 4 3 2 1

ACKNOWLEDGMENTS

This book would not have been possible without the assistance of dozens of generous people, some of them old friends, others met during the course of the project. Among the many who helped the project along, special thanks are due to: Rachel Monfredo, research assistant at the Boston Museum of Fine Arts; Philip Zea, curator at Historic Deerfield; Jane Beck, director of the Vermont Folklife Center; John Michael Vlach, director of the folklife program at George Washington University; Lisa Rebori, collections manager at the Houston Museum of Natural Science; Allison Eckhardt Ledes, editor of *The Magazine* ANTIQUES; Edwin Churchill, chief curator at the Maine State Museum; Patricia Kane, curator of American decorative arts at the Yale University Art Gallery; Harold and Florie Corbin, Jean Whitnack, Gene and Linda Kangas, Merle Glick, Peter Furst, Carole Wahler, Larry Ballard, Jackie Oak, Nol Putnam, and Louis Irion III.

A number of private collectors, craftspeople, and dealers generously allowed objects in their keeping to be shown. I am extremely grateful to all of them. Special thanks are due to Jim McCleery, David Schorsch, Steve Michaan, George H. Meyer, Joshua Baer, Paul Kebabian, Paul and Diane Madden, Linda Kohn, Joel and Kate Kopp, Thelma Hibdon, and Roddy Moore.

Roddy Moore, the director of the Blue Ridge Institute at Virginia's Ferrum College, jumped into the project at the last minute and enriched the book with wonderful ideas and objects. Mark Leithauser and Gaillard Ravenel, designers extraordinaire at the National Gallery of Art, offered many helpful suggestions about collectors and objects. Kate Adams and James Hastrich, crafters of exquisite miniature quilts and furniture respectively, directed my attention to the work of a number of talented contemporary craftspeople. Brian Cullity, chief curator at Heritage Plantation in Sandwich, Massachusetts, put me in touch with several key collectors in New England and the South.   Stuart Frank, director of the Kendall Whaling Museum, arranged the beautiful photographs of scrimshaw from his institution's extraordinary collection. Ken Burris, my second set of eyes, provided many of the book's most striking photographs.

I am eternally grateful to Hugh Levin, the publisher, who brought the idea for the book to me and supported it from start to finish, and to project manager Ellin Silberblatt, who held everything together with unfailing grace, skill, and good humor. Both have been a joy to work with. Thanks also are due to Debby Zindell, who ably edited the manuscript, Tonia Payne, who entered corrections and worried about myriad small but critical details, and Kathleen Herlihy-Paoli, who is responsible for the book's handsome design.

Finally, thanks to my girls: my daughters Emma and Georgia, who lovingly excused daddy's endless evenings and weekends at the computer, and my wife Nancy, without whose constant support and calmly balancing judgment nothing would have been possible.

ROBERT SHAW
Shelburne, Vermont

◄ FRONTISPIECE

A selection of traditional American craft works, made between 1800 and 1950, from the collection of The Shelburne Museum, Shelburne, Vermont.

Contents

EVERYDAY
MASTERPIECES

Craft has always been an important part of American life. Every community in eighteenth- and nineteenth-century America depended on its craftspeople—blacksmiths, potters, and weavers, among others—to supply essential tools, goods, and services necessary to daily life. Until the 1850s, when the sweeping changes brought about by the Industrial Revolution tipped the balance, America was a handcraft society in which the majority of goods in the marketplace remained the work of independent, self-directed handcraft people.

After the Civil War, manufactured goods, carried by a vastly improved transportation system, began to flood American society and displace many types of handcraftwork. In rural areas, however, where economic and cultural isolation often ensured a community's relative independence from the dramatic societal changes wrought by industrialization and growth, craft remained an important source of everyday needs well into the twentieth century.

The traditional crafts of many of these communities often played a major role in defining the region's relationship to society at large. In the Southern Highlands of Appalachia, for example, some rural enclaves became known in the twentieth century for their craft products, which were avidly sought by sophisticated urban tourists. This was also true of a number of Native American communities, whose pottery, baskets, and other crafts brought them much needed economic return from consumers and at the same time strengthened the identity of the community from within.

The works produced by early American handcrafters were, first and foremost, utilitarian objects, made for commercial or personal reasons, for profit or for pleasure. Although location and clientele had some influence on the final product, all these craftspeople remained loyal to regional traditions and values handed down from one generation to the next. Three basic groups of craftspeople were at work in early America. Professional tradesmen, such as cabinetmakers and blacksmiths, trained in a strict apprenticeship and earned their livelihood from their work. Itinerants and home craftspeople, including basket makers, weavers, potters, and tinsmiths, whose training was traditional but less formal and whose trade was often not their sole or primary source of income, carried on modest-scale production within a home workshop setting or, as itinerants, moved from town to town to practice their trade or ply their wares. Still other artisans, such as quilters, rug hookers, and scrimshanders, primarily produced works not to be sold but rather to embellish their own homes or to be given to friends and family members. Most home craftspeople learned their trade informally from their elders, working with a relative or neighbor who could teach the skills required of a particular craft.

◄ FOUR-PATCH CRIB QUILT

Unknown Amish artist. c. 1925. Holmes County, Ohio. Cotton. 39 x 30 in. The Esprit Collection, San Francisco, California.

Black was often used with dramatic effect in Holmes County Amish quilts. The four-patch blocks in this crib quilt are set off by solid-colored triangles and arranged in diagonal rows. The pink streak-of-lightning border keeps the eye moving constantly around the diagonals.

DOWITCHER DECOYS ▶

*Dr. Clarence T. Gardner and Newton Dexter. c. 1890.
Sakonnet Point, Little Compton, Rhode Island. Wood
with glass eyes. Collection of James M. McCleery, M.D.*

*Gardner, a prominent surgeon, and Dexter, a naturalist
who worked for the Smithsonian, were hunting and
fishing companions who carved many shorebird decoys
together. These dowitchers are evidence of their close
study of game birds, both mounted and in the wild.*

For the purposes of this study, craft and tradition cannot stand apart. Craft has always been linked to manual dexterity, skill, and attention to detail. Even in an age of nuclear energy and computer chips, it is still a compliment of the highest order to be called a craftsperson. Almost as important as the word *craft* is the word *tradition*, which might be defined as the accumulated knowledge and wisdom of many generations brought to bear on a particular task or problem. This knowledge largely defines the traditional craftsperson's patterns—his forms, materials, and methods.

Individual craftspeople are often said to work "within a tradition," meaning that they honor the time-tested parameters of the craft, often established over dozens, hundreds, or even thousands of years. The traditional craftsperson does not challenge the basic structure of the craft, but follows the path that tradition has defined, seeking only to make the object work better. He does not try to impose his will or personality on the product, but rather to follow the tradition through to its logical end, which is the perfect balance of style and function. The changes that the craftsperson brings to an object's form are always specific and usually slight—a different angle to the attachment of a pot handle, a variation in the lip of a basket, a different way of arranging the patterned pieces of a quilt top. Iona Opie, the English scholar of children's games and play, once described children as "Tories of the general and anarchists of the particular." The same might be said of the traditional craftsperson.

Function, the purposiveness of the craft, is central to the meaning of the crafts this book addresses; it both forms and informs them. Japanese society has long officially recognized its pre-eminent crafts-people as "living national treasures." Sōetsu Yanagi, who founded the Japan Folkcraft Museum in 1936, expressed the role of function this way in his book, *The Unknown Craftsman: A Japanese Insight into Beauty:*

> *Utility does not permit unsoundness or frailty, for between use and beauty there
> is a close relationship. Utility demands faithfulness in objects; it does not con-
> done human self-indulgence. In creating an object intended for practical use,
> the maker does not push himself to the foreground or even, for that matter, to
> the surface. With such objects, self-assertion and error—if present at all—are
> reduced to a minimum. This may be one reason why useful goods are beautiful.
> Objects whose makers remain anonymous have...an easy access to beauty; the
> fact that the finest examples of functional art existing in the world are mostly
> those that have had no opportunity to be marked by the maker's signature is
> worthy of very careful consideration.*

The emphasis of this book, then, is on functional objects, generally made of inexpensive and readily available materials, and intended for everyday use. High-style furniture, silver, glass, porcelain, and the like have been omitted both because they tended to be made by a few specialized people for an elite clientele and because they often employed expensive or exotic materials or required sophisticated methodologies. And, objects known as folk art, such as weather vanes, tobacconist figures, and trade signs, have also been excluded since, even though they certainly served a function, their purpose from conception was at least in equal measure decorative and artistic.

With few exceptions, the objects examined in this book were made to fill a particular need of the maker, the maker's household, or the maker's community. Most were common and democratic in the sense that they were one of many objects of their type made by many different craftspeople for the masses: in the words of Yanagi, "by the many, for the many." The beauty of these functional crafts does not derive, therefore, from their uniqueness, but rather from the perfect union between function and design. American craftspeople have created thousands of first-quality objects over the two hundred years of this country's independent existence. Out of necessity the pieces chosen for this book comprise a selective and somewhat arbitrary glimpse at a substantial body of work and only suggest the range and depth of each craft the study examines. An equally fine and representative grouping of objects could be selected several times over without any repetition or diminution of quality.

Decorative and functional motivations coexist in all craft, of course, and the boundaries are not clearly defined. Functional crafts often evolve into purely decorative forms. As demand for gunning decoys decreased in the early twentieth century, for example, many craftspeople began to create nonfunctional carvings of birds intended for the mantelpiece or living room rather than the marsh. Some crafts expressed both motivations from earliest times. Sgraffito-decorated redware, for example, was never intended to be used. Quilting also comes immediately to mind; surely the elaborately appliquéd Phebe Warner bedspread, completed around 1803, was not intended for everyday use. And many of today's crafts employ traditional methods to produce objects whose purpose is purely decorative and/or artistic. Some quilters and weavers now create wall hangings rather than bedcovers; some basket makers make completely nonfunctional "art" baskets. This study displays a few of these nonfunctional objects, both historic and contemporary, to show the broadening boundaries of traditional craftwork.

The role of craft has changed dramatically over the past two hundred years. Craft was once a necessity because most of the objects used by ordinary people in the course of their daily lives were made by hand. Today, craft is a luxury. While many contemporary craftspeople still make functional objects, very few of their wares are necessary to daily life; the vast majority can be found elsewhere. We no longer depend on the products of the craftsperson, but look instead to manufactured goods for our needs.

PLATE ▶

Artist unknown. c. 1800–1825. Pennsylvania. Red earthenware. Height: 1 7/8 in., diameter: 12 1/8 in. The Henry Francis du Pont Winterthur Museum, Winterthur, Delaware.

The stylized incised fish on this whimsical sgraffito plate swim not only in different directions but also in different orientations.

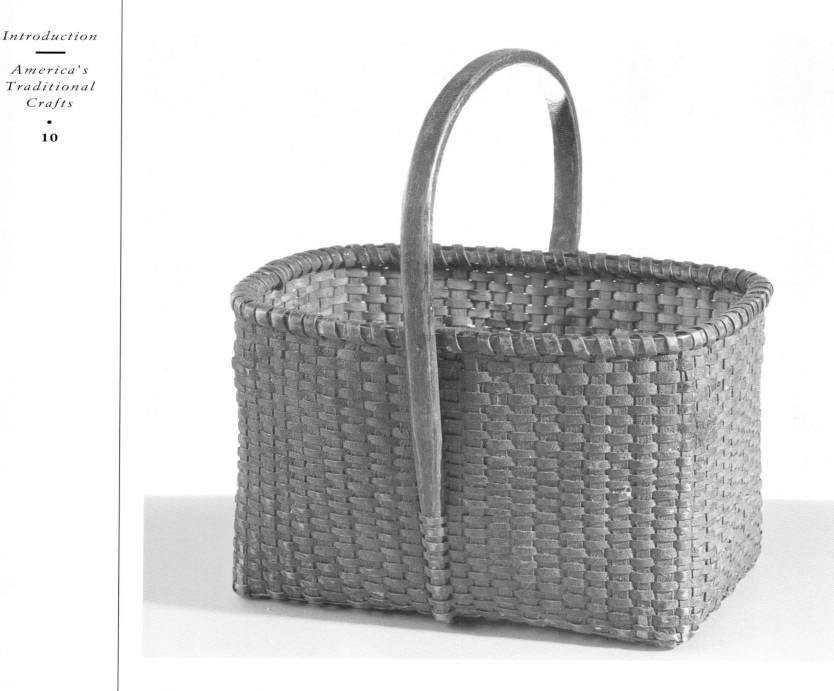

▲ GATHERING BASKET

Unknown Shaker artist. c. 1850. Alfred or Sabbathday Lake, Maine. Ash splint. 8 1/2 x 6 1/2 x 11 1/2 in. Private collection.

Few Shaker baskets are known to have been painted. The carefully carved tapered handles of this basket distinguish it as well.

In our digital society, time has become the most valued of commodities. Everybody knows that a machine can do the work more quickly and that machines have freed us from the drudgery of repetitive handwork. Indeed, most people's first question on looking at a handcrafted object will be, "How long did it take to make that?" Any traditional craftsperson will answer, "Just long enough to make it right." In other words, where we measure and value time, the traditional craftsperson first measures and values quality.

Ironically, craft today represents a luxurious attention to detail and quality of materials that most people do not need and often cannot afford. Many antique quilts, baskets, decoys, pots, and tools— indeed virtually all the older objects illustrated in this book—are too valuable to be used anymore and are therefore divorced from their original function and often appreciated solely for their aesthetic appeal. Skilled contemporary handwork, valued above even the finest machine work, also carries a higher price and therefore is often available only to a fairly well-to-do segment of society. Even if the contemporary craftsperson intends to create a functional object, its increased cost affects the buyer's attitude toward the piece. One is simply not inclined to put expensive objects to hard, everyday use. Many of today's retail catalogues of homewares, for example, offer American buyers well-made quilts, hand sewn in China where labor is cheap, at a fraction of the price an American quilter could demand. The imported covers go on the beds of the middle class, many of whom cannot justify the expense of equally fine handmade American quilts.

Craft has always had its champions, even in times when the quality of manufactured products has been reputedly sound and flawless. The English Arts and Crafts movement, a somewhat rarified reaction against the influence of the Industrial Revolution and its sometimes slipshod products, was the first modern attempt to emphasize the importance of beauty and craftsmanship in everyday objects. John Ruskin, the philosopher and theoretician whose 1851 book *The Stones of Venice* laid the conceptual groundwork for the Arts and Crafts movement, idealized handcraftwork, in which he found a dignity and humanity lacking in the relentless perfection of the machine. William Morris, an independently wealthy aristocrat and struggling painter, put Ruskin's ideas into practice, designing and creating such elements of interior design as wallpapers, furniture, carpets, and curtains. Morris and especially his disciple Charles Robert Ashbee, a gifted silversmith, set the standard for the artist/craftsman, who integrated fine art and craft in sophisticated design. The influence of the English Arts and Crafts movement, although felt primarily by the upper classes who had conceived it, traveled across the Atlantic in the later years of the nineteenth century, and touched a number of important American artist/craftspeople, such as Gustave Stickley, Louis Comfort Tiffany, and Frank Lloyd Wright.

The idealization of craft espoused by Ruskin and practiced a generation later by Morris, Burne-Jones, and Ashbee may be seen in part as a reaction against the dehumanizing effects of the Industrial Revolution. But the Industrial Revolution was not a monolithic destroyer of craft. In truth, the mythic age of handcraft died with the Renaissance, if not before. Machines and handcrafts are not, as many espouse, diametrically and ideologically opposed. They have coexisted for centuries, particularly in the case of textiles. The touch of the human hand is essential to craft, but does not negate the valuable contribution of the machine. Nor are mass-production and quality work inimical terms. One need only consider the high quality production of the Norton pottery of Bennington, Vermont, or Mason's Decoy Factory of Detroit, to offer but two American examples, to dispel this notion. Both companies produced massive numbers of objects in standardized forms and employed a number of workers. Handwork was an integral part of both companies' products, and machinery helped to facilitate production. The reputations of both firms grew from long-standing traditions, reflecting continuities of form and function that could be traced back for generations.

Tradition was also nurtured within religious sects, where it served to both define and reflect the community's values. Many sects deliberately chose not to embrace changes widely accepted in society at large. They often developed their own craft traditions, producing objects inseparable from the tenets of their faith. Indeed, the relationships between the objects and the craftspeople in such groups are often indivisible, so much so that several American sects—most notably the Shakers and the Amish— have come to be identified by outsiders as much by their craft products as their beliefs.

The most influential and creative of America's many nineteenth-century Utopian religious sects was the United Society of Believers in Christ's Second Appearing, better known as Shakers for their unorthodox, spirit-inspired dancing during religious services. The Shaker movement was founded by "Mother" Ann Lee, an illiterate English factory worker, who brought a small band of followers to America in 1772 to spread the gospel and prepare for the millenium. Espousing spirituality, celibacy, community, and hard work, the Shakers formed over twenty settlements, primarily in the Northeast, but eventually reaching as far west as Ohio and Indiana and as far south as Florida. At their peak, in the 1840s, the Shakers numbered over four thousand "Believers," as they called themselves; today, fewer than a dozen remain in the historic communities of Canterbury, New Hampshire, and Sabbathday Lake, Maine.

Craft was central to the Shaker way of life. Mother Ann's dictum, "Put your hands to work, and your hearts to God," was practiced six days a week, with the Sabbath reserved for community worship. Shaker "Brothers" and "Sisters" worked separately in a variety of community work places, including laundries, bakeries, kitchens, gardens, and agricultural harvest rooms, as well as in a host of handcraft shops. Since each community was basically self-sufficient, supplementing its own production of food and goods by selling herbs, seeds, and craft items to the "world," the Shakers were to a large extent free of the pressures of the outside marketplace. They built their work and dwelling places, grew their own food, and made their own hand tools, furniture, baskets, boxes, barrels, brooms, tin and wrought ironware, clothing, agricultural implements, and sewing accessories. The basic tenets of the Shaker faith—simplicity, modesty, grace, practicality, usefulness, durability, and a striving toward perfection—were manifested in the objects designed and created by Shaker craftspeople. The Shakers believed in excellence and practiced it in every aspect of their lives. Their crafts reflect that belief, revealed in three-dimensional form.

As early as the 1890s, a few far-sighted individuals realized the importance of preserving America's vanishing traditional handcrafts. Among the first and most influential was Dr. William Goodell Frost, president of Kentucky's Berea College, who soon after his appointment began to encourage the revival of Appalachia's "fireside industries," as he called them. Berea established the first school in Appalachia for the traditional arts; students were even allowed to barter fine old coverlets and other handcrafts toward tuition costs. The college supported the work of both its students and many local craftspeople, and became a model for the emergence of dozens of other schools and craft guilds, such as the Penland School of Crafts in North Carolina, between the 1890s and the early 1930s. These institutions continue as important centers for handcrafts today.

The 1920s and 1930s brought a broad resurgence of interest in the country's handcraft traditions. Collectors and dealers began to turn their attentions to American-made objects, finding aesthetic merit in long-neglected traditional handwork. During the Depression, the Index of American Design, a WPA (Works Project Administration) effort, employed hundreds of artists who researched thousands of traditional craft objects of every type and recorded them in detailed watercolor paintings. The Index, housed at the National Gallery of Art in Washington, D.C., remains the greatest single repository of traditional American craft design. In 1939 the publication of Allen Eaton's seminal study *Handicrafts of the Southern Highlands,* which profiled the work of dozens of craftspeople, also helped fuel interest in traditional crafts, as did his follow-up volume on New England crafts, published just after World War II.

◂ BLANKET CHEST

Artist unknown. Late eighteenth century. Cape Cod, Massachusetts. White pine. 27 x 44 x 17 in. Private collection.

This simple storage chest is distinguished by its decoratively scrolled skirt and fanciful all-over graining, executed in a hue that bears no resemblance whatsoever to nature.

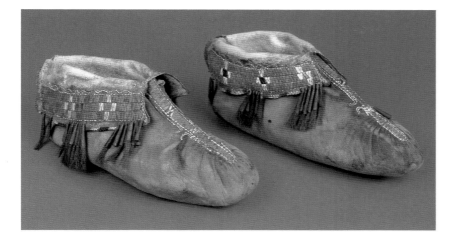

◄ MOCCASINS

Unknown Delaware Indian artist. c. 1780. Lower Hudson River Valley, New York. Deerskin with porcupine quill work, tin bangles with red-dyed deer hair. 10 1/4 x 4 1/8 in. National Museum of The American Indian, Smithsonian Institution, New York.

These early eastern Woodland moccasins were made from a single piece of buckskin.

RUSH-LIGHT HOLDER ►

Artist unknown. Late eighteenth century. New England. Wrought iron, ash burl stand. Height: 7 in. The Shelburne Museum, Shelburne, Vermont.

This simple, early lighting device, made to hold the burning stalk of a meadow rush, exemplifies purity of form following function to its logical conclusion. Rushes, which grew in swampy areas throughout New England, were gathered in late summer. The stems were cut into eight- to ten-inch lengths and the fibrous outer layer was peeled off. The remaining porous pith was then soaked in melted lard or tallow. After drying, the prepared rush was placed in the holder at an angle. Lit at the top, it burned like a cigar, lending its meager light to evening activities such as sewing or reading.

Despite the attentions of collectors, dealers, and artists, public support for traditional handcrafters dwindled. Although a number of innovative modern craftspeople began work just after World War II, society's view of craft sunk to its lowest level in the 1950s and often became identified with the nonskilled handwork of hobbyists and children. The powerful resurgence of interest began with the naivete and amateurism of the back-to-the-land movement of the 1960s. It left a dual legacy. To many Americans, craft still conjures images of macramé, poorly-thrown and undecorated pottery, and tie-dyed clothing. But many of the people drawn to craft in the 1960s, determined to reawaken interest in a disappearing art, began to organize major craft shows, seek out skilled but neglected older craftspeople, research and record traditional methodologies, and teach eager students. Although its survival is still threatened by a host of factors, many moribund and endangered traditions have been revitalized, and traditional craft remains very much alive.

One measure of the vitality of traditional craft is the number of annual events that focus on these handworks. Most notable of these is the Festival of American Folklife, sponsored by the Smithsonian Institution. This annual ten-day-long extravaganza, which begins at the end of June and runs through July 4th, celebrates America's traditional folk cultures in all their richness and diversity, offering the finest in regional and ethnic food, dance, and music in addition to featuring dozens of remarkable traditional craftspeople. Another Federal agency, the National Endowment for the Arts, administers the National Heritage Fellows program, which honors living traditional craftspeople of extraordinary achievement. Many of the 150 artisans honored since the program was initiated in 1982 have appeared at the summer festival in Washington. The Blue Ridge Folklife Festival, held each October at Virginia's Ferrum College, near

Roanoke, is a regional version of the Washington event that highlights the folkways of the Blue Ridge mountains and includes many traditional craftspeople. Other fine regional festivals are the Florida Folk Festival, held each Memorial Day weekend in White Springs, about sixty miles west of Jacksonville; Louisiana's Natchitoches-Northwestern Folk Festival, held in late July, and the Indian and Pioneer Heritage Fair, hosted by the Mississippi Crafts Center in Ridgeland in late October.

Hundreds of highly skilled craftspeople have been drawn to traditional crafts in the past twenty-five years. A number of these younger craftspeople are producing objects that rival any ever made in the traditions they have researched and learned to practice; many work with history and art museums around the country to reproduce historic traditional crafts. A small but outstanding show featuring such craftspeople is the Pennsylvania Traditional Crafts and Folk Art exhibition held each October in Stouchburg, Pennsylvania. Although the show is restricted to only eleven exhibitors, each ranks at the top of his or her particular craft, offering outstanding redware, tin, wrought iron, baskets, coverlets, furniture, and other traditional Pennsylvania crafts. Another, much larger, show, with 150 carefully selected craftspeople, is the Celebration of American Craftsmanship, held just before Thanksgiving in Wilton, Connecticut.

Beginning in the 1950s a modern craft movement began to take shape in America. A handful of pioneering craftspeople brought influences from contemporary abstract painting into their works, creating expressive, nonfunctional tapestries and ceramics. The American Craftsmen's Co-operative Council, now the American Craft Council, was formed; the new organization united modern craftspeople and championed innovative work through its publications and the formation of the American Craft Museum in New York, founded in 1956 and dedicated solely to twentieth-century crafts. Supported in recent decades by an explosion of galleries, museum exhibitions, and public interest, the modern craft movement has continued to grow increasingly more sophisticated and diverse. Contemporary craftspeople look backward and forward, experimenting with a host of techniques made possible by technological breakthroughs while drawing on craft and art traditions from throughout the world and spanning all periods of history. The ACC sponsors several annual craft events focusing on contemporary crafts, including a February show in Baltimore, Maryland (the biggest of the year, with five hundred juried exhibitors), and a late June fair in West Springfield, Massachusetts. Although these huge fairs do not include many strictly traditional craftspeople, they do provide access to a wide range of remarkable objects, some of which directly reflect their attention to traditional methods and models. The contemporary American craftsperson, whether modern or traditional, expresses, through his craft, a unique vision, a vision grounded in a deep reverence for a common heritage that values the beauty created by the perfect union of form and function.

◄ TEXAS HOOKED RUG

Molly Nye Tobey. c. 1950. Barrington, Rhode Island. Wool. 38 x 59 in. The Shelburne Museum, Shelburne, Vermont. Gift of Joel, Jonathan, and Joshua Tobey.

Mrs. Tobey's Texas rug includes a mule, a steer, a watermelon, and a ten-gallon hat on a background of wheat, corn, and blue bonnets. Before designing her state rugs, Molly Nye Tobey spent considerable time researching the products, minerals, flora, and fauna of each state. She learned that Texas was the largest producer of mules and watermelons in the country and combined these lesser-known products of the state with more familiar Texas icons in her design.

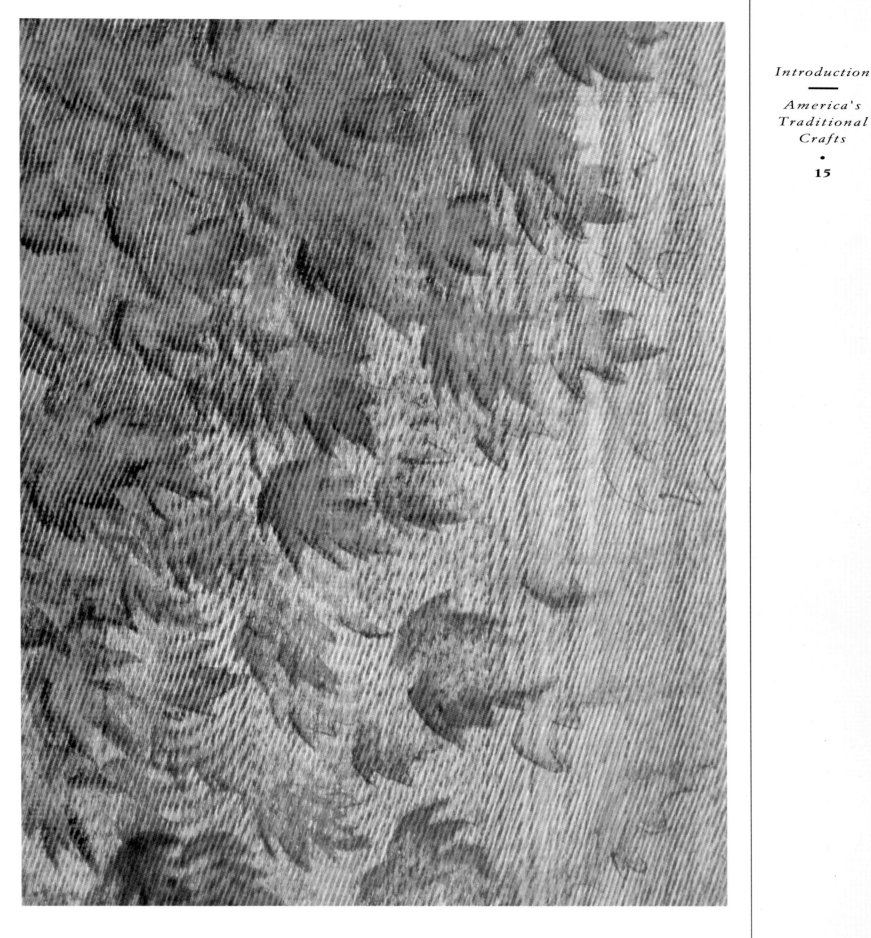

▲ LEAF RUG

Lyn Sterling Montagne. 1988. Atlanta, Georgia. Linen weft, rayon and linen warp: ikat-dyed, handwoven, and painted. 84 x 53 in. Private collection.

Lyn Sterling Montagne is a professional rug weaver who has incorporated the influence of Japanese textiles and painting into her work. Her Leaf Rug combines traditional handweaving techniques with complex but delicate use of color and a distinctly modern sensibility. The artist writes, "Since 1984, I have been working with a weaving structure which builds in a natural resist for painting. The rugs are woven with linen and rayon, fibers which have different absorption rates. This allows me to apply color to the rayon while resisting it with the less absorbent linen. Further experimentation involved various weave structures, pre-dyeing the linen surface to enrich the color, and a move from imagery determined by the geometry of the weave structure to more organic imagery."

Q U I L T S

Of all the crafts practiced in America, none has touched more lives than quilting. Generations of Americans have slept under quilts made by a mother, grandmother, sister, or aunt; hundreds of thousands of American women have expressed their creativity by patiently working designs and sewing layers of fabric together to warm their families and loved ones. No other craft is more closely identified with uniquely American values and mythology. Quilts also reflect our irresistible longings for the real or imagined comforts of home and family. They evoke feelings of nostalgia for a mythical golden age of America, an America of small towns, tightly knit communities, and solid, traditional values, where God and country reign supreme and every bed is covered in homemade patchwork.

The craft of quilting was brought to America by European settlers. The idea of encapsulating a warm, insulating layer of batting between pieces of fabric is an ancient one that was apparently practiced by many societies, from the ancient Egyptians to the Chinese. Quilted clothing and floor coverings predate quilted bedcoverings, and evidence suggests the existence of both of these types of textiles well before the birth of Christ. The oldest surviving quilted bedcovering is a very sophisticated Italian quilt dating to about 1400, which depicts, in intricate needlework, scenes from the legend of Tristan. The highly refined needlework strongly suggests that the quilt is representative of a craft already long practiced and well developed. Quilting in the British Isles can be traced back to the 1500s and was widely practiced in the seventeenth and eighteenth centuries. Commoners made simple, functional quilts of homemade wool, while the more privileged often dressed their beds with quilts made of decoratively patterned cotton chintzes imported from India, where quilting was also popular.

Quilts are defined as bedcoverings that are usually made up of three layers—a backing, a warm center filling, and a decorative top—put together into what has often been called a textile sandwich. The three layers usually are sewn together by hand with a needle and thread, often in elaborately stitched designs that can add an intricate and subtle decorative element to the top layer.

Quilts can be broken into three basic types—plain, pieced, and appliqué—named for the dominant technique used in fashioning the quilt top. Like their English antecedents, the earliest American quilt tops were most often plain or "whole cloth," wherein lengths of a single type of fabric were decorated with intricate quilt stitching in floral or geometric patterns. The top material was usually a glazed wool, solid-colored, imported from the mother country. Printed cottons were used occasionally; these were often left unquilted.

◄ DOUBLE WEDDING RING QUILT

Mrs. Andy G. Byler. c. 1920–1935. Midwestern United States. Cotton. 85 x 66 1/2 in. Museum of American Folk Art, New York. Gift of Cyril I. Nelson in memory of his grandparents, Guerdon Sterns and Elinor Irwin Holden, and in honor of his parents, Cyril Arthur and Elise Macy Nelson.

Carefully placed, jewel-like colors sparkle throughout the chains of this Amish quilt, keeping the eye in constant motion.

This trio of Appalachian quilters was photographed c. 1930 by Doris Ulmann. A typical Log Cabin quilt is seen hanging in the background.

Photograph, Berea College, Berea, Kentucky.

America's greatest contribution to quilting was developing the use of pieced work in creating quilt tops. Piecing, which builds tops from many small pieces of material sewn together, began as an art of necessity. It is hard to overestimate the difficulty and starkness of life in colonial and frontier America. Resources were extremely scarce and settlers simply could not afford to waste anything. The much maligned Puritan values of thrift, economy, and utility were as much practical necessities as religious mandates. Recycling of materials was absolutely essential. Clothing, which was often patched over and over and reworked to fit different members of a family, also provided the raw material for pieced quilts. Because large pieces of fabric were expensive and often simply unavailable, American women developed the idea of sewing together small scraps of material, either left over from newly sewn clothing or cut from worn clothing and other household textiles, to form entire quilt tops. The pieces were cut into geometric shapes and then carefully arranged, often into repeating blocks, to form overall patterns.

English quilters had employed piecing techniques as an element in their work, but Americans were the first to organize pieced tops into blocks, thus opening up an incredible array of organizing patterns. Successful pattern designs gained colorful and evocative names such as Log Cabin, Tumbling Blocks, Grandmother's Flower Garden, Rocky Road to Kansas, and Star of Bethlehem. Despite the seeming rigidity of the geometric patterns, slight variations in fabric color and placement could transform a design and allowed each quilter great opportunity for personal creativity. As patterns proliferated and spread across the country, a number of regional styles developed, each identified by patterns and color schemes determined by powerful cultural influences and preferences.

Pieced quilts were made for hard, everyday use. They warmed and decorated the beds of family members, wrapping the sleeper in the care and skill of the woman of the house. They stood up well to the wear and tear of daily household use. Since the worn pieces, being of fairly small size, could be replaced without great difficulty, mending was relatively easy. Piecing was an extremely democratic art; its techniques were simple to learn, and seemingly every nineteenth-century housewife made quilts. Depending on the inclination and skill of the craftswoman, the quilt that she created could be quite basic or wildly complex.

Appliqué quilts, in which the quilter applied and sewed cut pieces of fabric to a plain top to create an overall design, were generally fancier, more personal, and more formal in design than pieced quilts. Appliqué designs allowed for more freedom than pieced patterns because the quilter could place the cutouts in any arrangement on the top and was not locked into the strict geometric demands of pieced designs. Some appliqués featured large overall designs such as the Tree of Life, while others built up rhythmic patterns of repeated motifs. In later years, many followed a block format, repeating a pattern over and over to form an overall design. Both overall and block designs were often surrounded by a decorative border made up of such motifs as trailing vines, leaves, or flowers.

Because they lend themselves to pictorial designs, appliqué quilts can be imaginative and expressive; personal messages, visions, and experiences can directly inform the piece. Supreme examples of this personal, expressive quality include Harriet Powers's Bible quilt and Elizabeth Roseberry Mitchell's extraordinary graveyard quilt. Each of these quilts brings an intensely personal vision of religious belief into moving, palpable form; neither was ever meant to be seen by anyone other than its maker and her immediate family. Appliqué quilts were often made to commemorate rites of passage, such as engagements, weddings, births, and christenings. Such quilts were treated with special care by their owners. They might be put out for holidays or anniversaries or to honor special guests in the house, but they spent most of their time carefully folded and packed in a cedar chest.

The great age of pieced quilting spans approximately the first hundred years of the republic, with the greatest concentration of work occurring between 1820 and 1880, as America's cotton industry grew and the country's textile mills printed an ever-increasing array of fabrics. American women took enormous pride in their creations and availed themselves of the wide variety of fabric choices offered in stores to express their individual ideas, beliefs, experiences, and hopes. Rather than being defined by their limitations, quilters could now reach out to embrace the astonishing technological advances of a rapidly changing and growing nation. Quilt competitions were held at county fairs, and women worked long and hard to create unique designs, sometimes combining pieced work and appliqué in imaginative new ways, expanding the earlier prescribed boundaries of both forms. Hundreds of thousands of quilts were made during these years. They are perhaps the most visible and enduring documents of the everyday lives of nineteenth-century American women of every race and social class, and they represent an exuberant, expressive, and passionate parallel history of the growth of the burgeoning new country.

During the 1840s, block-style construction, which is ranked with piecing as

◄ THE PHEBE WARNER COVERLET

Attributed to Sarah Furman Warner Williams. c. 1803. New York City. Linen, with linen and cotton appliqués, silk embroidery thread. 103 1/4 x 90 1/2 in. The Metropolitan Museum of Art, New York. Gift of Catherine E. Cotheal, 1938.

This extraordinary decorative bedcover draws its inspiration from the central tree-of-life motifs common to palampore bed hangings imported from India, as well as from the needlework pictures often worked by young women of the period. The charming disregard for scale seen in the central panel's juxtaposition of massive birds with tiny trees, sheep, and human figures lends humbling naiveté to an overwhelming technical achievement.

This group of women gathered for a quilting bee was photographed in Mehama, Oregon, c. 1905.

Courtesy of the Oregon Historical Society, Portland, Oregon.

America's greatest conceptual contribution to quilting, became the norm. This innovative, time-saving technique allowed the quilter to fashion a quilt of equally sized, repeating square sections that could be made one at a time and later sewn together to form a top. Women often gathered in "bees" to sew blocks together; sometimes the blocks were the work of a single woman, and in other instances each member of the group contributed blocks to form the bedcovering. Bees sometimes pooled the talents and time of a community to make presentation quilts that celebrated a marriage or the departure of a minister or mutual friend. These quilts were sometimes made up of unrelated pieced or appliqué blocks, each one signed by its maker.

In the 1870s and 1880s, late Victorian preferences for decorative complexity led to so-called crazy quilts, which combined random arrangements of pieces, a wide variety of materials—especially the silks and velvets then popular as dress materials—and fancy embroidery stitches. The term "crazy" comes from the fractured, or "crazed," look of the quilts, in which pieces of many asymmetrical forms and sizes were joined together with prominent embroidery stitches, which only added to the broken look of the overall pattern. Most crazy quilts were not actually quilted but rather tied together because the fragile silk material did not lend itself to intricate needlework. Silk crazy quilts, often more decorative than functional, and usually small in size, were made to be used as a throw on the parlor couch or love seat rather than as a cover for an upstairs bed.

As the nineteenth century waned, the Victorian taste for extensive decoration overshadowed the unadorned geometry of the traditional pieced quilt. By 1875, Harriet Beecher Stowe, writing in *The Minister's Wooing*, one of her later and lesser-known novels, could look back with nostalgia to describe the art of piecing in a simpler, earlier America, already long passed.

> *The good wives of New England, impressed with that thrifty orthodoxy of economy which forbids to waste the merest trifle, had a habit of saving every scrap clipped out of the fashioning of household garments, and these they cut into fanciful patterns and constructed of them rainbow shapes and quaint traceries, the arrangement of which became one of their few fine arts....Collections of these tiny fragments were ready to fill an hour when there was nothing else to do; and as the maiden chattered with her beau, her busy flying needle stitched together those pretty bits, which, little in themselves, were destined, by gradual unions and accretions, to bring about at last substantial beauty, warmth and comfort.*

At the same time that the general American public was moving away from pieced quilting in favor of more decorative work, pieced work was being adopted and reinvented with extraordinary creativity and discipline by members of highly conservative Amish and Mennonite religious communities in Pennsylvania, Ohio, Kansas, Indiana, and other parts of the Midwest. Utterly distinctive in their use of color and design, Amish quilts represent what is arguably the single most impressive body of expression in American quilting.

The Amish religion is an outgrowth of the German Protestant Anabaptist movement of the 1500s. Jacob Ammann, a seventeenth-century Mennonite bishop, founded this small and strict fundamentalist sect that, like other German groups such as the Quakers, Schwenkfelders, Mennonites, and Moravians, came to William Penn's land to escape religious persecution. The Amish initially settled in the Lancaster area in the early 1700s, where some families still inhabit land deeded to their ancestors by Penn himself. These deliberately "Plain People," as they call themselves, seeking separation from the modern world of the "English," live in tightly interdependent communities centered around church and family. They follow the rigid dictates of the Ordnung, a set of instructions that eschews anything frivolous, ostentatious, or superfluous, including publicly generated electricity, motorized vehicles, and other distractions. The Amish farm with horse-drawn equipment and drive horse-drawn carriages. Most Amish children attend community schools only through the eighth grade. Prayer permeates their daily lives; there is no separation between thought and deed. They practice nonviolence and nonresistance in all aspects of their lives. The Amish wear simple, modest clothing that is plain and solid colored. Men wear black trousers and jackets, light-colored shirts, and broad-brimmed hats; women wear long dresses and aprons and don bonnets in public. Buttons are not allowed because these simple people consider them to be vain.

The Amish came late to quilting. The earliest Amish quilts date from the 1860s, and very few are known to have been crafted prior to 1900. These early Amish quilts were made of wool. Cotton became the preferred fabric by the 1920s, and rayon and other synthetics dominated by the 1940s. Amish quilters deliberately shunned the fancy, decorative quilts of the Victorian era, and as a result, Amish quilts simultaneously embody the tightly defined limits and enormous creative possibilities of both the Amish way of life and of pieced work itself. Their designs employed a limited number of rigid geometric patterns, such as center diamond, diamond-in-the-square, four-patch, nine-patch, bars, and sunshine-and-shadow, all made up of pieces cut into the three basic, angled shapes of the square, triangle, or rectangle. Within these boundaries, Amish quilters created works full of astonishing tonal variations, startling color juxtapositions, brilliant manipulations of pattern, and, seen particularly in many examples from Lancaster, Pennsylvania, minutely detailed quilting.

CONTAINED CRAZY QUILT ▸

Mattie Mast Kauffman. c. 1910–1920. Arthur, Illinois. Cotton. 71 x 80 in. Private collection.

In contrast to most crazies, which employed exotic fabrics and fancy embroidery stitches, this Amish quilt is made up solely of cotton rag-bag scraps. The pieces are arranged into forty-two squares, surrounded by a wide solid-colored border that contains their chaotic rhythms. Arthur's Amish quilters produced a number of noteworthy crazies in the early twentieth century, several decades after the idea had passed out of fashion in the outside world.

A completely uninhibited sense of color sets Amish quilts apart from all others. While most "English" quilters followed the traditional use of evenly balanced complementary colors, the Amish viewed color differently from the rest of the "world" and chose combinations that expressed that vision. Fabrics were almost invariably solid colored like their clothing, but colors of virtually the same value—dark purple and black, for example—or the same glowing, saturated intensity of color might be placed side by side, with results that range from somber and subdued to vibrant and dazzling.

African-American quilters also brought unique cultural sensibilities and influences to the pieced quilt. Their use of bold, asymmetrical designs reflected African textiles. Like Amish quilts, African-American quilts are immediately recognizable in their uniqueness—clearly, they are made by a cultural group that is removed from the mainstream of society and draws its inspiration from sources unfamiliar to, or ignored by, society at large. In marked contrast to the strict geometric regularity of traditional pieced quilts, many African-American quilts emphasize a playful, improvisational approach to design. Their free, asymmetrical rhythms give these quilts an engaging sense of spontaneity and immediacy. African-American quilts are often tied rather than stitched, using brightly colored yarn or floss to bind the layers of the quilt. Tying, which can be spaced fairly widely, is much less work than quilting. The tied yarn can also be used as an integral part of the design by emphasizing the rhythm of a repeated motif or by bringing a balance of color to a seemingly random pattern.

The increasing availability and popularity of inexpensive manufactured woven bedcoverings in the late 1800s dramatically reduced the number of quilts being made and used. However, quilting remained important in more culturally isolated communities throughout the late nineteenth and early twentieth centuries, and the hard years of the Great Depression brought a strong revival of interest in quilting to American society at large. Driven once again by necessity, many resourceful American women rediscovered the deceptively simple joys of pieced work and appliqué. The then fashionable pastel colors were incorporated into traditional patterns and motifs, often with results that breathed new life into the old designs. Popular homemaking magazines, which were read by millions of women all over the country, published patterns and instructions. Creative quilters, influenced by contemporary design trends, experimented with new combinations and patterns that reflected the fast moving and increasingly complex times in which they lived.

Quilting is vibrantly alive today. More than any other folk craft, it has weathered and absorbed changes in fashion and continued to attract attentive practitioners to the present day. There has been a tremendous resurgence of interest in quilting and needlework in the past twenty-five years, from both practical and historical standpoints. Hundreds of thousands of American women are making quilts for use in their homes, often following patterns published in specialty magazines and in dozens of how-to books. The Great American Quilt Festival, a gathering of contemporary quilters, quilt dealers,

This quilter was photographed working in a smokehouse near Hinesville, Georgia, in April 1941.

Courtesy of the Farm Security Administration Collection, Prints and Photographs Division, Library of Congress.

THE CREATION OF THE ANIMALS QUILT ▸

Harriet Powers. c. 1895–1898. Athens, Georgia. Cotton, appliquéd and pieced, with plain and metallic yarns. 69 x 105 in. Museum of Fine Arts, Boston. Bequest of Maxim Karolik.

Harriet Powers (1837–1911) was born a slave in Georgia. Her two extraordinary Bible quilts, preserved at the Boston Museum of Fine Arts and the Smithsonian, represent powerful and moving statements of an intensely personal faith.

Hard pressed for cash, Powers reluctantly sold the earlier of the two quilts to an artist and art teacher named Jennie Smith from Athens, Georgia, in 1891. Through Jennie Smith's efforts, the second quilt, pictured here, was purchased by the faculty wives of Atlanta University.

and suppliers of materials held annually in New York since 1986, draws over one hundred thousand enthusiasts each year. Interest in historic quilts is also burgeoning, as they are increasingly recognized as compelling documents of women's lives in earlier times. Beginning with a seminal 1973 exhibition at the Whitney Museum of Art in New York, numerous museums and historical societies around the country have organized exhibitions and undertaken scholarly studies devoted to American quilts. A number of states, including New York, North Carolina, Arizona, and Vermont, have conducted statewide quilt searches, seeking historic regional examples, researching local documents and tracing family histories, gathering information on their makers, and subsequently organizing exhibitions and compiling extensive catalogues.

Today, quilts are everywhere. They pervade homemaking magazines and are virtual clichés of the "country" look popularized in the late 1970s after the Bicentennial. Most national mail-order homeware catalogues offer traditionally patterned quilts alongside their sheets, pillowcases, and down comforters. These icons of Americana are, ironically, often made in the Far East, where hand labor is extremely cheap. They can be of extremely fine quality; all too many have deceived knowledgeable dealers and entered the marketplace in recent years claiming to be genuine examples of the handwork of early quilters.

Quilting has also become a self-conscious art form, completely divorced from its functional aspects and practiced by textile artists who create unique designs intended to be displayed on gallery walls. Some of the most interesting contemporary quilters, such as Nancy Crow and Michael James, transform traditional pieced work into sophisticated modern "textile painting." Like many contemporary quilt artists, Nancy Crow does not use a frame but rather assembles her quilts on the walls of her studio. She draws from a vast and diverse array of modern fabric patterns and colors she keeps on hand to create geometrically based works of great visual and technical complexity. She is a virtuoso colorist who constantly tries new color combinations and says that one of her goals "is to have hundreds and hundreds of colors in one quilt." After she has finished piecing the top of a quilt, a process that can take months or even years to complete, a traditional needleworker hand quilts the piece. At least one of her works was quilted by an Amish quilting bee from Holmes County, Ohio, home to the largest concentration of Amish in the country. Like Nancy Crow, Michael James uses the strip piecing method and often produces works in series, experimenting with highly disciplined variations on a particular intellectual theme or design concept. Both artists' works are represented in the collections of a number of major art museums.

▲ MEDALLION BLOCK QUILT

Artist unknown. c. 1820–1840. Connecticut. Wool and wool yarns, pieced, embroidered, and appliquéd. 88 x 84 in. The Shelburne Museum, Shelburne, Vermont.

Cut to fit a four-poster bed, this early quilt combines elements of English, framed medallion block-style design with pieced work. The quilter has embellished the blocks with embroidered flowers that break up the rhythms established by the piecing. The large flowers in the framed central sections each cover nine small squares, while each of the smaller flowers outside the center has a larger block of its own.

▼ HONEYCOMB QUILT

Elizabeth Van Horn Clarkson. c. 1830. New York City. Multicolored calicos and white cotton, pieced and quilted. 107 5/8 x 98 1/4 in. The Metropolitan Museum of Art, New York. Gift of Mr. and Mrs. William A. Moore, 1923.

This large and intricate early pieced-work quilt is made from hundreds of small hexagonal segments of fabric, pieced together and quilted. Each of the many flowers is made up of seven hexagons, six of one fabric surrounding a central piece of a different fabric.

MARINER'S COMPASS QUILT ►

Artist unknown. c. 1830–1850. Possibly New Jersey. Cotton. 100 x 96 in. The Shelburne Museum, Shelburne, Vermont.

The cutting and piecing of this intricate design required enormous skill and precision. The many-pointed, pieced compass designs are balanced with delicate hickory leaf and orange slice medallions, and the centers of both designs are quilted in diamond patterns.

◄ GRAVEYARD QUILT

Elizabeth Roseberry Mitchell. c. 1839. Lewis County, Kentucky. Cotton. 85 x 81 in. Museum of the Kentucky Historical Society, Frankfort, Kentucky.

According to family tradition, Mrs. Mitchell made this quilt after visiting the graves of two of her sons. A picket fence borders the outside of the Lemoyne Star pattern quilt as well as the central graveyard and path. The nineteen coffins that ring the edges of the quilt are marked with the names of then living family members. Two coffins representing Mrs. Mitchell's sons were originally placed in the graveyard; two others were subsequently moved from the edge to the center sometime after the quilt was made.

▼ TUMBLING BLOCKS CROSS QUILT

Margaret Younglove Calvert. c. 1850–1870. Bowling Green, Kentucky. Cotton, wool, silk, and mohair. 77 x 72 in. The Kentucky Museum Collection, Western Kentucky University.

The quilter used the dimensionality of the tumbling or baby blocks pattern to create the illusion of three different planes in this quilt: the plain blue field, the six-sided field on which the cross rests, and the cross itself. The blocks seem to float freely across and between fields through three dimensions, creating a powerful and unsettling overall composition.

▲ SUNFLOWERS QUILT

Carrie M. Carpenter. c. 1860s. Northfield, Vermont. Cotton. 84 x 75 in. The Shelburne Museum, Shelburne, Vermont. Gift of Ethel Washburn.

This quilt is cut to fit a four-poster bed, making it appear that the three sunflowers grow from the foot of the bed. The boldly designed quilt includes a number of ingenious details; Mrs. Carpenter, who must have been an avid gardener, cut the seed pods of her flowers from a printed brown calico fabric and quilted them in a diamond pattern, stuffed the stalks to raise them slightly, and quilted the leaves as well.

◄ LOG CABIN QUILT (BARN RAISING VARIATION)

Artist unknown. c. 1860. Region unknown. Wool challis. 82 x 80 in. Collection America Hurrah, New York.

The predominately blue and white color scheme and one-square deep border of alternating dark and light set this Log Cabin quilt apart. The cool tonality of blue and white is banded in red and accented by the red centers of the small blocks that form the pattern. The pattern variation is named for its long, undulating lines, which are reminiscent of post-and-beam barn frames.

LOG CABIN QUILT (LIGHT AND DARK VARIATION) ►

Artist unknown. c. 1870. Region unknown. Cotton. Collection America Hurrah, New York.

The squares of this Log Cabin variation are arranged so that each group of four contains a central diamond composed solely of dark strips of cloth. Pulsating rows of dark and light diamonds seem to alternate across the quilt.

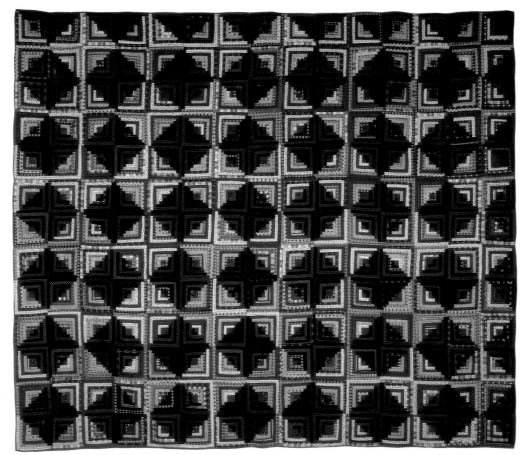

▼ LOG CABIN QUILT (WINDMILL BLADES VARIATION)

Artist unknown. c. 1870. Region unknown. Cotton. Collection America Hurrah, New York.

The dramatic sawtooth border enhances an already powerful choice of color and pattern in this Log Cabin pattern variation. The strips of fabric are arranged to form intersecting "windmill blade" crosses, while the triangular corners of each group of four squares meet to form a light and dark diamond.

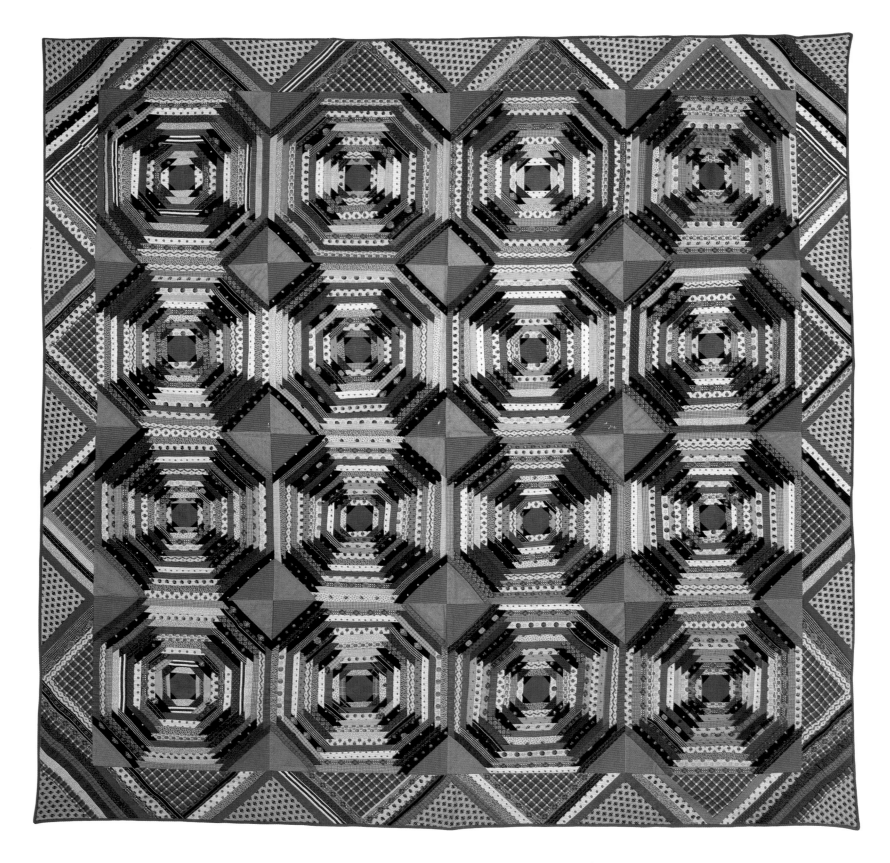

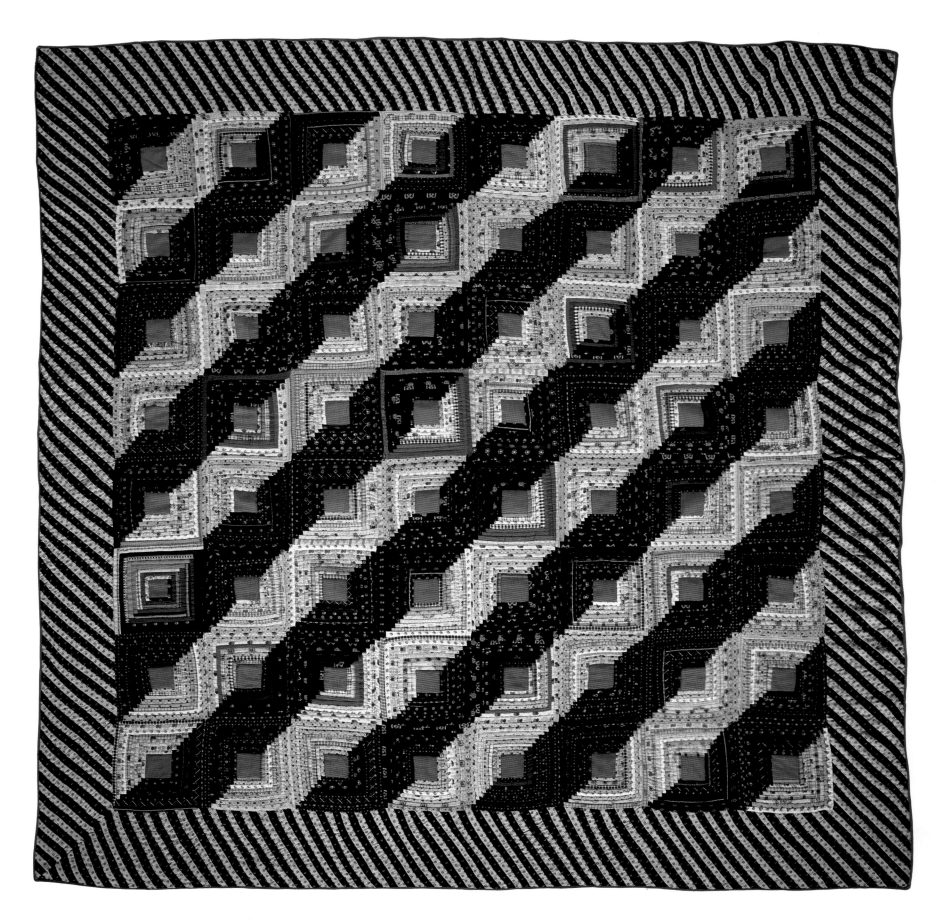

▲ LOG CABIN QUILT (STRAIGHT FURROW VARIATION)

Artist unknown. c. 1865. Region unknown. Printed wool challises and cotton, pieced and quilted. 87 1/2 x 88 1/2 in. The Metropolitan Museum of Art, New York. Purchase, Eva Gebhard-Gourgaud Foundation Gift and funds from various donors, 1974.

The blocks of Log Cabin quilts were always made up of equal diagonals of light and dark fabrics centered on a solid-colored square. In the Straight Furrow variation, the blocks were aligned to create alternating rows of light and dark punctuated by the usually red centers of the cleverly disguised blocks. In this quilt, the thick, central rows are framed by a border of thin black and white lines that run in the opposite direction, adding another dimension to the already complex visual rhythm.

▲ CONTAINED CRAZY QUILT

Nancy Doughty. 1872. Probably Maryland. Printed cottons, pieced and quilted. 89 1/2 x 72 in. The Metropolitan Museum of Art, New York. Purchase, Mr. and Mrs. Edward Scheider Gift, 1989.

This early crazy quilt is inscribed in ink on the center piece of striped fabric: "Made by/ Mrs. Nancy Doughty/ in the 82nd year of her age/ for her friend/ Miss Lizzie Cole A.D. *1872." Unlike most crazy quilts, which were made from silks and velvets, this example uses household cottons, probably saved in the family rag bag. Its subdued palette and strongly containing diagonals give the quilt a very different feel and appearance from later and more florid crazies.*

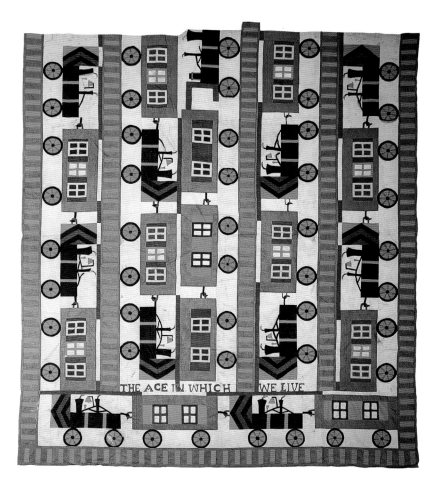

◄ TRAIN QUILT TOP

Mrs. M. J. Saunders. c. 1880. Kosciusko, Mississippi. Pieced and appliquéd cotton. 101 1/4 x 90 1/4 in. Collection of the Mississippi State Historical Museum, Jackson, Mississippi. Gift of Adele Foster Benson.

Mrs. Saunders made this vibrant quilt top after taking her first train ride to the Gulf coast. The wheels of the trains are pieced and appliquéd so they rest on tracks that form the sides and borders of the quilt.

STAR OR SUN VARIATION QUILT ►

Nancy Miller Grider. c. 1880. Russell County, Kentucky. Wool. 75 x 62 in. Private collection.

The maker's family called this unique pattern "Kentucky Sun." Eschewing the geometric regularity of most pieced work, Mrs. Grider created a vivid and painterly overall composition accented by many irregularly shaped pieces of rag-bag fabric. The quilt vibrates with the quick energy and improvisational daring with which it most certainly was made.

BARS QUILT ▸

*Unknown Amish artist. c. 1880. Lancaster County,
Pennsylvania. Wool. 76 x 86 in. The Esprit Collection,
San Francisco, California.*

This early Amish Bars employs the subdued palette common to pre-1900 Lancaster County quilts. The unusual
corner blocks are made up of triangles of four contrasting
fabric colors. Intricate quilting, typical of the Lancaster
Amish, covers the entire quilt.

BROKEN STAR OR CARPENTER'S WHEEL QUILT ▾

*Artist unknown. c. 1880. Illinois. Cotton. 80 x 80 in.
General Foods Corporate Collection.*

This whole quilt pulsates with movement, as the quilter's clever manipulation of color and design has left no
place for the viewer's eye to rest. The broken star that
surrounds the central star, like the accordian or folding
paper chain it resembles, seems to be constantly in movement, collapsing in on itself and then expanding again.
All the motion is effectively contained by the quilt's two
outside borders.

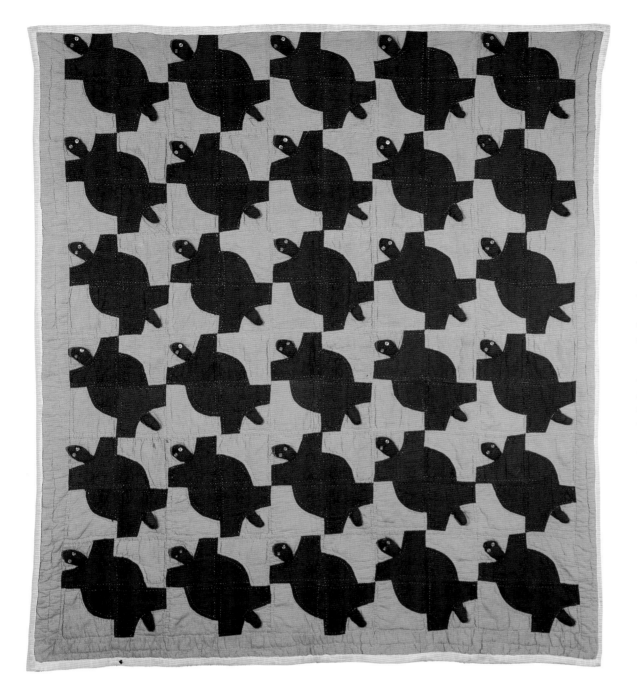

◄ TURTLE QUILT

Unknown African-American artist. Late nineteenth century. Probably Georgia. Stuffed and pieced cotton and silk. 76 x 64 in. Hirschl and Adler, New York.

This clever variation of the traditional Drunkard's Path pattern was probably made by an African-American quilter. The stuffed heads and tails and button eyes of the turtles, probably added to delight a child, complete the transformation of the pattern from geometric to representational.

FANS QUILT ►

Artist unknown. c. 1900. Region unknown. Cotton, pieced and quilted. 76 1/2 x 75 3/4 in. The Metropolitan Museum of Art, New York. Purchase, Mrs. Roger Brunschwig Gift, 1988.

Fan quilts, influenced by the late Victorian interest in anything of Japanese origin, were quite popular in the last decades of the nineteenth century. This example of the genre is cleverly composed, with a single, circular, fanned sunburst filling the four blocks at center, surrounded by a complex rhythm of large and small mirrored images. Fan pattern quilting adds a subtle thematic reinforcement to the entire composition.

CRAZY QUILT ▶

*Artist unknown. c. 1900–1910. Lancaster,
Pennsylvania. Wool and flannel. 78 x 73 in.
Collection America Hurrah, New York.*

*Although its maker could not have known, this
rag-bag quilt's pattern clearly resembles cultivat-
ed farmland seen from the air. Not unlike a
modern abstract painter, the maker manipulated
rhythms of color, size, and pattern to produce a
brilliantly successful composition.*

◀ MELON PATCH QUILT

*Mary Midgett Bridgman. 1902. Hyde
County, North Carolina. Home-dyed sugar
sacks with cotton print backing. 76 x 78 in.
North Carolina Quilt Project, Durham, North
Carolina. Collection of Annie B. Lowry.*

*This sugar-sack quilt demonstrates how thrifty
Carolina quilters made use of any readily
available scrap materials. The sacks were
bleached and then dyed. The simple but effective pattern of oblong, oval "melons" breaks
the quilt into nine groups of four blocks each.
The melon patch is contained by alternating
dark brown and orange borders.*

▼ TIED SCALLOP PATTERN QUILT

*Unknown African-American artist. c. 1910. Southern United States. Tied cotton. Collection
America Hurrah, New York.*

*Instead of quilting, African-American quilters often chose to hold the layers of their quilts
together with tied yarn or embroidery floss. As in this quilt, the ties often became an important
and decorative design element, accenting the irregular rhythms of the piecing.*

BARS VARIATION QUILT ▸

Unknown Amish artist. c. 1910. Lancaster County, Pennsylvania. Wool. 63 x 76 in. The Esprit Collection, San Francisco, California.

This is a rare variation of the classic Amish Bars pattern, with the normally solid-colored bars broken into segments of different colored wool fabrics.

▾ TIED TRIANGLES AND RECTANGLES QUILT

Unknown African-American artist. c. 1910. Southern United States. Tied cotton. Collection America Hurrah, New York.

The careful placement of the brightly colored ties punctuates and enhances the unusual geometric pattern of this African-American quilt.

◄ DIAMOND-STRIPES CRIB QUILT

Unknown Amish artist. c. 1910–1920. Kansas. Cotton percale, cotton sateen, plain-weave wool. 37 x 45 in. Collection of Michael Oruch.

Groups of four intersecting blocks at right top, right bottom, and left center are organized to create slightly off-center diamond frames pulsating outward from a solid black center diamond. Like cracked glass, the stripes in many blocks and groups of blocks mirror each other. The border, composed of strips of unequal size and asymmetrical placement, continues the quilt's vibrant, skewed rhythms.

RAILROAD CROSSING CRIB QUILT ►

Unknown Amish artist. c. 1915. Holmes County, Ohio. Cotton and wool. 43 x 50 in. Collection of Scott and Cindy Albright.

Shining like lights flashing against the dark black field, the crossings are composed of triangles that are illuminated by a variety of color rhythms. The five stars serve as focus points, anchoring the quilt's gentle motion.

▾ FOUR PATCH VARIATION QUILT

Unknown Amish artist. c. 1920. Lancaster County, Pennsylvania. Pieced wools. 72 x 74 in.
The Esprit Collection, San Francisco, California.

The brilliant, pulsating, red central cross unifies the four four-patch blocks it bisects and is seem-
ingly contained by the contrasting black border. A less imaginative or daring quilter would have
used only black borders, resulting in a far more predictable and static visual rhythm.

DIAMOND-IN-THE-SQUARE QUILT ▸

Unknown Amish artist. c. 1920–1930. Lancaster County, Pennsylvania. Wool. 77 x 77 in. The Esprit Collection, San Francisco, California.

Patterns built around a central diamond were very popular among Lancaster County quilters. This deceptively complex example, which uses six different fabric colors, accentuates the central diamond by surrounding it with a vibrant red border anchored by corner pieces of the same dark purple fabric used in the square's subtly contrasting corners.

◂ BROKEN DISHES QUILT

Artist unknown. c. 1920. Possibly Ohio. Silk and cotton. 77 x 76 1/2 in. The Metropolitan Museum of Art, New York. Sansbury-Mills Fund, 1973.

This brightly colored, sophisticated, and exuberant post–World War I quilt mixes yellow, pink, and orange dress silks with contemporary printed cottons in a freely composed pattern that reflects the attitudes of the time in which it was crafted.

PINWHEEL QUILT ▶

J. L. 1930. Indiana. Wool and cotton. 84 x 71 in. The Metropolitan Museum of Art, New York. Friends of the American Wing Fund.

This midwestern Amish quilt, while not so rigidly geometric as Amish quilts from Pennsylvania, is still very carefully composed. The blocks are arranged so that the left and right halves of the quilt are almost exact mirror images, both in form and color.

UNNAMED PATTERN CRIB QUILT ▼

Unknown Amish artist. c. 1930–1935. Pennsylvania. Cotton. 38 x 55 in. Collection of Barbara S. Janow and Barbara Ross.

This unique quilt is built from a simple pattern of cleverly arranged squares and triangles. The repeating colored forms seem to be mirrored in solid black.

▾ BOW TIES CRIB QUILT

Unknown Amish artist. c. 1930–1940. Middlefield, Ohio. Cotton. 38 x 54 in. Private collection.

This jaunty little quilt with its rows of bright bow ties was probably made for a boy. As was often the case in Amish quilts, the purple background is not uniform in color.

▼ Pyramid Tumbling Blocks Quilt

Unknown Amish artist. c. 1935. Ohio. Cotton. 108 x 94 in. Collection America Hurrah, New York.

This midwestern Amish variation on the popular, but technically demanding, tumbling blocks pattern arranges the blocks into an inverted pyramid. The blocks seem to cascade down and back up along the strong repeating diagonals. The pattern variation also is called Stairway to Heaven.

▲ STARS CRIB QUILT

Unknown Amish artist. c. 1935. Holmes County, Ohio. Cotton and cotton sateens. 35 x 41 in. Private collection.

The many different shades of blue used in this little quilt provide a subdued contrast to the more dramatic color variations in the stars.

▼ RAINBOW MONOGRAM AND INITIAL QUILT

Ida W. Beck. 1952–1954. Easton, Pennsylvania. Cotton. 90 x 94 in. The Shelburne Museum, Shelburne, Vermont.

In a letter to The Shelburne Museum, Miss Beck described her needlework masterpiece this way: "On the central panel is a 24 x 14" alphabet monogram, also seven other alphabets—script, block, Old English, etc. and the side pieces are joined to the central panel by a 2 1/2" script alphabet on one side and block alphabet on the other. Each side has six large scallops, each one contains a month of the year and the flower of the month, in natural size and color, either solid embroidery or buttonholed appliqué. In all there are about 400 letters, all hand embroidered in assorted colors, about fifty flowers, all different; it is hand quilted, was several years in working (quilting) it. It is quite original and I was several years in planning and making it. I am over 70 years old—a shut-in since childhood, so have always done needlework, and monogramming was my speciality for many years."

Amber Densmore. c. 1985. Chelsea, Vermont. Cotton. Private collection.

Amber Densmore's version of this old traditional pattern is notable for its many subtle variations of fabric and color.

AMBER DENSMORE, QUILTER

Amber Densmore was born on a farm in Berlin, Vermont, in 1902 and spent her long life until her death in 1992 working with her husband Sabin on a farm they bought during the Great Depression in the small and somewhat isolated central Vermont farming community of Chelsea. She recalled that "in those days if you had a pair of horses, a plow, a harrow, and a cultivator, then come haying time a mowing machine to rake, that's all the machinery you needed. The rest of it came out of the strength of your body—pitch the hay, chop the wood, and everything."

As a girl, Amber Densmore learned needlework and quilting skills from her family and neighbors. Like generations of frugal Vermont farm wives before her, she crafted her carefully designed and stitched pieced and appliquéd quilts from household rag-bag materials, following traditional patterns she had learned from her family and friends.

Jane Beck, director of the Vermont Folklife Center in Middlebury, describes Mrs. Densmore and her quilts this way: "Her work is truly exceptional. She personifies the term folk artist in its most complete sense. She is a visual spokeswoman for a tradition that is endangered in Vermont—the farm wife who works beside her husband and yet manages to find time for those quiet moments of artistic pleasure so necessary to create beauty of leftovers and scraps and the well-worn traditions of every day."

Mrs. Densmore was honored as a National Heritage Fellow by the National Endowment for the Arts Folk Arts Program in 1988.

PIECED STRIP QUILT ▸

Lucinda Toomer. c. 1975. Dawson, Georgia. Cotton. 82 x 61 in. International Folk Art Foundation Collection at the Museum of International Folk Art, a unit of the Museum of New Mexico, Santa Fe.

Lucinda Toomer was honored in 1983 as a National Heritage Fellow by the Folk Arts Program of the National Endowment for the Arts. Her playfully composed pieced strip quilt is full of the seemingly improvised rhythms typical of twentieth-century African-American quilts. While each of the twelve blocks is made up of four rows of four diamonds, the sizes of the diamonds vary slightly within the blocks; none of the twelve blocks is exactly the same, nor are they evenly spaced, as would be expected in an Anglo-American quilt. The unique mixture of black and green diamonds in the bottom left-hand corner block and the balancing strip of red beside it complete the offhanded composition.

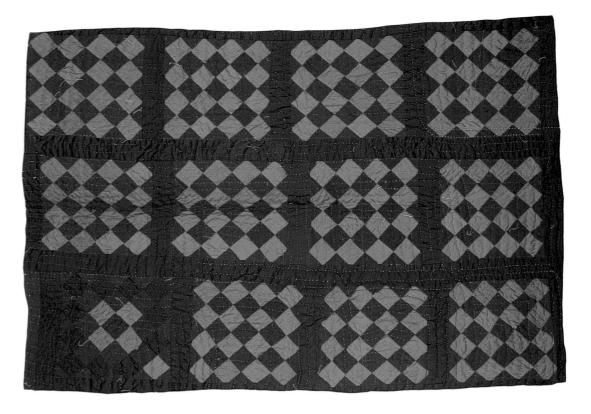

◄ BITTERSWEET XIV

Nancy Crow. Hand quilted by Rose Augenstein. 1981. Baltimore, Ohio. Cotton. 68 1/2 x 68 1/2 in. Collection of the American Craft Museum, New York. Museum purchase with the aid of funds from the National Endowment for the Arts, 1984. Donated to the American Craft Museum by the American Craft Council, 1990.

Nancy Crow did not take up quilting until relatively late in life. After studying ceramics and weaving at Ohio State University art school, she practiced tapestry weaving before turning to contemporary quilting full time in 1979.

Like a traditional quilter, Crow usually builds her quilts in block formats. Choosing from the enormous range of contemporary textiles she maintains in her studio, Crow sews pieces of fabric together in strips before adding them to a quilt in progress. She works intuitively to find the right color and pattern combinations. Crow's Bittersweet series of twenty-two quilts explores the ebb and flow of human emotions and energies through a host of rhythmic and color variations.

▲ RHYTHM/COLOR: SPANISH DANCE

Michael James. 1985. Somerset Village, Massachusetts. Machine-pieced cotton and silk, machine quilted. 100 x 100 in. Collection of the Newark Museum, Newark, New Jersey. Purchased in 1985 with funds granted by the Louis Comfort Tiffany Foundation.

The striped border and four blocks of diamonds suggest traditional pieced patterns and anchor the swirling rhythms of color and line in this remarkable modern quilt.

N A T I V E
A M E R I C A N
B E A D W O R K   A N D
Q U I L L   W O R K

Prior to the arrival of Anglo-European explorers and settlers, the native peoples of the vast eastern Woodlands, which stretched unbroken from the New England coast to the Great Lakes, decorated their clothing, moccasins, pouches, and other personal accessories primarily with dyed porcupine quills. The porcupine, which subsists on a diet of tree bark, leaves, and tender branches, was a prominent member of the northern forest animal community, and, before the nineteenth century, was most commonly found from upstate New York into the upper Midwest. Its barb-ended quills defended the slow-moving and rather dim-witted rodent from enemies such as wolves, martens, and, in later years, the dogs of fur trappers. Indians carefully removed the hollow, cylindrical quills from the porcupine's body and tail (sometimes without killing the animal, for which they had great respect), sorted them by size (they could be up to four or five inches long), and dried them. The dull white and tan quills were then colored with natural dyes, among the most common and striking being buffalo berry and the suggestively named bloodroot that produced shades of red, wild sunflower that gave yellow, and wild grapes that produced a true black. Finally, the quills were softened by being chewed, then were flattened and attached to the leather or, as was sometimes used in later years, cloth surface being decorated. The flattened quills were worked in a number of ways. They could be wrapped around strips of sinew (cut from animal tendons) or thread and sewn to the surface, or could be woven over and under warp threads on a loom to produce an effect very much like beadwork. Some gifted quill workers took quills, which could be as much as 1/8-inch wide before flattening, and spliced them together to form long, seemingly unbroken pieces.

Quill work apparently spread from the Woodland nations to the Plains, where the porcupine was not native. Quills became, therefore, one of the chief items of commerce between nations as Plains Indians had to trade with their eastern neighbors to obtain the undyed materials. This dynamic changed rapidly, however, when trappers and traders introduced glass beads to both groups in the early 1800s. Indians were fascinated by the shimmering and colorful glass. The relative ease of working with beads, which required no dyeing and were far easier to thread and sew than quills, brought them ready and enthusiastic acceptance from all but the die-hard traditionalists who thought them a cheap substitute. Although beadwork soon became dominant, quill work retained its champions and never completely died out, and the two mediums were sometimes combined very successfully.

◄ SHOULDER BAG

Unknown Chippewa Indian artist. 1851. Michigan. Wool fabric and yarn, cotton fabric and thread, silk ribbon, glass and metallic beads. Length: 31 1/4 in., width: 7 in. © The Detroit Historical Museum, Detroit, Michigan.

The intricate geometric designs on this shoulder bag were woven on a loom, which made a very tight weave structure possible. The name "Joseph Lantre," probably the person for whom the bag was made, and a date, "Mars 21 1851," appear on the bag.

Alice New Holy Blue Legs of Grass Creek, South Dakota, is a Lakota Indian porcupine-quill artist. She is shown here with some of her work and a pile of quills.

Photograph courtesy Museum of International Folk Art, Santa Fe, New Mexico.

The first beads brought by trappers and traders were large "pony" beads, so-called because they were transported by pony teams. Pony beads were usually blue or white. By the 1840s, much smaller and more versatile "seed" beads, available in a wide range of colors, were introduced and quickly gained favor. Beads were so highly regarded by Indians that traders, who were primarily interested in beaver and other fur pelts, found them far more effective as barter than many of the more practical items, including pots and pans, clothing, fabric, or even guns and ammunition.

Virtually all quill work and beadwork was created by women, and both crafts therefore reflect a distinctly feminine point of view. Indian societies of the Woodlands and the Plains practiced a sharp division of labor; the men hunted and made war, while the women cared for the children and elders, tended and gathered crops, cooked, and made the clothing. Within the Woodland nations, particularly among the mighty and warlike Iroquois, women held much of the political power as well; they appointed and could dismiss chiefs and owned all the property of the community. When a captive was brought to an Iroquois village, it was the women who decided whether he was to be adopted by the tribe or tortured and killed.

Beadwork reached its highest level of sophistication among the Plains Indians, particularly the western Sioux. In the later years of the nineteenth century, some craftswomen went to extraordinary lengths to produce buckskin war or ceremonial shirts and dresses covered with elaborate, decorative beadwork, paint, shells, or hairlocks, and edged with rawhide fringe. When covered with beadwork, such a garment could be impractically heavy, the beads alone weighing from four to seven pounds. However, as the native civilizations declined, the shirts became more and more elaborate and were worn with enormous pride by their makers and owners as emblems of their oppressed and vanishing cultures.

Both beadwork and quill work are still practiced among Native Americans today. Alice New Holy Blue Legs of the Lakota people of South Dakota, for example, is descended from a long line of quill workers. She is a skilled quill worker who has taught many others how to prepare and work

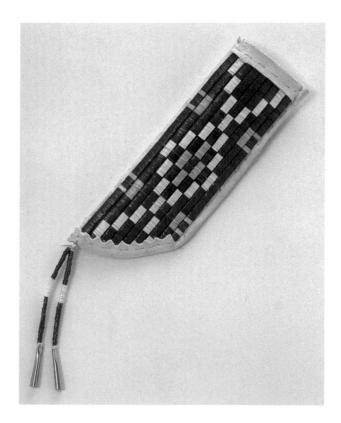

KNIFE CASE ▸

Alice New Holy Blue Legs. c. 1988. Grass Creek, South Dakota. Porcupine quills on deer hide. Length: 7 1/2 in. International Folk Art Foundation Collection at the Museum of International Folk Art, a unit of the Museum of New Mexico, Santa Fe.

Alice New Holy Blue Legs, a Lakota Indian, was honored as a National Heritage Fellow by the Folk Arts Program of the National Endowment for the Arts in 1985. A descendant of many generations of porcupine-quill workers, she has helped keep the tradition alive by passing on its secrets to her daughters and granddaughters as well as many nonrelatives.

with porcupine quills in the hope that this venerable and rather difficult traditional Indian craft will continue into the next century. Similarly, Maude Kegg of Minnesota carries on the Ojibwa tradition of loom weaving beads into the intricate leaf, floral, and geometric patterns that have characterized the masterful decorative work produced by Great Lakes Indian women for hundreds of years.

▾ MOCCASINS

Unknown Yanktonai Sioux Indian artist. c. 1870. Poplar, Montana. Buckskin, porcupine quills, tin bangles. Length: 9 1/2 in. Peabody and Essex Museum/ Peabody Museum Collection, Salem, Massachusetts.

These elaborately decorated moccasins, completely covered with brightly colored quill work, feature the geometric designs that were favored by Plains Indians.

▲ POUCH AND CLOAK

Unknown eastern Woodland Indian artist. Late eighteenth century. Hudson River Valley or Connecticut. Dyed buckskin embroidered with porcupine quills. Height of pouch: 9 in. New York State Museum, Albany, New York.

The simple, somberly colored decoration of this early pouch and cloak is typical of eastern Woodland Indian quill work.

CRADLE BOARD ▶

Unknown Sioux (probably eastern Dakota) Indian artist. c. 1830. Probably near Falls of St. Anthony, Upper Mississippi River. Wooden backboard, buffalo (?) skin, porcupine quills. Length: 31 in., width: 17 1/2 in. National Museum of Natural History, Smithsonian Institution, Washington, D.C. Gift of Mrs. Sarah Harrison.

This cradle was originally collected by the early explorer, artist, and author George Catlin, who noted that it "was purchased from a Sioux woman...as she was carrying her infant in it." Catlin traveled "amongst the wildest tribes of Indians in North America" between 1832 and 1839; his book of letters and notes, first published in 1841, remains one of the most important documentations of what he described as the "manners, customs and conditions of the North American Indians."

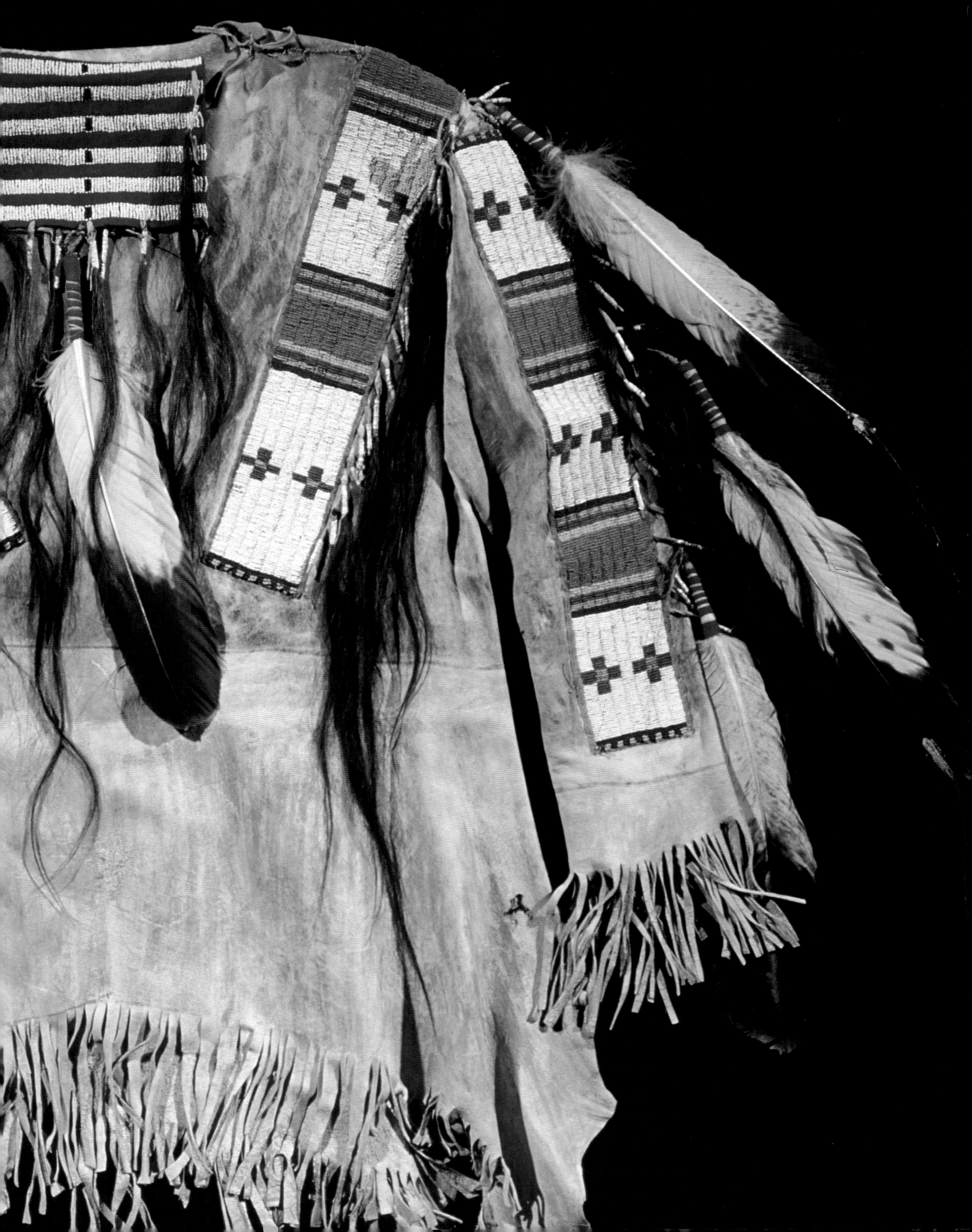

◂ KICKING BEAR'S WAR SHIRT

Unknown Sioux (Dakota) Indian artist. c. 1875. South Dakota. Buffalo skin, glass beads, porcupine quills, human hair. Length: 40 in. National Museum of Natural History, Smithsonian Institution, Washington, D.C.

This shirt belonged to the famous Sioux war chief Kicking Bear, who fought against Custer at the Little Bighorn. The shirt is decorated with locks of hair taken from his rivals in battle. In 1889 Kicking Bear became a founder of the Ghost Dance religion, a messianic cult that invoked the Great Spirit to purify the Plains in anticipation of the return of the buffalo and all Indians killed by sickness and war with the white man. After Sitting Bull was killed in December 1890, Kicking Bear and his followers fled into the South Dakota badlands, surrendering the day before the fateful Wounded Knee Massacre that marked the end of Indian resistance. Kicking Bear was held as a prisoner of war in 1891, traveled to Europe with Buffalo Bill in 1892, and became a delegate to Washington in 1896.

◂ HALF-LEGGINGS

Unknown Metis-Sioux Indian artist. c. 1880. South Dakota. Buckskin, cotton fabric, glass beads. Length: 20 in., width: 12 in. © The Detroit Institute of Arts, Detroit, Michigan. Founders Society Purchase with funds from Richard Manoogian.

Metis communities were made up of descendants of marriages between Canadian trappers and Indian women. Caught between cultures, the Metis drew from both sides of their heritage, often creating clothing that was based on European styles but decorated with Indian designs. Encounters with Mexican vaqueros may have influenced the creation of these chap-like half-leggings, which were worn over pants. The beaded decoration includes tiny American flags.

MOCCASINS ▶

Unknown Sioux Indian artist. c. 1870. Possibly South Dakota. Buckskin, porcupine quills, seed beads, paint, rawhide. Length: 9 1/2 in. The Shelburne Museum, Shelburne, Vermont.

The interior leathers of these moccasins are painted with brightly colored geometric designs similar to those found on the painted rawhide bags called parfleches that sometimes were made by Plains Indians.

◀ STORAGE BAG

Unknown Sioux Indian artist. 1890. South Dakota. Cowhide, porcupine quills, glass beads, tin, horsehair. Length: 14 3/8 in., width: 24 1/4 in. Buffalo Bill Historical Center, Cody, Wyoming.

In the late nineteenth century, Sioux quill workers sometimes incorporated pictorial elements into their designs. This Sioux bag depicts a mounted warrior "counting coup"—hitting his living opponent with a specially carved coup stick. Among most Plains Indian nations, personal glory was an essential element of warfare, and a warrior's stature in battle was measured by an elaborately codified system that awarded highest merits for acts involving the greatest daring, bravery, and personal risk.

◀ MAN'S SHIRT

Unknown Winnebago Indian artist. c. 1880. Wisconsin. Wool fabric, silk ribbon, velvet ribbon, glass beads. Height: 27 1/8 in., width (shoulder to shoulder): 19 3/4 in. © The Detroit Institute of Arts, Detroit, Michigan. Museum Purchase with funds from the state of Michigan, the city of Detroit, and the Founders Society.

This formal dress shirt is decorated with bold, embroidered floral bead designs typical of the Great Lakes area. All of the materials, including the wool broadcloth from which the shirt is made, were foreign to Indian culture and were gathered in barters with Anglo-American traders.

▲ Dress

Minnie Sky Arrow. c. 1890. Western Dakotas. Cowhide, glass beads. Height: 39 in., width: 48 in. National Museum of Natural History, Smithsonian Institution, Washington, D.C.

This dress, which is entirely covered with beadwork on both sides, weighs 13 1/4 pounds. According to her son, Minnie Sky Arrow was a graduate of Carlisle and an accomplished pianist, who, in her later years, gave concerts around the country. She wore this masterpiece of beadwork during her recitals.

◄ TOBACCO BAG

Unknown southern Arapahoe Indian artist. c. 1890. Oklahoma. Buckskin, glass beads. Height: 29 in. Buffalo Bill Historical Center, Cody, Wyoming. Gift of William D. Weiss.

To Indians of the Plains, pipes were sacred objects, invested with deep symbolic meaning, and smoking, however pleasurable, was a religious act. Specially carved and decorated pipes were reserved for ceremonial occasions related to healing, hunting, making war, or making peace. Pipe bowls and stems were usually separate pieces. They were carried in bead- or quill-decorated bags like this example along with smoking materials made of a mixture of tobacco and other herbs, such as sumac leaves, dried barks, and mullein.

LANCE CASE ▲

Unknown Crow Indian artist. c. 1890. Montana. Rawhide, buckskin, glass beads, wool stroud, porcupine quills. Length: 51 1/2 in. Buffalo Bill Historical Center, Cody, Wyoming.

This lance case, crafted after the Crow had been moved onto reservations, was made for ceremonial use in parades and was carried empty.

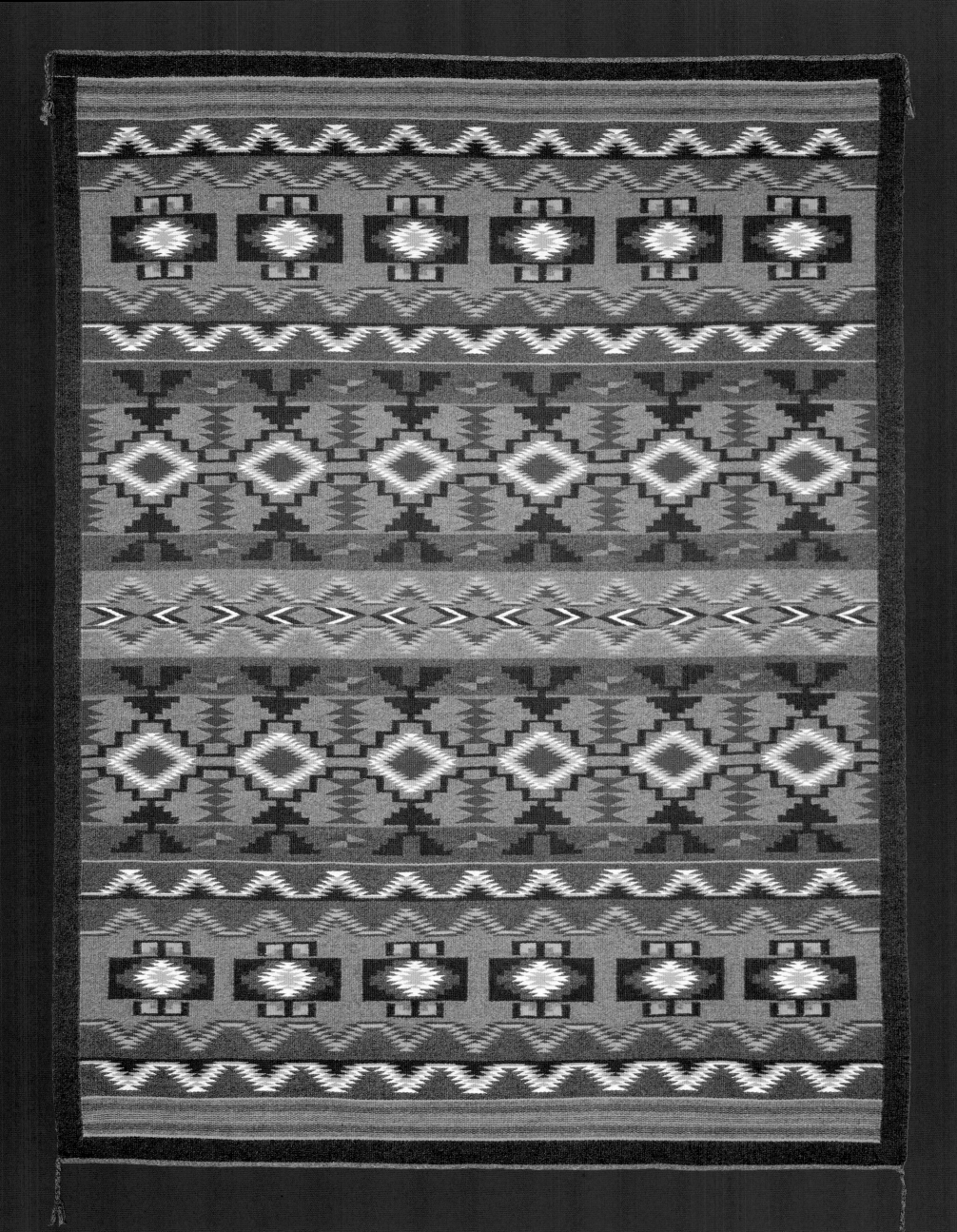

W E A R I N G B L A N K E T S, C O V E R L E T S A N D O T H E R W E A V I N G S

W E A R I N G B L A N K E T S

The most notable Native American weavers are the Navajo, whose weaving tradition results from the collision of three very different cultures in the Southwest: the Pueblo, an agricultural people native to the region since prehistoric times; the Navajo, a nation of nomadic hunter-gatherers who migrated from the North to the desert country sometime between 1300 and 1500; and the Spanish, who arrived shortly after the Navajo. The Navajo are relative newcomers to weaving, having learned the craft in the late 1600s from their neighbors the Pueblo, who had been weaving for centuries. Because of the threat of Spanish subjugation after the conquest of the Rio Grande Valley in 1598, many Pueblos fled to live with the as yet unconquered Navajo, taking their craft with them to their new home. The Navajo embraced the craft of weaving, and by the end of the seventeenth century their creations were sought by Pueblo and Spanish alike.

Among the many changes that the Spanish brought to the Southwest in the 1600s was the introduction of sheep, specifically the churro, a breed that easily adapted to the difficult environment of the high desert country of northern New Mexico. The long, thick, non-oily wool of the churro absorbed dye readily and did not require washing, a blessing in a climate where water was scarce. Indigo, also brought to the Southwest by the Spanish, was the most commonly used dye, although unfortunately it could not be grown in the desert. No source of red dye was ever found in the desert, so the resourceful Navajo traded for bayeta, a deep-red, wool flannel material made in England and Spain, and then painstakingly unraveled the fabric to obtain red yarn for their weavings.

While Navajo weavings have long been thought of as rugs, the weavings made for their own use and for trade with the Pueblo and Spanish were not rugs but rather blankets, made to be worn for warmth and protection from rain, cold, wind, and the extremes of the high desert climate. The Navajo made two basic blanket forms, a longer-than-wide form adapted from the Spanish serape, which was worn draped around the shoulders like a shawl, and an almost square, wider-than-long form that came to be

◄ STANDARD RUG

Irene Clark. 1990. New Mexico. Wool yarn. 63 1/2 x 47 in. Denver Art Museum, Denver, Colorado.

The vividly colored eye-dazzling geometrics of this contemporary rug are set against a cool background of grays and tans to create a textile that successfully combines traditional design ideas with a modern color palette.

known as a chief's blanket and could be worn draped around the body in various ways depending on the severity of the weather. The chief's blanket was also used as a ground cover for sitting and often hung in doorways to prevent drafts.

Serapes, which typically carried bold white and/or blue geometric designs set against a vivid red background of bayeta, were favored both by Mexicans, who found they compared favorably with the Saltillo serapes woven in northern Mexico, and by the Anglo traders who first came to the region in the 1820s. The red, white, and blue serapes were, not surprisingly, popular with officers of the U.S. Army, who were among the Navajo's best customers from the mid-1820s through the mid-1850s. The much more subdued chief's blankets, which prior to 1840 featured only parallel stripes of white, blue, and brown (accented occasionally by bayeta stripes), were greatly esteemed by the many Indian nations with whom the Navajo traded, including the Blackfeet, Nez Perce, Crow, and Cheyenne. The Navajo chief's blanket commanded a premium as a trade item (as many as twenty horses might be demanded for a fine piece), and thus only men and women of considerable material wealth could afford them.

At the end of the Mexican-American War in 1848, the United States took control of the Southwest and, like the Spanish before them, almost immediately came into armed conflict with the defiantly independent Navajo. The clash between cultures reached a head in 1863 when Colonel Kit Carson defeated the Navajo in a guerilla war, destroying their villages and killing their sheep. Some eight thousand Navajo, virtually the entire population, were captured and interred in eastern New Mexico, where they were kept for five years before being allowed to return to their devastated homeland.

After the defeat, the Navajo focussed on weaving as a commercial venture, making many changes in their products in an attempt to appeal to new customers. Elements of both Navajo and Saltillo serape designs were combined in the chief's blanket, which became the dominant form in the 1870s. Brightly colored, commercially dyed yarns became widely available and were juxtaposed in clashing jig-jag patterns called "eye dazzlers." Traders encouraged the Navajo to incorporate pictorial elements familiar to Anglos, such as cows, trains, eagles, and flags, into their weavings. Traders noticed that many settlers were using Navajo blankets as rugs, and encouraged the Indians to follow the market, sometimes even to the point of copying Oriental carpet designs, which were becoming increasingly popular. By the turn of the century, the Navajo were weaving almost entirely for the Anglo-American tourist market and the now famous Navajo rug was their dominant product.

Navajo weaving is still practiced, although fewer young people are interested in learning the craft than

This Navajo weaver is working at a typical outside loom.

Courtesy of Rae Burnette, American Indian Services.

◄ PICTORIAL RUG

*Unknown Navajo Indian artist. c. 1915–1925.
Wool. 71 1/2 x 44 1/2 in. Collection America
Hurrah, New York.*

*Early twentieth-century Navajo weavers,
encouraged by the traders who marketed their
rugs to the expanding tourist trade, began to
produce pictorial designs.*

might be hoped. Navajo weavers
work at looms similar to those of the
Pueblo. The looms are very simple.
They are made of logs and set up outside, partially buried in the sandy soil
and tied together for stability. The
weaver sits on the ground in front of
the loom and works from the bottom
up, weaving as many as 50 to 100
weft (horizontal) threads per inch
through the warp (vertical), which is
strung on the loom first to provide a
strong foundation for the dense weft.

In addition to traditional styles,
which are still produced by some
weavers, a number of modern styles
have been developed in this century.
Among the most prized of contemporary Navajo rugs are the so-called
Two Gray Hills rugs, named for a
trading post where the style was
developed around 1915. This subdued style uses only gray, black,
brown, tan, and white colors derived
from natural dyes to create intricate patterns based on motifs adapted from Oriental rugs. Two Gray
Hills rugs are prized for their high-quality weaving; their very high weft counts and innovative designs
are evidence of the artists' ability to adapt to a changing world while still preserving the finest traditions of Navajo weaving.

COVERLETS AND OTHER WEAVINGS

Writing in 1937, Allen Eaton observed, "Of all the folk arts of the Southern Highlands...the coverlet has from time immemorial held first place not only in the hearts of the pioneer women to whom it was the happiest outlet for creative expression, but of kinsfolk and friends whom in one way or another have felt its many services of use, sentiment, and beauty. Even today, far back in the mountains of every Highland state, are families whose meager incomes do not exceed a few dollars a year, but who treasure the old 'kivers' and would never consider selling one of them except 'for to get the doctor.'"

Weaving is an ancient craft that has been practiced widely from medieval times in Scotland, England, Ireland, and Germany, and came to America with the first settlers. Handwoven coverlets, made of wool, cotton, or linen, were made in early colonial days and became extremely popular for use as bedcovers and warm throws in the early nineteenth century. Coverlets are the homiest, most traditional, and most independent of American textiles. Unlike quilts and rugs, which, despite nostalgic reports to the contrary, almost always employed store-bought material, coverlets could be crafted strictly from materials at hand. Some were entirely homemade, from plant or animal fiber grown, spun, and dyed on the family farm. In early New England, New York, and Pennsylvania, home weavers often worked in a back room or outbuilding to make coverlets for the family, employing traditional technology that had changed little over hundreds of years. Home production of coverlets continued in the Southern Highlands of Kentucky, Tennessee, West Virginia, and North Carolina throughout the nineteenth century.

Both home and professional weavers made coverlets. Early home weavers worked at massive "barn-frame" looms, so-called because they were made from the same heavy hewn timbers used to build houses and barns. These somewhat crude and cumbersome looms were operated with a hand shuttle and typically had four harnesses. Professionals, who usually wove on a commission basis, often used more complicated multi-harness looms with up to twelve harnesses, allowing finer, more intricate and elaborate weave structures. Although most professional weavers worked out of their own shops, some traveled from farm to farm to weave on their customers' looms. Most professionals worked with their customers, who often provided the

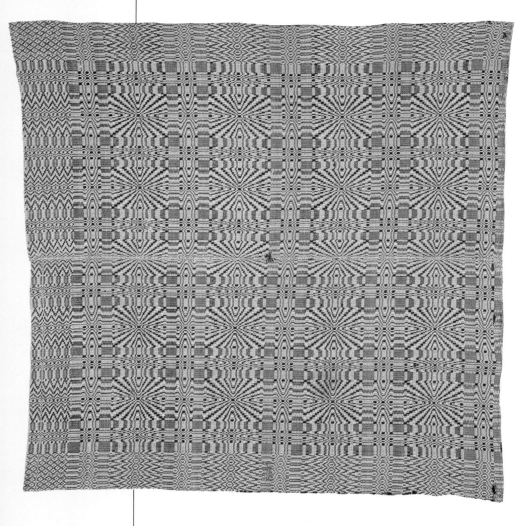

◄ OVERSHOT COVERLET

Artist unknown. c. 1825–1850. Probably Pennsylvania. Red, green, and dark blue wools with natural cotton. 70 x 68 in. Abby Aldrich Rockefeller Folk Art Center, Williamsburg, Virginia. Gift of Mrs. William John Bovaird.

Overshot coverlets, woven on hand looms, are named for the long lengths of weft thread that pass over the plain weave foundation to form the coverlet's geometric pattern. Overshot is the simplest of weave structures and was widely used by early American weavers. The main design of this coverlet is known as the Sunrise Pattern. The seven-inch green border at one end is in a pattern known as Bonaparte's March.

Aunt Lou Kitchen of Shootin' Creek, North Carolina, was a spinner and weaver. One of her coverlets hangs behind her in this c. 1930 photograph by Doris Ulmann.

Photograph, Berea College, Berea, Kentucky.

fiber for the piece and, in many cases, chose a pattern from the weaver's book of "drafts," a collection of designs drawn on paper and passed like quilt patterns from one craftsperson to the next.

The simplest and most common weave structure, used extensively by both home and professional weavers, is "overshot." In this technique, horizontal wool weft threads are passed over several strands of vertical cotton warp at regular intervals to form geometric patterns. "Summer and winter" weave also floats weft over warp but at much closer intervals, thus creating a tighter weave structure. This technique creates reverse sides that are mirror images of each other, one dark and one light in color. It is believed that the name *summer and winter* comes from the juxtaposition of light and dark sides that characterizes these coverlets. While both overshot and summer and winter coverlets were made by home weavers, the more complex "double" weave, which required a multiharness loom, was the realm of the professional. As the name implies, the double weave technique creates a two-layered textile made up of double sets of warp and weft threads joined together at regular intervals. Like summer and winter weave, double weave produces a mirror image textile, with one side the reverse of the other in color and pattern.

The introduction of the Jacquard loom in the 1820s revolutionized textile production. The new loom used a binary system of punched cards, often cited as a forerunner of the computer, to regulate the lifting of warp threads. The Jacquard facilitated the weaving process enormously and also allowed the creation of complex curved patterns. Most Jacquard coverlets included elaborate borders, often made up of repeating figurative designs such as trains, birds, buildings, or trees, as well as signature blocks at each of the four corners where the weaver could fashion a design around his unique logo including the name and address of his patron and the date of completion. Harry Tyler of Jefferson County, New York, for example, identified his coverlets with a lion, and David Haring of Bergen County, New Jersey, with a rose and four leaves.

Coverlets were not the only type of weaving practiced in the nineteenth century. Among the most interesting resulted from the attempt by the Shaker communities of Pleasant Hill and South Union, Kentucky, to establish silk production in this country. Beginning in the 1830s, both communities grew silkworms and laboriously spun and dyed the silk thread that had been harvested from the cocoons. A few beautifully colored and finely woven kerchiefs remain to document the aesthetic, if not financial, success of the venture.

Coverlet weaving, which greatly declined in popularity in the late 1800s, was at the forefront of the revival of traditional American crafts in the early decades of the twentieth century. Throughout the rural South, where a number of older weavers had continued the tradition, men and women were again attracted to both the creative challenge of weaving and its potential as a source of income. By the late 1930s, hand weaving, helped by the introduction of smaller and easier-to-use looms, was the dominant home "industry" of the Southern Highlands. It was taught at dozens of schools and colleges, and handmade coverlets were offered for sale to outsiders by many craft guilds. The back-to-the-land freethinkers of the 1960s generated widespread interest in hand weaving as they stubbornly sought to immerse themselves in the do-it-yourself charms of making one's own clothes and bedding from start to finish. Hand weaving's intimate connections to our culture's most basic longings for self-reliance, independence, and creative expression have engaged thousands of craftspeople to continue the tradition, and its survival now seems assured.

▲ WOOL BLANKETS

Artists unknown. Nineteenth century. Western Virginia. Wool and linen. Collection of Roddy and Sally Moore.

Home weavers throughout the country made blankets and a variety of other household textiles, often using wool sheared from their own sheep. These blankets made in German settlements in western Virginia are notable for the intense colors of the dyed wool from which they were woven. The green, yellow, and purple blanket is from Shenandoah County, while the middle two are from nearby Rockingham County, both located in the west central region of the state. The plaid blanket at the bottom is from Wythe County, and the gray, purple, and red striped blanket resting on top is from Botetourt County, both located in southwest Virginia.

NECKERCHIEFS ▶

Unknown Shaker artists. c. 1830–1850. South Union, Kentucky. Silk. Shakertown, South Union, Kentucky.

Shakers in Kentucky, who began importing and cultivating silk worms in the late 1820s, were among the first Americans to grow their own silk. Shaker historian Henry Blinn wrote of Pleasant Hill in 1873, "[We] visit[ed] the house where they [were] feeding silk worms. Several thousand were laid upon shelves and fed with the leaves of the mulberry. The sister who had charge of them would pick them up and call them 'pretty little creatures.' " Shaker weavers created subtle, shimmering, iridescent effects by using different color threads for warp and weft.

This c. 1930 photograph by Doris Ulmann shows a weaver working at a typical barn-frame loom. These massive, homemade looms were used throughout the United States to make overshot coverlets and other household textiles.

Photograph, Berea College, Berea, Kentucky.

CHIEF'S BLANKET ▶

Unknown Navajo Indian artist. c. 1840. New Mexico. Wool. 55 x 70 in. Joshua Baer and Company, Santa Fe, New Mexico.

Early Navajo wearing blankets like this rare example were renowned in their time for their extremely fine and dense weave structures, which repelled water, wind, and dust, keeping the wearer warm and dry. They were called chief's blankets because their high cost and trading value made them accessible only to those men and women of high rank.

▲ SERAPE

Unknown Navajo Indian artist. c. 1880. New Mexico. Wool. 75 x 50 in. Joshua Baer and Company, Santa Fe, New Mexico.

Serapes were longer-than-wide blankets adapted by the Navajo from Mexican precedents. This "eye-dazzler" is woven from brightly colored, analine-dyed Germantown wools, named for the Pennsylvania town where much of the commercially spun wool originated.

▼ CHIEF'S BLANKET

Unknown Navajo Indian artist. c. 1870. New Mexico. Wool. Height: 61 7/16 in. Denver Art Museum, Denver, Colorado.

So-called Phase III chief's blankets like this example combine bold quarter-, half-, and full-diamond forms with the simple traditional striping of the classic Phase I pattern.

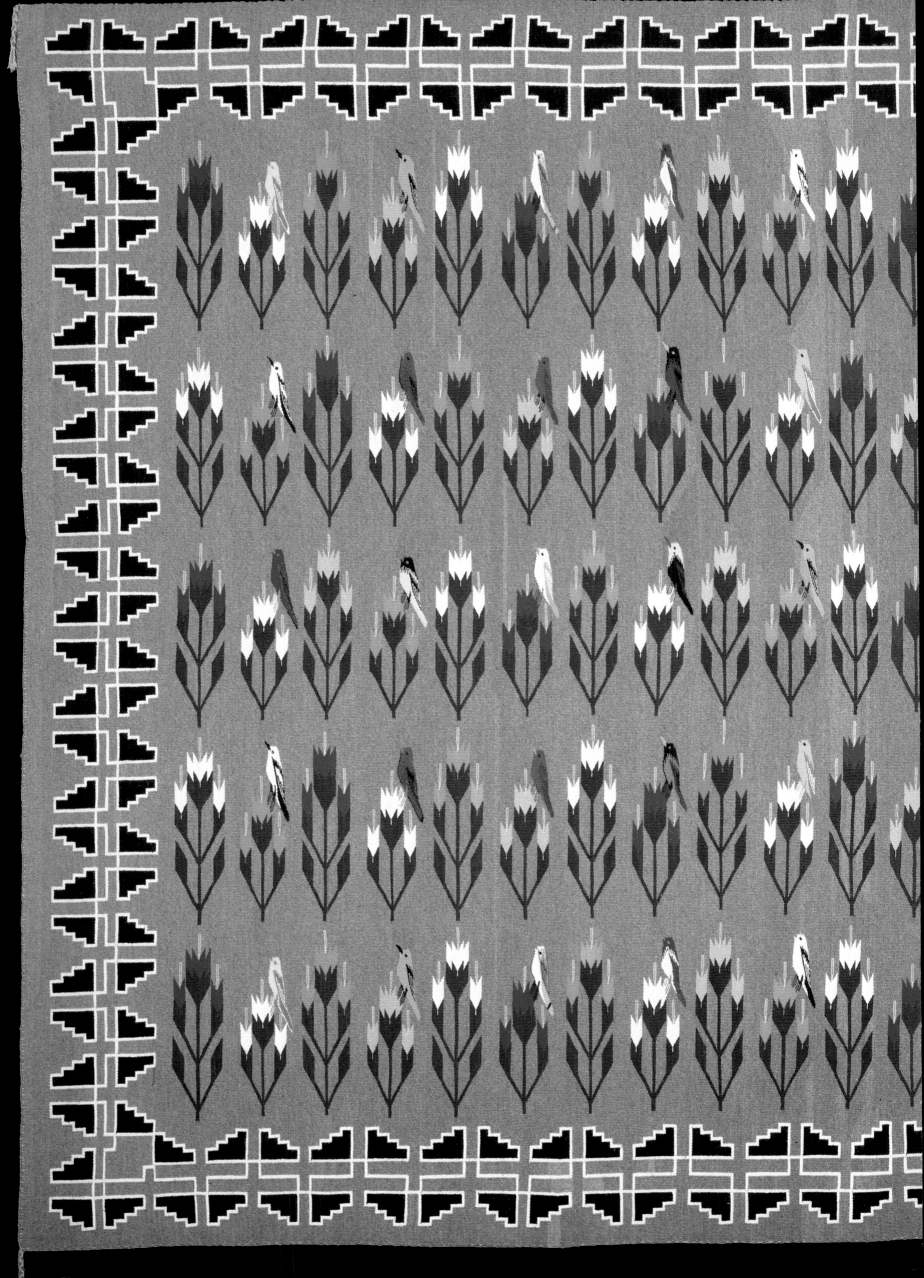

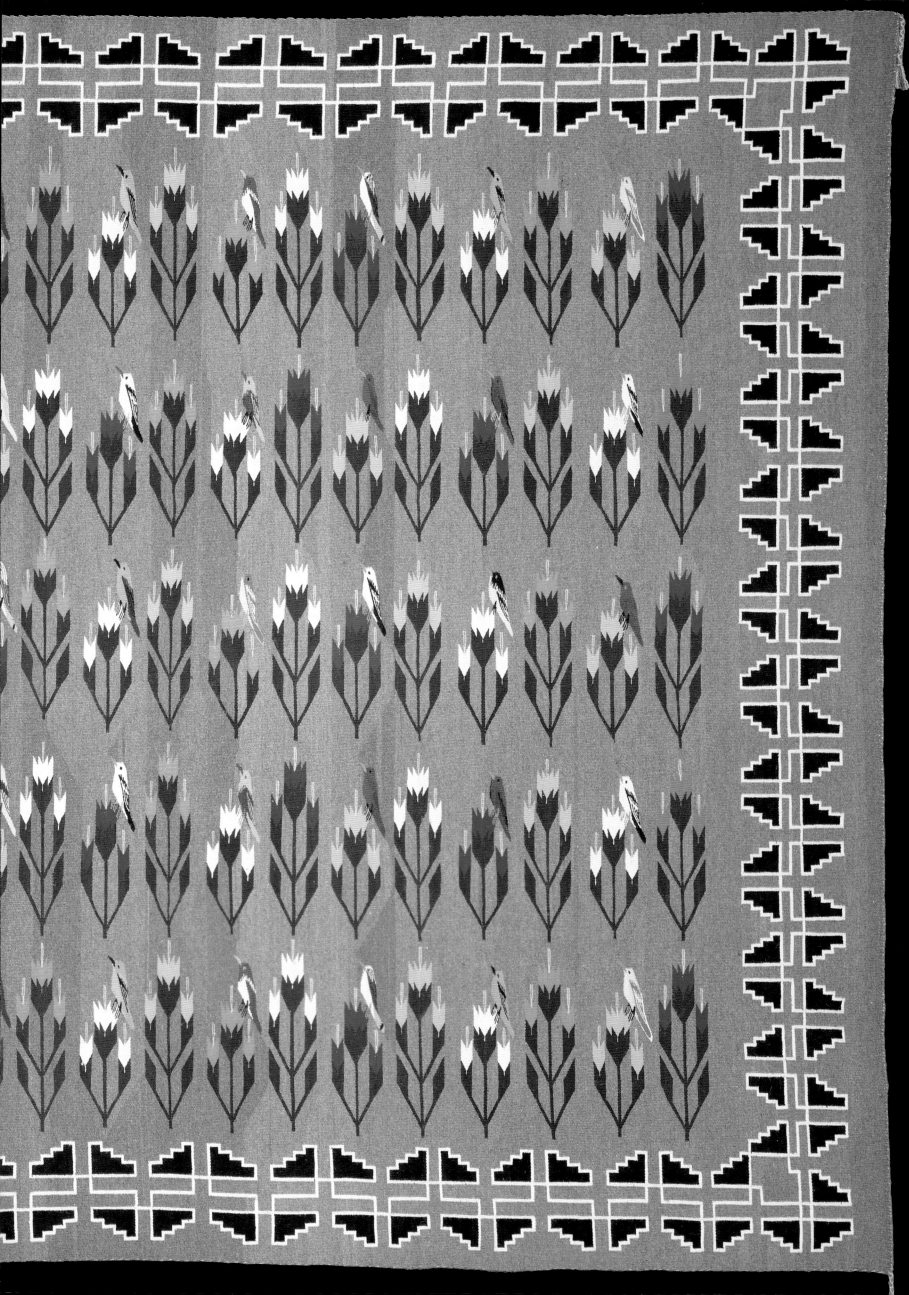

▲ CHARM BAG

Unknown Mesquakie Indian artist. c. 1880. Tama, Iowa. Wool yarn, cotton cord, glass beads. Height: 3 7/8 in., width: 5 3/8 in. © The Detroit Institute of Arts, Detroit, Michigan. Museum Purchase with funds from the state of Michigan, the city of Detroit, and the Founders Society.

Small, handwoven charm bags, decorated with intricate geometric and pictorial designs, were used by some Prairie Indians to hold sacred personal objects. Like sashes, these bags were woven without a loom.

◄ BIRD AND CORNSTALK RUG

Asan Yellowhair. 1983. New Mexico. Wool and commercial dyes. 94 x 131 in. Denver Art Museum, Denver, Colorado.

This large, contemporary rug features an original repeating pattern of colorful finches and tanagers perched on cornstalks topped with red, yellow, gold, or white ears. The bold geometric border seems to be on a different plane than the birds and flowers it contains. All the patterns are set against a subdued, neutral-colored field.

SASH ►

Unknown Osage Indian artist. c. 1890. Oklahoma. Wool yarn, glass beads. Length (including fringe): 84 1/8 in., width: 5 in. © The Detroit Institute of Arts, Detroit, Michigan. Museum Purchase with funds from the state of Michigan, the city of Detroit, and the Founders Society.

Sashes, worn around the waist, over the shoulder, or wrapped around the forehead, were a traditional item of clothing woven by many eastern Woodland peoples. Sashes were woven without a loom using a technique similar to braiding. Strings of tiny glass beads were often mixed into the patterns of the yarns. In the late 1800s, the sash was adopted by Prairie peoples like the Osage, who favored brightly colored commercial yarns.

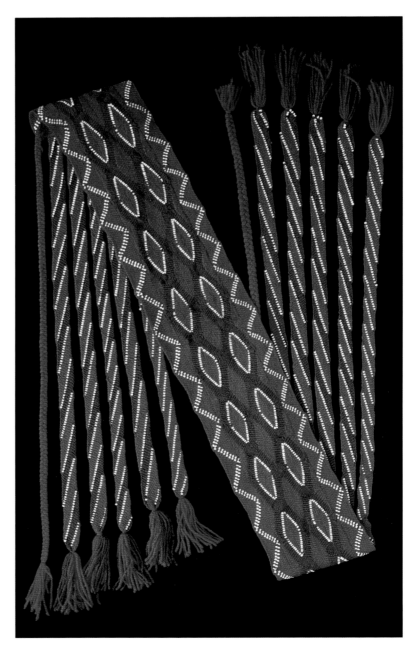

▾ DOUBLE CLOTH COVERLET

Artist unknown. c. 1825. Possibly New York. Cotton and wool. 91 x 75 in. The Metropolitan Museum of Art, New York. Gift of Margaret and Richard Parish, in memory of their paternal grandparents Rebecca and Festus Parish, 1984.

Double cloth coverlets, usually the products of professional weavers, were made of double sets of warp and weft threads, woven simultaneously on a multiharness loom. The layers were joined by interweaving at set intervals. This process created a warm, thick, reversible bedcover, usually with dark-colored wool on the top and light-colored cotton on the reverse side. This example uses the Virginia Beauty pattern with a Pine Tree border.

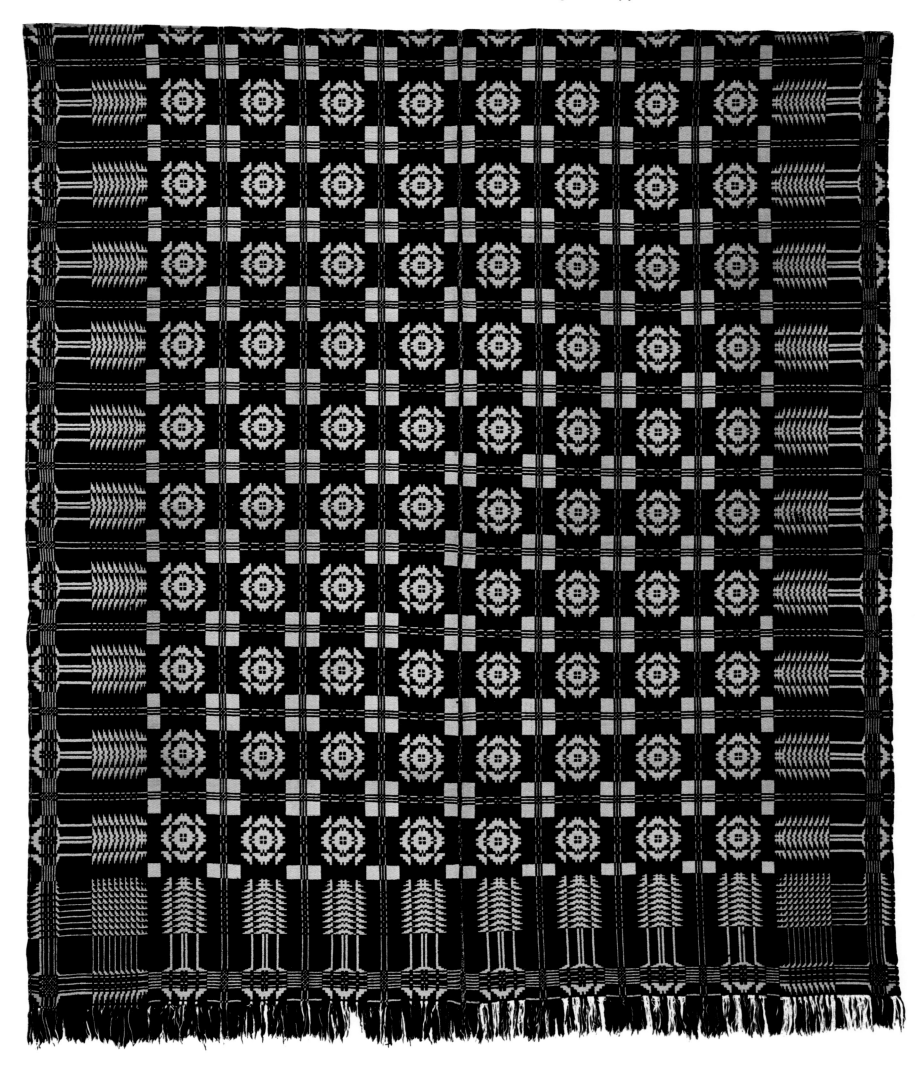

FOUR ROSES CENTERFIELD VARIATION COVERLET WITH LION AND TREE BORDER ▸

Gottfried Kappel. c. 1830–1850. Zoar, Ohio. Warp: natural cotton, weft: natural cotton and dark blue and red wool. 79 x 77 in. Illinois State Museum Collection, Springfield, Illinois. Gift of Benjamin and Evangeline Hunter.

Gottfried Kappel was the master weaver at Zoar, site of a German religious sect's communal settlement. His tied-Beiderwand coverlet, in which two layers of fabric are completely tied together in the weave, was woven on a Jacquard loom.

DOUBLE BOWKNOT AND WINDOW SASH COVERLET ▾

Artist unknown. c. 1830–1860. Region unknown. Warp: natural cotton, weft: dark blue and magenta wool. 88 x 68 in. Illinois State Museum Collection, Springfield, Illinois.

This pattern is sometimes called Ladies' Delight or Gentleman's Fancy. The beautiful magenta color was achieved with natural dye, which was either cochineal, a pigment derived from a type of beetle, or brazilwood.

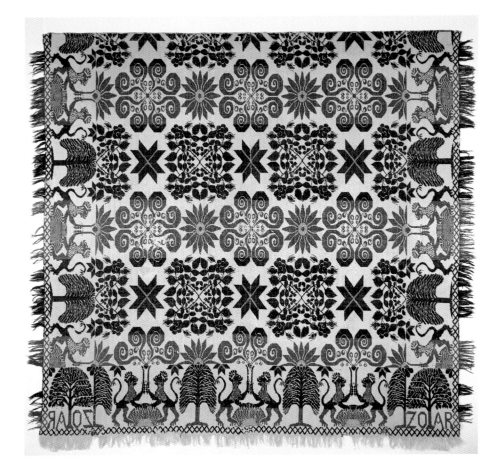

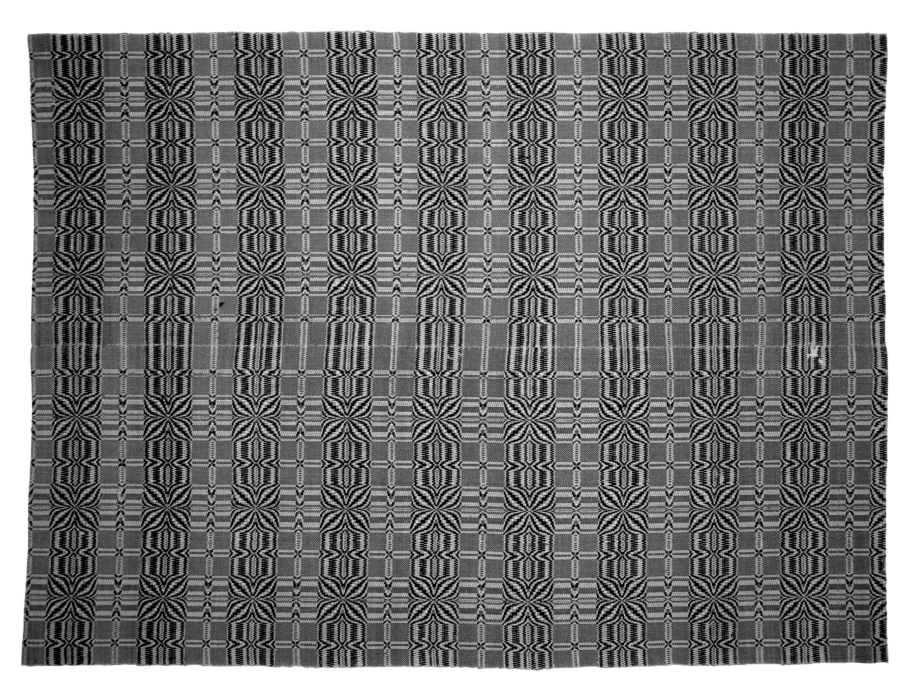

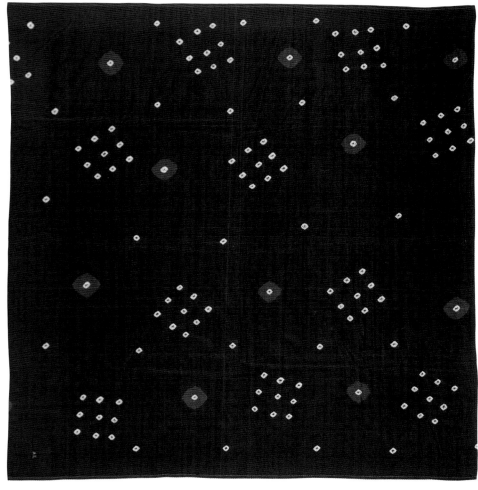

▲ JACQUARD COVERLET (DETAIL)

Harry Tyler. 1840. Butterville Township, Jefferson County, New York. Cotton and wool. 83 x 74 in. The Shelburne Museum, Shelburne, Vermont.

Many professional Jacquard weavers used representational corner block designs to identify their work. Tyler's signature was the bold, stylized lion. This coverlet was made for Ruth C. Clark.

◄ TIE-DYED NECKERCHIEF

Unknown Shaker artist. c. 1840–1875. Probably woven at South Union or Pleasant Hill, Kentucky; tie-dyed at Alfred, Maine. Silk. 32 x 33 1/4 in. Collection of Julio C. Caro.

Silk produced and woven in Kentucky was sold or bartered to other Shaker communities. A handful of strikingly modern-looking tie-dyed neckerchiefs are known to have been made at Alfred.

H O O K E D ,   S E W N , A N D   E M B R O I D E R E D   R U G S

In early America, floors were bare and ruggs (*sic*) were reserved for beds. Bed rugs were in common use until after the Revolution; lighter weight and equally warm quilts did not become the dominant bedcover until the early 1800s. The now quaint and curious expression "snug as a bug in a rug" recalls that early era when thick and rarely washed layers of bedding sometimes housed unpleasant and unwelcome company.

Bed rugs were heavy and bulky. They were made of thick wool yarn looped in running stitches through a woven wool or linen fabric ground. Making a bed rug was a complicated project. The elaborate overall floral designs favored for bed rugs demanded careful planning. Yarn was made at home and dyed to the desired hues using natural dyes. Then the pattern was laid out and many hours were spent stitching the yarn through the ground. Of the fewer than fifty existing bed rugs, many are signed and dated in needlework by their makers—a gesture signifying well-deserved pride in the completion of an extraordinary task.

Floor rugs came into common use in the early years of the nineteenth century, just as the bed rug, perhaps coincidentally, was falling from favor. The earliest floor rugs were made in the same way as bed rugs, that is, by sewing yarn in a running stitch through a woven backing. Unlike bed rugs, however, in which the stitched yarn was most often left uncut, most yarn-sewn floor rugs had clipped surfaces. Thick, yarn-sewn rugs were usually fairly small in size and were used primarily as hearthrugs and decorative table covers.

Another early rug-making method called "shirring" became popular in the 1830s as manufactured fabrics became more widely available and women sought to reuse scraps of clothing and other household fabrics in their rugs. Cotton scraps were far too thick to sew through a foundation so rug makers developed an appliqué technique in which the scraps of cloth were sewn onto, rather than drawn through, the backing. Three different shirring variations were developed. The easiest, and therefore most common, was chenille or "caterpillar" shirring, named for its puckered, gathered surface, which resembled a hunched inchworm. The caterpillars were created by sewing a running stitch down the

◄ KNIT CARPET

Unknown Shaker artist. c. 1890–1895. Probably Hancock, Massachusetts. Wool yarn with braided cloth border. Diameter: 19 in. Collection of George W. Sieber.

This late Shaker rug was possibly knitted by Sister Elvira Curtis Hulett (1807–1895) of Hancock. The rug reflects the less austere and more worldly attitude of late nineteenth-century Shaker society. The knitted patterns are quite complex throughout and include a variety of plied combinations, achieved by knitting two or more color yarns together.

*Mrs. Anderson and her son of Saluda, North Carolina, are
shown hooking a rug from rag-bag scraps in this c. 1930 photograph by Doris Ulmann.*

Photograph, Berea College, Berea, Kentucky.

center of a strip of cloth and then pulling the
thread to gather the fabric. The resulting caterpillars were then appliquéd to the backing. In
bias shirring, strips of cloth were cut on the bias
(across the grain of the fabric) and folded lengthwise. The folded edges of the strips were then
sewn to the foundation, leaving the loose edges
facing up to create the pile. In pleated shirring,
the most technically difficult and therefore most
infrequently used variation, strips of cloth were
folded sideways many times, then attached to the
backing by sewing between each pleat.

Hooking, destined to become the dominant rug-making method, first became popular in the 1840s.
Like shirring, hooking allowed the use of readily available rag-bag material to make rugs. Instead of
sewing the fabric to the ground, however, hookers used a small tool to pull thin strips of rag through
the backing material. The first surge of interest in hooking was buoyed during the 1840s when
resourceful housewives discovered they could recycle loosely woven burlap grain sacks as backing for
their hooked rugs. These sacks made an ideal ground for hooked rugs
because they were strong and durable and it was relatively easy to draw bits
of rag through their coarse weave. Many Americans could not afford to buy
the fashionable, new factory-made carpets for their homes. The combination
of the grain sack and the rag bag made attractive rugs accessible to anyone
with needlecraft skills, which meant virtually any woman in America in the
mid-nineteenth century.

Unlike yarn sewing and shirring, both of which had been practiced in
Europe, hooking seems to have originated in America. Several researchers
have suggested that sailors in the seaside communities of New England used
tools similar to the rug hook to work with strands of rope. Many outstanding
early homemade examples of rug hooking have been found in Maine in
particular, as well as the neighboring provinces of the Canadian Maritimes.
The region's early interest in rug making evolved into the establishment
of cottage industries late in the nineteenth century, and hooking continues to
the present day.

RAINBOW AND HOUSE RUG ▸

*Lucy Barnard. c. 1860. Dixfield Common, Maine. 29 x 60 in. The Metropolitan Museum of Art,
New York. Sansbury-Mills Fund, 1961.*

*Three remarkable rugs by Lucy Barnard are preserved at the Metropolitan Museum of Art. All
three feature a large white house on a hill with connected stables. This one, with a rainbow encir-
cling the house and a pair of bold trees framing it, is the most dramatic of the three. In the left
foreground, a couple rows a canoe on a pond.*

Like the quilter, the rug hooker usually worked at a frame, which could be oriented either vertically or horizontally. The design was often drawn on the backing with pencil or charcoal as a guide. Although some hookers adapted the repeating geometric patterns popular for quilts, most designed their rugs as overall pictures, using appealing and familiar scenes for inspiration. Not surprisingly, flowers, animals, and houses were among the most common design elements chosen for rugs. While, like pieced quilts, the majority of hooked rugs were attractive but unimaginative, a number of successful rug designs may be seen as fabric paintings, in which scraps of material function as an artist's palette to create original and expressive visual statements.

As rug hooking grew in popularity many housewives sought designs they could copy. Several entrepreneurs supplied this need by offering easy-to-follow patterns, which provided the design and left the choice of material up to the hooker. Beginning in the late 1860s, Edward Sands Frost, a Maine tin peddler, designed an extremely successful group of patterns for hooked rugs. His designs were imprinted on metal templates and then stenciled in color on burlap. A woman had only to hook directly through the stenciled design to create the piece. The most popular of the 180 available designs featured stiffly posed animals, both wild and domestic, and/or flowers; several patterns also included floral borders, and a number imitated expensive Oriental rugs. Frost's "color-by-number" rug patterns were first marketed door-to-door and later, after he had sold the company, by catalogue. E. S. Frost & Co. remained in business until 1900.

Other rug-making methods using fabric scraps also were devised, including braiding, crocheting, and knitting. Because these methods did not require the use of a backing, the resulting rugs had the distinct advantage of being reversible and therefore were longer wearing. Braided rugs, made by wrapping strips of rag around each other in long, thick oval or circular bands, were extremely versatile and

Molly Nye Tobey of Barrington, Rhode Island, was a professionally trained textile designer. However, she found more creative satisfaction in hand-hooked rugs than in factory design. She is shown at work in her living room in this c. 1930 photograph.

Courtesy of The Shelburne Museum, Shelburne, Vermont.

especially durable. While braided rugs were made throughout the nineteenth century, they became a particular favorite of early twentieth-century rug makers and, while most are now machine made, they are the most commonly encountered traditional American rug today.

Despite the increasingly widespread availability and affordability of manufactured carpets in the later years of the nineteenth century, many rural craftspeople continued to make rugs for their own use. In the 1920s hooked rugs rode a wave of renewed popular interest. Many homemakers learned the craft so that they, like generations of women before them, could supply handmade rugs for their homes. Old rugs, many of which had been set aside for years, were recovered from families' barns, back rooms, and attics (a large floral rug now in the collection of The Shelburne Museum had been relegated to serving as a cover for the woodpile) and touted as important American handcrafts by curators, collectors, and dealers. Rugs were featured in the new *Magazine* ANTIQUES alongside Chippendale high chests and Sandwich glass. Collectors sought outstanding examples, which sold for record prices at auction until the onset of the Depression when the burgeoning market in early American antiques slowed drastically. At the same time, rural entrepreneurs took advantage of the resurgent interest in traditional handcrafts by organizing cooperative groups of hookers and offering rugs made by members of the group in home decorating magazines and city marketplaces. Rug-making co-ops, organized in Maine, northern Massachusetts, Kentucky, North Carolina, and several other states, offered a stock set of designs to their customers; handcrafted quality, not individual creativity, was the selling point. Many rural men and women took up the craft as a means of income, thus rekindling and perpetuating the tradition, albeit on a more uniform and commercial basis. Some sophisticated city designers also became fascinated with the possibilities of the craft. Molly Nye Tobey, for example, a graduate of the prestigious Rhode Island School of Design and a successful textile designer, turned her attention to hooked rugs in the 1940s and over time executed a series of fifty state rugs, emphasizing flora, fauna, minerals, and other phenomena commonly associated with each state.

Like many other traditional handcrafts, rug hooking has enjoyed a tremendous burst of popularity in the past fifteen years. Among traditional textile arts, hooking is second only to quilting in popularity and is practiced by tens of thousands of women in all areas of the country. As was the case one hundred years ago, predesigned patterns are readily available, many in kit forms that include material, hook, and instructions. A number of talented professional handcrafters offer traditional rugs, many of original design, for use and display. Creative home hookers and textile artists are also stretching the limits of traditional design and, as their forerunners did, discovering ways to use the techniques to express contemporary ideas.

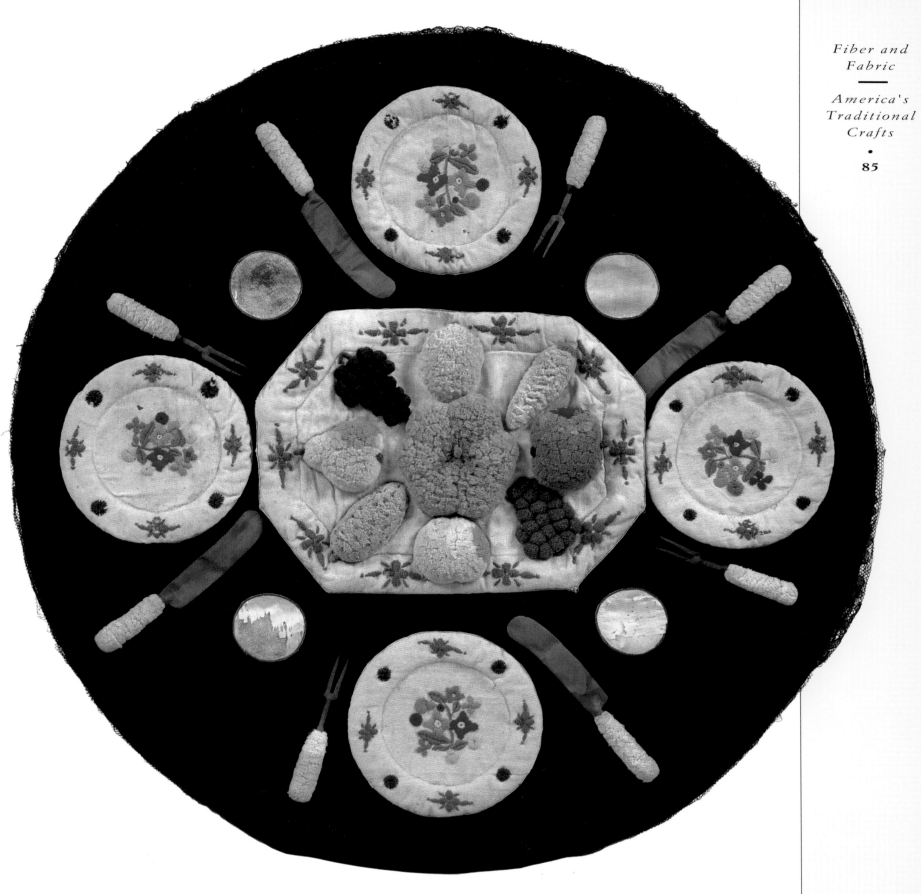

▲ TROMPE L'OEIL TABLE RUG

Artist unknown. Second half of the nineteenth century. Southeastern Pennsylvania. Appliquéd cotton and silk on wool. Diameter: 33 in. The Schwenkfelder Library, Pennsburg, Pennsylvania.

Although the eye at first refuses to accept the fact, the place settings, complete with detailed floral pattern china, are actually made up of pieces of fabric appliquéd into place, as is the mouthwatering platter of fruits and vegetables at center.

BED RUG ▶

*Artist unknown. c. 1800–1820. Lower
Connecticut River Valley. Wool yarn hooked
on handmade wool blanket. 92 x 81 in.
Hempsted House Collection, The Antiquarian
and Landmarks Society, Hartford, Connecticut.
Gift of Katherine Prentis Murphy.*

*This bright, sunny bed rug has a relaxed and
open design, with a pleasing array of meander-
ing vines and cheerful flowers.*

▼ FANTASY GARDEN RUG

*Artist unknown. c. 1800. Northeastern United States. Yarn sewn on madder-dyed linen. 17 1/4 x 29 1/4 in. Collection of Jonathan
Holstein and Gail van der Hoof.*

*Tiny houses are overwhelmed by gigantic flowers in this imaginative yarn-sewn rug. Additional flowers, framed in black squares at
the upper corners, and randomly placed triangles add complexity and intrigue to the design.*

MARY COMSTOCK'S BED RUG ▸

Mary Comstock. 1810. Shelburne, Vermont. Handspun wool yarns sewn on handwoven wool twill blanket. 84 1/4 x 76 in. The Shelburne Museum, Shelburne, Vermont. Gift of Mrs. Henry Tracy.

Heavy, wool bed rugs were popular bedcoverings in early New England. Mary Comstock was sixty-six years old when she completed her rug on January 30, 1810. Like the majority of bed rugs, this rug's design is dominated by a central image of enormous flowers growing from a small pot, a motif related to the tree-of-life found in many early quilts.

SHIRRED SPIRALS RUG ▶

Artist unknown. c. 1825. Region unknown. Bias shirring, yarn sewn, and wool embroidery on linen. 35 1/2 x 55 1/4 in. The Henry Francis du Pont Winterthur Museum, Winterthur, Delaware.

This rug's stars and circles are shirred, while the animals are embroidered. The black horse in the border upsets the expectations of regularity created by the fairly consistent rhythms of the other design elements.

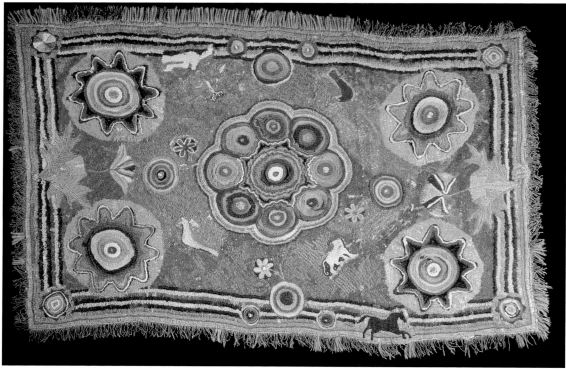

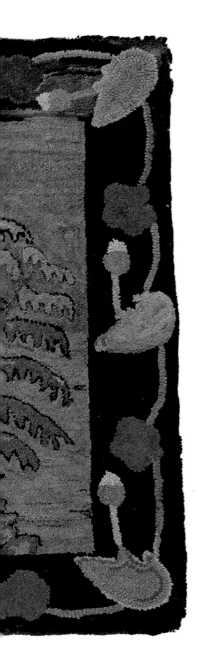

◄ LEOPARD RUG

Artist unknown. c. 1820–1830. New England. Wool yarns sewn on plain-weave wool ground. 37 x 70 in. The Shelburne Museum, Shelburne, Vermont.

This rug probably served as a hearthrug: a decorative cover for the stone in front of the fireplace, used during the warm summer months. The ferocious beast and coconut tree may have been inspired by an illustrated natural history book.

▼ PICTURE BLOCK TABLE RUG

Artist unknown. c. 1845. Region unknown. Wool appliqué on woolen ground. 37 x 54 in. Collection America Hurrah, New York.

Table rugs dressed early American tables for company or special occasions. This table rug was probably made by an experienced quilter who organized it in appliquéd blocks surrounded by a border of trailing vines. Both techniques were common in contemporary quilting, but rarely used in rugs. The scalloped outside border echoes the rhythm of the vines and provides a welcome contrast to the straight edges of the central blocks.

▼ THE CASWELL CARPET

Zeruah Higley Guernsey Caswell. 1835. Castleton, Vermont. Wool embroidery on wool. 13 ft. 3 in. x 12 ft. 3 in. The Metropolitan Museum of Art, New York. Gift of Katharine Keyes, 1938, in memory of her father, Homer Eaton Keyes.

This monumental embroidered rug is the undisputed masterpiece among American carpets. It is an incomparable technical and imaginative tour de force. Zeruah Caswell sheared the wool used in the rug from her own sheep, dyed it herself, and spun it on a wheel made by her father. Each of the over seventy different blocks is embroidered with a unique, original floral or representational design.

The carpet was made specifically to fit the Caswell family's living room. The long floral panel at the far left, set at a right angle to the rest of the blocks, was used to cover the hearthstone during the summer months and could be removed in winter when it was not needed and might have been burned by sparks from a blazing fire.

▲ HOOKED RUG WITH STARS, CRESCENT, AND FRETS

Artist unknown. After 1850. Region unknown. Hooked wool on burlap. 30 1/2 x 48 1/4 in. National Museum of American Art, Smithsonian Institution, Washington, D.C. Gift of Herbert Waide Hemphill and museum purchase made possible by Ralph Cross Johnson.

This unique rug's design is both charming and perplexing. The eleven stars and crescent moon are seemingly of some significance, as is the amorphous silhouetted shape at lower right. All these elements must have had clear and special meaning to the maker, but unfortunately their sense is lost to modern viewers.

SPANIELS RUG ▶

Artist unknown. c. 1870–1900. New England. Wool. 31 x 46 in. The Shelburne Museum, Shelburne, Vermont.

This richly colored and shaggy-fringed rug was probably based on a commercial pattern, although the woman who hooked the rug made a number of imaginative changes that bring movement and interest to the typically stiff and impersonal composition offered by the original pattern. Farm animals and pets were among the most common subjects for pictorial rugs.

HEART-IN-HAND RUG ▶

Artist unknown. c. 1875. New Jersey. Wool on burlap. 38 x 22 in. Collection America Hurrah, New York.

The heart-in-hand was a common motif of the Independent Order of Odd Fellows, one of the most prominent of the many fraternal organizations in eighteenth- and nineteenth-century America. All eight hands in this rug hold a heart, and the inner and outer hands are connected by the vines.

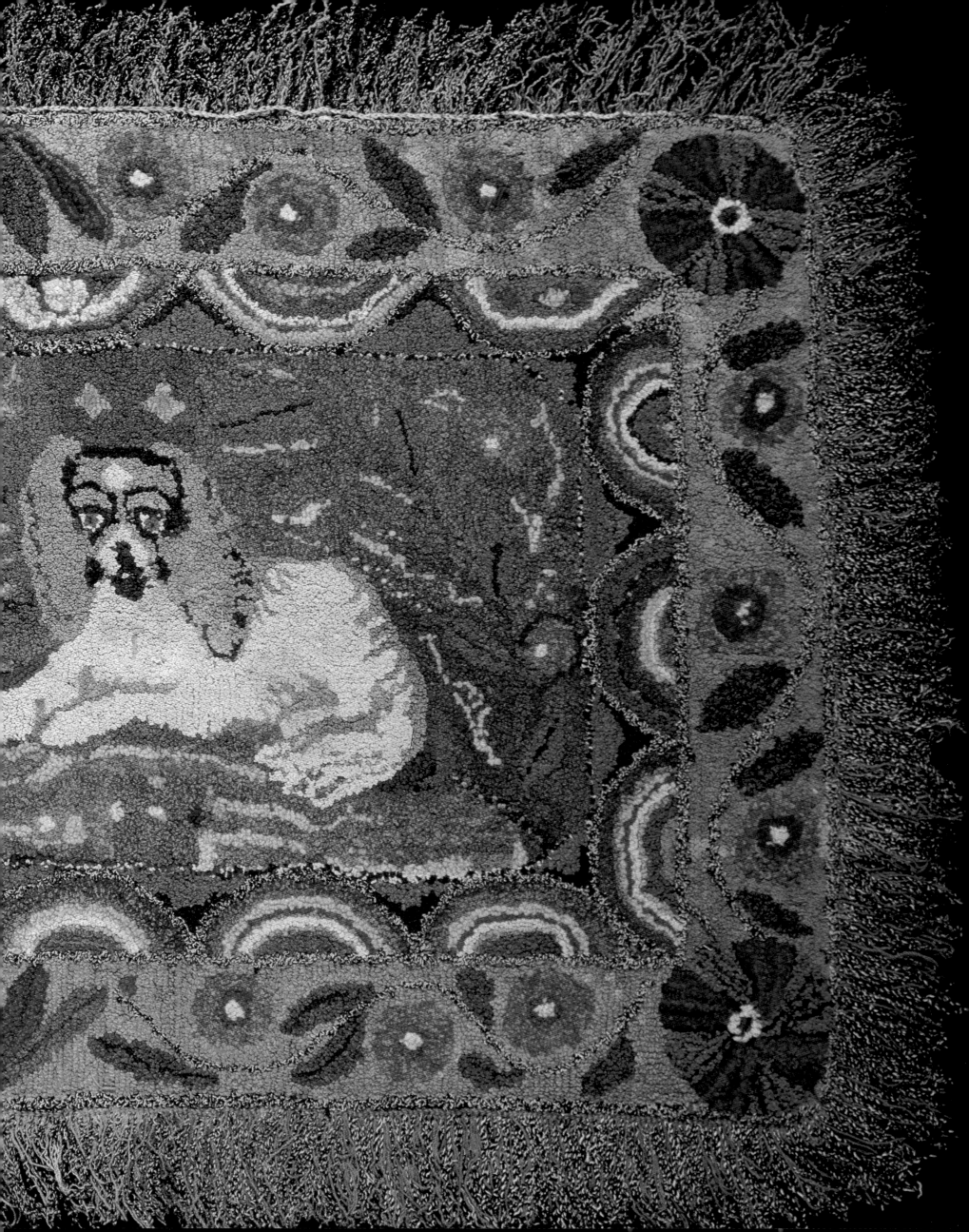

BLACKSTONE FAMILY RUG ▶

Eleanor Blackstone. c. 1885. Lacon, Illinois. Wool, cotton, and human hair. 94 x 117 in.
Henry Ford Museum and Greenfield Village, Dearborn, Michigan.

This enormous rug is one of several worked by Mrs. Blackstone during the 1880s. Three are pre-
served in public collections (two at Greenfield Village and the third at the Metropolitan
Museum of Art), and a fourth remains in private hands. Portraits of Mrs. Blackstone's six chil-
dren, which go so far as to incorporate locks of each child's hair, fill the rugs, along with images
of favorite toys and pets. Two of the Blackstone daughters, Blanche and Anne, are believed to
have assisted in making the rugs, which commemorate family milestones and events and include
a number of Biblical verses.

▼ KNITTED "SAMPLER" RUG

Attributed to Sister Elvira C. Hulett. c. 1892. Hancock, Massachusetts. Wool. 36 x 27 in.
Collection of Mr. and Mrs. George Shaw.

In the late Victorian age, dwindling Shaker communities were compelled to relax their strin-
gently ordered codes of behavior in order to attract (and keep) new members. With the loosen-
ing of restrictions came more worldly tastes in decoration. A rug as freely designed and colorful
as this one would have been unthinkable among Shakers a generation earlier.

BRAIDED CIRCLES RUG ▶

Artist unknown. c. 1890. New England. Wool and cotton. 79 x 105 in. The Shelburne Museum, Shelburne, Vermont.

This unusual room-sized rug combines small and large braided circles with a geometric hooked background in a vibrant overall composition.

▲ "PENNY" TABLE RUG

Artist unknown. 1893. New England. Appliquéd and embroidered wool on machine-pieced cotton backing. 42 x 47 in. The Shelburne Museum, Shelburne, Vermont. Gift of Mrs. Evelyn W. Lamplough.

This "penny" rug, so named for its many fabric circles, was used as a cover for a round Victorian parlor table. One wonders if the design, which moves from the thirty-six mittens in the outside ring to the six birds surrounding the central date, reflects the changes in season as work on the rug progressed.

CALIFORNIA HOOKED RUG ▶

Molly Nye Tobey. c. 1950. Barrington, Rhode Island. Wool on burlap. 72 1/2 x 40 in. The Shelburne Museum, Shelburne, Vermont. Gift of Joel, Jonathan, and Joshua Tobey.

Mrs. Tobey's California rug, one of fifty state rugs she hooked between 1943 and 1961, includes a colorful array of fruits and vegetables grown in the state, and top and bottom borders full of blue whales.

B A S K E T S

Basketry is the oldest and most widely practiced of all handcrafts, outdating pottery by thousands of years. Virtually every society on earth has employed readily available plant fibers to create such vital and useful objects as food gathering and storage containers, clothing, and even shelters. Plant fibers such as grass, cane, twigs, branches, and bark provided early peoples with strong, durable, lightweight, flexible materials that could be woven, twisted, or coiled into a variety of forms that retained or even amplified the highly desirable properties of the medium. Basketry requires only the simplest of wood-splitting and cutting tools, used to gather and shape the plant material to be worked. It is truly a "hand" craft, dependent only on the work of strong and skillful hands in the manipulation of the medium for results of even the highest quality.

America's basketry traditions are ancient. Native American basket fragments, discovered in Utah's Danger Cave and carbon dated to be at least nine thousand years old, represent the earliest known examples of basketry in the world. Nomadic North American hunter/gatherers developed lightweight baskets and packs to gather and transport food, tools, clothing, and young children. The development of basketry is also closely linked with permanent human settlements and the practice of agriculture, which necessitated the availability of a variety of containers to assist in the planting, cultivation, harvesting, and storage of foodstuffs as well as the safekeeping of other material goods.

The earliest American baskets were made by Native Americans of the Southwest and were their most important material possessions. The ancient ancestors of the Anasazi and Pueblo people, who flourished from before the birth of Christ until about A.D. 700, are known to anthropologists as the Basket Makers because of the dominant role that the craft held in their societies. The Basket Makers' coiled and stitched baskets, often decorated with bold, geometric designs, served a variety of domestic and agricultural functions and set the high standard for basketry in the region, which continued for centuries among descendants such as the Pueblo, Hopi, and Zuni. Hopi basketry persists at a very high level of quality to the present day. Other unrelated nations that developed later in the Great Basin, such as the Navajo, Havasupai, Papago, and Pima, and most notably the Apache, also produced magnificent baskets that were of central importance to their cultures. The most common technique employed in southwestern basketry was coiling, achieved by sewing or weaving thin fibers around stationary horizontal hoops or circles. Initially, willow was the most favored material, followed, especially in later years, by yucca.

Europeans and their slaves brought influences from their own cultures to the practice of basketry, adapting American materials to their native traditions. The isolated African-American culture of the

◄ CAT-HEAD BASKET

Unknown Shaker artist. c. 1850. Probably New Lebanon, New York. Black ash splint. Height: 11 1/4 in., diameter: 10 1/4 in. Fruitlands Museum, Harvard, Massachusetts.

This small fancy basket, with its distinctively shaped bottom, was formed over a carved wooden mold. The use of molds allowed Shaker basket makers to create many virtually identical baskets of a particular style, which could be advertised and offered for sale to the "world." The lid of the basket slides up and down the handle but does not come off, thereby ensuring that the lid is not lost. Small, lidded baskets like this were often used to collect down or feathers.

Datsolalee, a Washo Indian basket maker, world-renowned in her lifetime, was photographed here in 1897.

Nevada State Museum, Carson City, Nevada.

▼ DEGIKUP (FOOD BOWL)

Datsolalee. 1917–1918. Oklahoma. Willow twigs, bracken fern stems, and redbud bark. Height: 12 in., maximum diameter: 16 1/4 in. Clark Field Collection, Philbrook Art Center, Tulsa, Oklahoma.

Datsolalee (meaning Broad-in-the-Hips) was a Washo Indian basket maker who achieved international recognition in her own lifetime for her extraordinary baskets. This basket, considered by many to be her masterpiece, was begun March 26, 1917, and completed February 16, 1918. A technical and artistic tour de force, the basket, which has an extremely tight weave structure, contains over 100,000 stitches—about thirty stitches per inch.

*Unknown northeastern Indian artist.
c. 1840–1860. New England. Brown
ash with paint decoration. 10 x 11 x
9 in. Collection of David A. Schorsch,
Inc., New York.*

*The crossed double handles of this
paint-decorated Indian basket are
quite unusual. Indian basket makers
of New England very often dyed or
painted the ash splints with which
they worked.*

South Carolina and Georgia
sea islands, for example, pre-
serves forms and methods
that may be traced to origins in west central Africa, while Pennsylvania Dutch baskets often show the
influence of Germanic coiled straw work or decorative painting traditions. Splint basketry, a technique
employing thin, flat strips of wood or other plant fiber, may have been introduced by either Latin
Americans or Europeans or both; however, the existence of several early seventeenth-century Indian
splint basket fragments suggests that precontact Indians may have understood the principles of splint
basketry as well.

Wood splint was the material most favored by European settlers for making baskets in nineteenth-
century America and was eagerly adopted by many Native American nations, most notably those in the
Northeast. Splint was gathered principally from ash in the Northeast and white oak in the South; both
trees provided strong but readily workable material. Wood splint was gathered and worked while still
wet, green, and pliable. Basket makers carefully selected trees for the straightness of their growth and
grain. After felling, each young tree yielded about six feet of usable wood, enough for six to eight baskets. The log was then split into vertical sections (usually quarters or eighths) and the bark removed.
After each vertical section had again been quartered, splints could be started with a knife and then
torn horizontally with the grain of the wood, parallel to the growth rings of the tree. Tearing, or *riving,*
splints was hard work and required great hand strength. Finally, the splints could be smoothed with a
knife or spokeshave.

Eastern Woodland Indian nations such as the Mohegan, Pequot, Micmac, Penobscot, Algonquin,
Passamaquoddy, and Wampanoag made many types of sturdy, functional splint storage and work baskets for their own use. The baskets were often covered and usually decorated with brightly colored
stamped or painted designs. Nineteenth-century northeastern Indians also adopted a wide range of
largely decorative European basket forms, which they sold to tourists. Catering to the Victorian preference for elaborate decoration, they made "fancy" sewing and trinket baskets with such special touches as braided sweetgrass embellishments, protruding "warted" and "porcupine twist" weave structures,
decorative handles, and dyed splint. The tourist trade continues to contribute to the vitality of Native
American basket-making traditions in the Northeast as well as in many other areas of the country.

*Fiber and
Fabric*

—

*America's
Traditional
Crafts*

•

102

Another notable Indian splint basket-making tradition is that practiced for generations among the Chitimacha people of Louisiana. Historically, the Chitimacha were the most advanced of southeastern basket makers, producing lidded, double-woven baskets with intricate and colorful twill-plaited weave patterns. Chitimacha baskets are made of river cane and feature tight-plaited geometric interweavings of dark brown, red, and natural splint. The natural splint is dyed red with bloodroot and dark brown with black walnuts or butternuts. Another southeastern people, the Cherokee of North Carolina, practice a related style of splint work using white oak. The most common decorative elements in these weave structures are diamond shapes, which also interweave red, brown, and natural splint. A number of craftspeople in both regions, such as Ada Thomas, a Chitimacha basket maker in Charenton, Louisiana, carry on the traditions today.

The Shakers, so accomplished at many types of handwork, began producing baskets for their own use soon after the first communities were established. Basket-making shops were an integral part of many Shaker communities, and by the 1840s the Shakers had established a firm reputation for their superbly made baskets. Most Shaker baskets were woven over wooden molds, using ash or hickory splint, and included a wide variety of sewing, work, and agricultural forms. Like all Shaker-made objects, they have clean, spare lines and crisp, symmetrical forms.

The quality of Shaker basketry remained so consistently high that it has often been a target for misattribution. For many years virtually any well-made basket with origins in New England or New York was dubbed Shaker. Recent scholarship has begun to sort what is truly Shaker made from what is not

and to accurately identify the source of the product's aesthetic value. For many years baskets made in the Taconic region of upstate New York were misidentified as Shaker; today the Taghkanic (the spelling of the original Indian word) basket-making tradition is recognized as important and distinct. Unlike other craftspeople, Taghkanic basket makers had access to oak, ash, and hickory and used all three woods in their work, often mixing woods in a single basket. Typically, Taghkanic baskets are round bottomed with wide rims that extend slightly out from the top of the basket. Taghkanic makers also developed a unique form of swing handle. Rather than attach the handle directly to the basket, they drilled holes at either end of the handle and then attached it to wooden loops set into the rim of the form.

From the 1850s until around 1895, another extraordinary group of baskets was made on Nantucket Island, thirty miles off the south coast of Cape Cod, where imported rattan was used to create distinctive, handled oval and circular forms with extremely tight and fine

◄ TALL STORAGE BASKET WITH BOWED SIDES

Unknown Shaker artist. c. 1850. Possibly Enfield, New Hampshire. Maple and ash splint. 25 x 15 x 15 in. Collection of David and Yvette Schorsch.

This unusual tall basket may have been used as a clothes hamper in a Shaker laundry room.

*Fiber and
Fabric*

*America's
Traditional
Crafts*
•
103

*Mitchell Ray made baskets on Nantucket until after World War II,
almost single-handedly keeping the tradition alive after it had stopped
aboard the lightship.*

*Collection of Nantucket Historical Association, Nantucket,
Massachusetts.*

weave structures. These so-called Nantucket lightship
baskets were first made by keepers of the New South
Shoals lightship, anchored off the treacherous coast of
the island where the building of a permanent lighthouse
was impossible. A tour of duty on the lightship might
last several months, with few responsibilities other than
the tending of the light. The time-consuming and intricate workmanship involved in crafting Nantucket lightship baskets helped some of the keepers pass their time
and also gave them a secondary source of income.
Lightship baskets have wooden bottoms and hickory or
oak ribs. They were formed around molds and were
often made in nested sets of three to eight baskets, with
incrementally smaller baskets made to fit tightly together. These baskets continued to be made on Nantucket
Island itself well into the twentieth century. Several contemporary craftspeople have revived and
updated the tradition in recent years, using traditional techniques to create such new forms as cradles
and women's pocketbooks.

Farther south, Appalachian basket makers worked with native white oak to create ribbed baskets for
agricultural and household uses. The most common ribbed form is built around two flat hoops that
intersect at right angles to form the handle and rim or spine of the basket. Ribs, often made of thin,
round strips of wood, splay off from the spine to form the rest of the basket's substructure and are
then interwoven with flat splints to complete the form. Appalachian makers often extended the ribs
out beyond the vertical hoop of the handle to form a "buttocks"-shaped bottom. These baskets are
especially lightweight and sturdy; they make extremely durable, long-lasting work baskets.

Basket making is very much alive today. Indeed, it ranks with quilting as the most widely and contin-
uously practiced of all traditional folk crafts. Perhaps this popularity can be linked to the fact that basket making has always been considered a "woman's craft" in most traditional communities. In these
communities, women remain, as a group, relatively isolated from the changes occurring in the population at large, and therefore often serve to protect their traditions. Today, dozens of makers all over the
country, men and women, white, African-American, and Indian alike, carry on family and local traditions unbroken from generation to generation. Appalachia in particular remains a center of traditional
basket making with many craftspeople carrying on long family traditions of white oak basket work.
Similarly, dozens of basket makers in the South Carolina low-country centered around Mt. Pleasant,
just north of Charleston, carry on the three-hundred-year-old sweetgrass basket-making tradition of
the region, selling their wares to tourists in city markets and shops as well as to travelers from stands
along Highway 17.

Today, contemporary craftspeople, such as Connie and Tom McColley, employ traditional techniques
to create exciting new forms. The McColleys, who live in West Virginia, are masters of the Appalachian white oak basket-making tradition, who began by making faithful renditions of the typical buttocks form. In recent years, however, they have concentrated on purely decorative baskets, experi-

menting with forms suggested by such natural objects as seashells, or incorporating the natural shapes of branches to use as handles or other structural elements. They call themselves "weavers of wood" rather than basket makers. Tom McColley says, "We have been making baskets for about seventeen years. We are primarily self-taught, learning by studying old baskets and photographs of baskets. Our earlier work was more traditional in style, basically copies of well-designed traditional white oak baskets. As we gained skill in using the material, we began to push the limits of what had been done before us, expanding the possibilities and redefining our definition of 'basket' in a more contemporary context. Although our baskets deal more with ideas than function, they still maintain a link to the tradition."

▼ WORK BASKET

Artist unknown. c. 1850–1900. Northeastern United States. Ash splint. Height: 9 1/2 in., diameter: 24 in. The Shelburne Museum, Shelburne, Vermont.

This large, open work basket was probably used inside for carrying laundry, yarn, or other lightweight items or outside for gathering fruits and vegetables.

LIDDED RYE-STRAW BASKET ▶

Artist unknown. c. 1900. Rockbridge County, Virginia. Rye straw with white oak handle. Height: 14 1/2 in., diameter: 14 in. Collection of Roddy and Sally Moore.

Rye-straw baskets were made in German communities throughout Virginia and southern Pennsylvania. To make the baskets, bundles of tough rye straw were lashed together and then coiled into the desired shape. The oak handle of this lidded basket is lashed with thin strips of white oak and attached with cut nails.

*Fiber and
Fabric*

*America's
Traditional
Crafts*

•

106

▼ Round Melon-Shaped Basket with Carved Bail Handle

Artist unknown, possibly Cherokee. Early nineteenth century. North Carolina. Painted white oak splint. 9 x 7 1/2 x 7 1/2 in. Private collection.

Melon-shaped baskets were among the most common forms crafted in the Appalachian region throughout the nineteenth and early twentieth centuries. Many basket makers continue to make the form, using the traditional white oak splint techniques of the region. The deceptively strong and durable baskets are built around a framework of ribs that radiate from the wide intersecting hoops of the handle and rim.

UTILITY BASKET ▸

Artist unknown. c. 1840. New England. Painted wood splint. 7 x 9 3/4 x 5 in. Private collection.

Despite its small size, this perfectly proportioned basket projects a feeling of monumentality. New England basket makers often painted their baskets in solid colors, both for decoration and to protect the surface.

◂ CHEESE BASKET WITH CARVED BAIL HANDLE

Artist unknown. c. 1830. New England. Wood splint. 11 x 10 x 9 1/2 in. Collection of David A. Schorsch, Inc., New York.

Cheese baskets were used to separate curds and whey. The basket was lined with permeable cloth, and when the curd mass was dropped in, liquid whey dripped through into containers that were placed below.

▼ ROUND SWING-HANDLED GATHERING BASKET

Artist unknown. c. 1900–1925. Columbia County, New York. Ash splint with tinned iron. 17 x 14 1/2 x 14 in. Private collection.

Most Taconic swing-handled baskets are attached to ears set across rather than parallel to the rim. A round tin disk attached to the bottom of this basket carries the pencil inscription, "Oct 7 1923 Saybrook Mr. Hubbard near Bridge," possibly a reference to the maker and place of purchase.

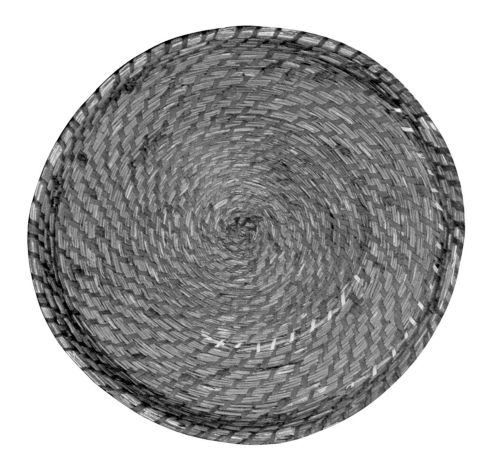

◄ RICE FANNER

Artist unknown. c. 1850. South Carolina. Rush and oak. Height: 2 in., diameter: 20 3/4 in. The Charleston Museum, Charleston, South Carolina.

Coiled basket fanners were used by slaves working on coastal rice plantations to sift grain from chaff. The lightweight chaff was blown away when threshed rice was tossed into the air.

▼ COVERED SEWING BASKET

Unknown Shaker artist. c. 1870. Mount Lebanon, New York. Poplar splint. 3 1/2 x 5 3/4 in. Private collection.

This small and delicate lady's fancy basket was made to hold needles, thimbles, spools of thread, and other sewing accessories.

Fiber and
Fabric

———

America's
Traditional
Crafts

•

112

◂ NANTUCKET LIGHTSHIP BASKETS

Artists unknown except right front by George Washington Ray.
c. 1875. New South Shoals lightship, Nantucket, Massachusetts.
Hardwood, rattan. Diameter of smallest basket: 8 1/2 in.
Collection of Paul and Diane Madden.

The New South Shoals lightship was moored near the South
Shoals, about twenty miles off Nantucket Island, to provide a
warning beacon to ships trying to navigate past this treacherous
area. From 1856, when the lightship was first moored, to 1892,
when the vessel was relocated, keepers serving on the lightship
crafted distinctive rattan baskets during their leisure hours.

◄ ROUND NANTUCKET LIGHTSHIP BASKET

George Washington Ray. c. 1875. New South Shoals lightship, Nantucket, Massachusetts. Hardwood, rattan. Diameter: 8 1/2 in. Collection of Paul and Diane Madden.

As a major seaport, Nantucket supported many coopers throughout the eighteenth and nineteenth centuries. Nantucket baskets, which, like barrels, are constructed from staves set into a circular bottom, are believed to have been influenced by coopering. This basket has a wooden swing handle attached to an eared stave.

▼ DYED SPLINT BASKETS

Artists unknown. c. 1875–1925. Left: Pulaski County, Virginia. White oak splint. Height: 13 3/4 in., diameter: 13 1/2 in. Right: Botetourt County, Virginia. White oak splint. Height: 14 in., diameter: 15 in. Collection of Roddy and Sally Moore.

Color was applied only to the outside of the oak splint staves and weavers of these unusual southern white oak baskets. By alternating plain and colored weavers, the basket makers created distinct vertical lines of color. The basket at left has a square bottom and is similar in form to New England "cat-head" baskets but, unlike them, was not woven over a mold.

◄ OVAL NANTUCKET LIGHTSHIP BASKET

Artist unknown. c. 1875. New South Shoals lightship, Nantucket, Massachusetts. Hardwood, rattan. Maximum diameter: 13 3/4 in. Collection of Paul and Diane Madden.

Unlike most lightship baskets, this example has a fixed handle. Oval baskets were much less common than round ones.

Fiber and
Fabric

———

America's
Traditional
Crafts

•

114

▼ SPLIT-HANDLED OVAL TRAY BASKET

Artist unknown. c. 1900. Wythe County, Virginia. White oak. Height: 12 in., length: 17 in. Collection of Roddy and Sally Moore.

The split handle is attached solely with nails, and the flat bottom is structurally unsupported, making the basket suitable for only the lightest of loads. It may have been used to hold food on the table.

Ida Pearl Davis and Thelma Hibdon. 1988. Woodbury, Tennessee. White oak splint. Height: 14 1/2 in., diameter: 13 3/4 in. Collection of Thelma Hibdon.

Ida Pearl Davis has been making traditional white oak baskets since she was a child. She now works with her daughter Thelma Hibdon, to whom she has passed the skills she learned from her mother, who in turn had learned from her mother and grandmother. To make their baskets, Mrs. Davis and Mrs. Hibdon weave flat strips of split white oak through a framework that is built of the wide, flat intersecting hoops of the rim and handle and a number of thin rod-shaped ribs.

IDA PEARL DAVIS AND THELMA DAVIS HIBDON, SPLINT BASKET MAKERS

Mother and daughter Ida Pearl Davis and Thelma Hibdon of Woodbury, Tennessee, make traditional, ribbed white oak baskets. Basketry having been mainly woman's work in earlier times, Mrs. Davis traces her maternal craft tradition to her great-grandmother Adeline Barrett. Mrs. Davis made her first basket (an egg basket) under her mother's tutelage at age seven and traded it at the local general store for a twenty-five-cent cap. She remembers hard times when she and her mother and her three sisters all made baskets to sell for groceries, and also recalls feeling ashamed of making baskets because it seemed to publicize the family's poverty.

Mrs. Davis laid the craft aside for a number of years during mid-life while she worked at local textile plants, but became active again in the early 1970s, partly because of revived popular interest in baskets. Besides, she says, "It gets in your blood and you won't never quit." Mrs. Davis enjoys the more exacting work of show baskets, which,

unlike common work-baskets, have finer splints and more numerous ribs. She specializes in them today, finding that collectors prefer them to common baskets. Working with her daughter, Thelma Hibdon, to whom she has taught the craft, she produces show baskets in seven different sizes. Mrs. Davis and Mrs. Hibdon still prepare all their own materials, searching local woods for promising-looking white oak trees and then laboriously cutting splints, handles, and ribs from the logs with draw and pocket knives. The mother and daughter team feels its greatest honor was being invited to participate in the 1986 Smithsonian Festival of American Folklife located in Washington, D.C.

Fiber and
Fabric

———

America's
Traditional
Crafts

•

116

▲ OLLA

Unknown Apache Indian artist. c. 1900. Arizona. Willow.
Height: 28 in. New York State Museum, Albany, New York.

The large baskets made by Apache basket makers to store seeds and
grains closely resemble traditional Pueblo pottery storage jars in
form. The range of common decorative motifs used by southwestern
Indian potters, rug makers, and basket makers expanded in the late
nineteenth century to include human and animal forms in addition
to traditional geometric patterns.

◄ TRIPLE-POCKET WALL BASKET

Artist unknown, probably Penobscot Indian. c. 1890. Maine.
Painted wood splint. 30 x 18 x 7 in. Private collection.

Probably made for sale to the tourist trade, this hanging basket is
distinguished by its carefully planned proportions. The repeating
rhythms on the three stacked baskets are beautifully accented with
blue paint.

TOURIST BASKET ▾

Unknown Abenaki Indian artist. Early twentieth century. Northern New England. Willow, sweet or holy grass, dye. 12 3/8 x 10 1/4 in. Hood Museum of Art, Dartmouth College, Hanover, New Hampshire.

This brightly colored basket was made to appeal to the tourists who flocked to New England's many summer resorts in the early years of this century. Although it employs traditional Abenaki basket-making techniques, the form is not one used by Indians.

◄ **BASKET WITH LID**

Ada Thomas. 1980. Charenton, Louisiana. Swamp cane, plaited in double weave. Height: 11 in. U.S. Department of the Interior, Indian Arts and Crafts Board.

Ada Thomas, who died in 1992, was a master of the Chitimacha Indian basket-making tradition. Both her grandmother and an aunt were also basket makers; Mrs. Thomas learned her craft from them as a child. In later years she shared her knowledge, helping to keep the tradition alive. She was honored as a National Heritage Fellow by the Folk Arts Program of the National Endowment for the Arts in 1983.

◄ TWILL BASKET

Jennifer Heller. 1992. Owensboro, Kentucky. White oak. 14 x 12 in. Collection of Owensboro Museum of Fine Art, Owensboro, Kentucky.

Twill weave, in which horizontal splints are passed over two or more vertical elements before being passed under one or more elements, was a technique commonly used by many southeastern Indian peoples and more rarely by Anglo-American basket makers. The most common twill weave was over two, under two, which created a diagonal pattern. Both the handle and basket of this contemporary basket are woven in twill patterns.

▲ BASKET WITH BRANCH HANDLE

Connie and Tom McColley. 1991. Chloe, West Virginia. White oak, cherry, white oak branch. 16 x 25 x 22 in. Private collection.

Many of the McColleys' white-oak baskets are worked with found materials such as the branch handle used for this piece. The artists also have experimented with form, creating baskets shaped like shells and a variety of other natural forms.

T O O L S   A N D
W O O D E N W A R E

T O O L S

The wide variety of specific tasks performed by traditional hand tradesmen of the eighteenth and nineteenth centuries, such as coopers, carpenters, sawyers, joiners, shipwrights, sailmakers, wheelwrights, and carriage makers, required specialized hand tools. Coopers, for example, used curved sun planes to even and smooth the tops of barrels, and wheelwrights shaped and hollowed the hubs of wheels using enormous reamers. Many craftspeople also required specialized tools. Tinsmiths, for example, cut and shaped sheet metal with shears, punches, and hammers; basket makers cut strips of ash or oak with aptly named crooked knives; and bowl makers hollowed burls with circular scrapers known as scorps.

Until well into the nineteenth century, when industrial production began to make inexpensive cast metal parts readily available to tool manufacturers, most early American tools were entirely handmade. Wood was the preferred material. Wooden hayforks, rakes, and grain shovels were found on every farm; wooden woodworking planes, calipers, bit braces, clamps, and mallets were in every carpenter's tool box. Only "edge" tools such as axes, adzes, froes, and saws demanded the use of sharp and durable metal edges and required the work of a blacksmith or other specialized metalworker.

Independent toolmakers, who worked alone in small home shops or with the help of one or two assistants, usually specialized in making particular types of tools, such as planes, rules, or bit braces, to satisfy local demand. Planes, for example, offered rich possibilities for toolmakers. Early American joiners and cabinetmakers used a wide variety of planes. A typical tool box might include anywhere from twenty to more than sixty different plane variations used for specific jobs such as shaping moldings and cornices, cutting grooves for feathered drawer edges, molding window sashes, and creating tongue-and-groove fittings. Because so many different types of planes were needed, plane making began in America relatively soon after the colonies were settled. The earliest known American plane maker was Francis Nicholson of Wrentham, Massachusetts, who died in 1752 at the age of seventy. He is one of at least twenty pre-1800 American plane makers whose work has been identified. Working primarily with native yellow birch, these early American toolmakers created distinctive tools that are notable for their high quality, graceful forms, and nonstandardized individuality.

◄ DIPPERS AND PAIL

Unknown Shaker artist. c. 1850. New York or New England. Dippers: unidentified wood. Length: 7 1/2 in. Pail: pine staves and bottom, hardwood handle, iron hoops and wire. Height to rim: 8 3/8 in., diameter (top): 11 in. Hancock Shaker Village, Pittsfield, Massachusetts.

Dippers were used by merchants and householders to measure dry goods such as flour and grains and also could be used to measure or simply drink liquids. The beautiful, curved handles of these Shaker dippers, which must have been extremely pleasing to hold, allowed the dippers to be hung with ease. Shaker woodenware was often painted in rich, solid colors.

▲ WHEELBARROW

Unknown Shaker artist. c. 1825–1850. New Lebanon, New York. Ash(?) handles and wheel, birch legs, pine headboard and bed, wrought iron braces and wheel rim. 18 3/4 x 67 x 26 in. The Shaker Museum, Old Chatham, New York.

This low-bodied barrow was used to remove stones small enough to be lifted by one man from rocky fields. The rocky soil of New York and New England had to be cleared before planting was possible. This barrow was probably built by a master wheelwright.

The Shakers were among the most innovative toolmakers of the nineteenth century. The circular saw, which revolutionized the preparation of lumber in the mid-nineteenth century, is said to have been invented in 1810 by a Shaker woman named Tabitha Babbitt, who, convinced that the Brothers' up-and-down saws wasted motion, looked to her spinning wheel and devised the prototype of the constantly cutting, circular saw. Conversely, the flat broom still found in every house today is the 1798 brain child of Shaker Brother Theodore Bates of Watervliet, New York, who, after observing Sisters sweeping with traditional round brooms, realized that a reconfiguration of the broom straw would greatly improve the tool's efficiency. The new design was so successful that broom making became an important cottage industry in several Shaker communities. Shaker toolmakers redesigned virtually every tool used in their communities, streamlining and simplifying designs of everything from yarn-winding swifts to wheelbarrows, always with an eye to refining and improving the tool's function.

Because tools were essential to all other pursuits, they were some of the first products that were mass-produced by American industry. By the end of the Civil War, the handmade tool was an anachronism, and by the turn of the century, factory machinery had assumed much of the work formerly performed by hand, thus eliminating the demand for hand tools. Today, with the exception of the carpentry trades, hand tools are most widely used by amateur handymen, and virtually all tools, whether for professional or home use, are factory made.

WOODENWARE

Native Americans, particularly those of the eastern Woodland nations, used the abundant wood that surrounded them to make many of their tools and implements. Men carved bowls, ladles, and utensils for daily use by their families, as well as for ceremonial occasions. Some of the few remaining early pieces have totemic animal forms, such as bears or frogs, carved into their handles. Anglo settlers, emigrating from an island nation whose forests had long ago been depleted, were overwhelmed by the plentiful supply of wood in America. They admired and were interested in the Indians' use of wood for everyday objects that would have been made only of metal or ceramic in England, and they soon began to emulate the ingenious and often beautiful work of the native people.

Treen (tree + n) ware was the most common tableware in many rural communities from early colonial days through the end of the nineteenth century. Wood was the most readily available and therefore least expensive material in early America and was used for virtually every sort of household implement, including mortars and pestles, rolling pins, spoons, ladles, dippers, plates, bowls, dough trays, pie crimpers, and cookie molds. All of these objects were carved or turned from single pieces of wood. Larger containers made to hold liquids, such as pails, buckets, churns, and barrels, usually required the hand of the cooper, a craftsman expert in shaping and joining staves of wood into watertight, circular forms, most often held together with iron hoops.

Burl, the large, extremely dense, and often beautifully patterned semicircular growths that form on the trunks of many trees, was favored from early days for bowls by Native Americans and settlers alike. To form a bowl, the burl growth was cut from the tree trunk and hollowed out with a sharp stone or, in later years, with a scorp, a handled tool holding a ring of sharpened wrought iron. Burl is very hard and created a durable and long-lasting bowl with a naturally attractive grain.

Bowls were often turned on a lathe, a device used by woodworkers for centuries, which allowed the craftsman to achieve perfectly symmetrical forms, inscribe decorative lines, and cut grooves and rims on the outside of the bowl. Early lathes were turned by hand or foot power. By the late 1700s, horse- and water-powered lathes were relatively common, allowing time-saving machine production of such curved objects as the barrel staves and bottoms used by coopers.

Wood was adapted to many uses. Hand-carved butter prints were made to decorate home products or to mark and identify butter made for sale by a particular dairy. Most were circular with incised designs that were pressed into the top of a tub of butter. Designs ranged from the simple to the elaborate and included such images as cows, wheat sheaves, flowers, and patriotic motifs

CROOKED KNIFE ▶

Unknown Passamaquoddy or Penobscot Indian artist. c. 1825. Maine. Wood, metal blade. Length: 9 in. Collection of William E. Channing.

Crooked knives, named for the angle at which the blade is attached to the handle, were the principal tool that Indian and Anglo-American basket makers in the Northeast used to cut and shape ash splint. Indians also used crooked knives for many other types of carving; indeed, the hand-shaped handle of this knife might have been carved with another crooked knife.

such as eagles and shields. The pineapple, a symbol of hospitality in early America, was a favorite of homemakers who were entertaining guests. Carved wooden prints also were used to decorate cakes and cookies, especially the traditional German springerle, an anise-flavored bar cookie.

Woodenware fell from favor for general use as the nineteenth century progressed. It was replaced by handmade tin and especially manufactured ceramic, both of which became widely available, were more practical and more versatile. Woodenware continued to be made, but primarily in factories that mass produced identical forms such as bowls, cooking spoons, and rolling pins.

Wood turning has enjoyed a renaissance in recent years. In the hands of a number of talented crafts-people, turning has become a highly sophisticated art form. James Prestini, who studied mechanical engineering at Yale, is generally credited as the seminal figure in the resurgence of the craft. Prestini began making lathe-turned vessels in the early 1930s while teaching mathematics at Lake Forest Academy. Working with common woods such as birch, cherry, and walnut, Prestini used the industrial lathe to create simple, functional forms, mainly bowls and plates, with uncommonly beautiful grain patterns. Prestini's work influenced many subsequent artisans, including Bob Stocksdale. Stocksdale turns exotic woods, such as macadamia wood, zebra wood, and teak, and, unlike Prestini, allows the grain of the block to dictate the ultimate orientation and form of the turning.

By contrast, Rude Osolnik, for many years a teacher at Berea College in Kentucky, where the teaching of traditional crafts is championed, has been instrumental in exploring the use and possibilities of found materials. Osolnik has also been a pioneer in turning veneered wood, using such basic wood as birch plywood to create highly figured and powerful forms. Ed and Philip Moulthrop, father and son turners from Georgia, use woods native to their region, such as red maple, magnolia, tulipwood, and even American chestnut, to create bowls and vases of unusual figure and often massive size. Ed Moulthrop began turning in the 1950s, designing and hand forging specialized tools he needed when he discovered they were not available commercially. The Moulthrops turn smoother cutting green wood, soaking rough cut pieces in polyethylene glycol to discourage warpage and bring out the grain. Philip Moulthrop takes eight months to a year to complete a bowl.

◄ LUMBER CALIPER

William Gardner Greenleaf. c. 1880. Littleton, New Hampshire. Wood and brass. Overall length: 54 1/2 in. Collection of Paul Kebabian.

Lumber calipers were used by loggers to measure cut trees. Each turn of the wheel measured five linear feet, while the caliper measured the log's diameter in inches.

Greenleaf was a carriage maker by trade who probably made his calipers on the side. He built the first weather station atop Mount Washington, the highest peak in New England, and also built a dam and wooden bridge in Littleton. Greenlief (as he sometimes spelled his name) was an eccentric, a tall man with a long white beard who always wore a knee-length cape fastened with a safety pin. His daughter Flossie, an accomplished violinist who played with the Boston Symphony Orchestra for a time, also made calipers, carrying on the family business after her father's death in 1916.

BOWL ►

Bob Stocksdale. 1980. Berkeley, California. Macadamia wood. Overall height: 3 3/8 in., diameter (top): 3 3/4 in. Museum of Fine Arts, Boston. Harriet Otis Craft Fund.

Stocksdale's turned bowls are made from highly figured wood. This tiny decorative bowl focuses on the dramatic starburst figure of the exotic tropical California-grown wood from which it was turned.

QUILTING FRAME ▸

Artist unknown. c. 1800. Deerfield, Massachusetts. Pine and ash. 98 x 97 1/2 x 33 in. Historic Deerfield, Inc., Deerfield, Massachusetts.

This rare, early quilting frame, made to hold the textile while it was being pieced and quilted, represents a superb example of a form successfully reduced to its essential elements. The legs are made of single pieces of ash split by triangular pine wedges fastened with hand-wrought nails; the horizontal elements are pine.

▾ DADO PLANE

Joseph Fuller. c. 1780. Providence, Rhode Island. Yellow birch. Length: 10 in. Collection of Paul Kebabian.

Dado planes were used to cut a flat groove across the grain of a piece of wood. In addition to the main cutting blade, they have a smaller "nicker" iron mounted at the front, which first scores the edges of the groove to avoid splitting the wood. Dado planes were used primarily by cabinet-makers to cut grooves that would hold fixed shelves in case pieces. Fuller is one of the earliest known American plane makers.

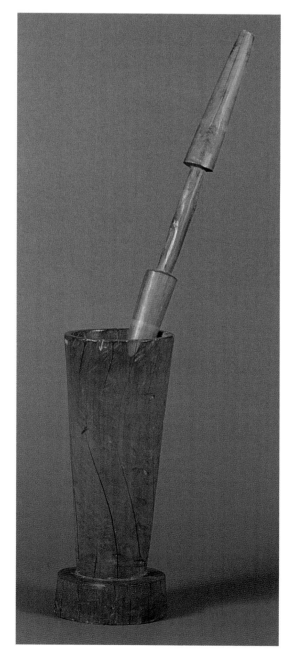

◄ MORTAR AND PESTLE

Artist unknown. Late eighteenth century. Used at Midway Plantation, Waccamaw, South Carolina. Carved cypress. Mortar: height: 28 5/8 in., diameter: 10 5/8 in. Pestle: length: 42 in. The Charleston Museum, Charleston, South Carolina.

This large, floor-standing mortar and pestle was made and used by slaves to grind rice, which was widely grown on coastal plantations.

▲ **BOOTJACK**

*J. C. Hern. 1831. Springwood Community, Botetourt
County, Virginia. Walnut, brass tack eyes. Length: 15 in.,
width: 3 3/4 in. Collection of Roddy and Sally Moore.*

*The artist's name and the date of completion are carefully
incised on the back of this bootjack along with a star-
shaped pattern similar to those often found on carved butter prints. The jack has a tapered cut in the back so it
would sit high enough off the floor to slip a boot into it.
Bootjacks allowed a person to remove wet or muddy boots
without having to touch them.*

◄ GRAIN SHOVEL

Unknown Shaker artist. c. 1825–1850. New Lebanon, New York. Walnut with tin patch and copper rivets. 43 1/2 x 10 1/4 x 2 1/2 in. The Shaker Museum, Old Chatham, New York.

This elegant shovel was carved from a single piece of walnut. Its bottom edge was repaired by the Shakers. Grain shovels were traditionally made of wood, although most were much cruder than this example. Wood was thought not to contaminate the grain; it also would not spark as a metal shovel would, thus eliminating the everpresent risk of fire in a hay-filled wooden barn.

▼ PLOW PLANE

Emanuel W. Carpenter. c. 1840. Lancaster, Pennsylvania. Boxwood. Length: 11 1/2 in. Collection of Paul Kebabian.

The appropriately named Carpenter worked as a plane maker in Lancaster from 1829 until his death in 1857. Carpenter ran a small but successful shop, taking on three to five teenaged apprentices at a time to assist. Carpenter received a patent in 1838 for a new method of making and applying the adjustable screw arms seen on this plane. From 1841 to 1848, Carpenter's planes were sold by the Philadelphia hardware store of Yarnell and McClure.

Although they look complicated, plow planes were used simply to cut a groove that would receive a tongue, feather-edge, or spline to join two pieces of wood. The adjustable fence of the plow plane, which rested against the edge of the lumber being cut, served as a guide in placing the groove.

▲ YARN WINDER

*Artist unknown. c. 1840. Probably Maine. Maple and
hickory. Height: 36 in. Collection of David A. Schorsch,
Inc., New York.*

*The craftsman cleverly organized the composition of this
tool so that it suggests a human form.*

◄ CABBAGE SHREDDER

*Artist unknown. Nineteenth century. Rockingham County, Virginia. Maple, iron blade.
Length: 21 1/2 in. Collection of Roddy and Sally Moore.*

Cabbage, which was easy to grow and kept well, was a staple of the early American diet, especially in German communities. This simple tool was used to shred heads of cabbage for slaw.
The maker of this shredder cleverly carved silhouetted human features into the top, using the
hanging hole as an eye.

▼ WASH OR SCRUBBING BOARDS

*Artists unknown. c. 1840–1870. Regions unknown. Left to right: carved and doweled pine,
carved fruitwood, pine with wire, carved and doweled pine. Private collection.*

Scrubbing boards were found in every laundry room in nineteenth- and early twentieth-century
America. Soiled clothes were soaped and then rubbed against the ridges of the board, which
stood with its legs in a tub of wash water. The fruitwood board second from left is of one-piece
construction; all the other boards are jointed.

▼ FOOTED BOWL WITH LID

*Artist unknown. c. 1820–1840. New England. Maple burl. Old Sturbridge Village,
Sturbridge, Massachusetts.*

This handsome, footed bowl, turned from maple burl, may have served as a sugar bowl for table
use. The acorn-shaped finial on the lid is an unusual decorative touch; knob handles, shaped
like the base of the acorn, are far more typical.

◄ COVERED CUP

Artist unknown. c. 1820–1850. Probably Pennsylvania. Maple. Height: 7 1/8 in. The Henry Francis du Pont Winterthur Museum, Winterthur, Delaware.

Pennsylvania Dutch artisans often decorated woodenware such as cups and even water buckets with stylized floral and representational designs.

▼ BEAVER EFFIGY BOWL

Unknown Kaskaskia Indian artist. c. 1795. Illinois. Wood. University Museum, University of Pennsylvania, Philadelphia.

Small ceremonial or eating dishes like this one often were carved by eastern Woodland Indian men for their intended brides. This example was made by a member of the Kaskaskia, once the dominant people of the Illinois nation. The Kaskaskia were renowned for their woodcarving skills, which were rivaled only by northwest coast peoples such as the Kwakiutl. Beavers were a symbol of plenty to many peoples of the eastern Woodlands region, as much a symbol of the area as the buffalo was to the Plains. Although wooden effigy bowls were once common, very few have survived.

BOWL ▸

*Unknown Shaker artist. c. 1825–1850.
New Lebanon, New York. Ash. Height:
9 1/2 in., diameter: 28 1/2 in. The
Shaker Museum, Old Chatham, New
York.*

*Because Shakers ate communally, this
huge bowl probably found much use in
New Lebanon kitchens. Despite its size,
it is delicately worked, with three incised
lines from the turning chisel adding a subtle decorative element.*

▾ LIDDED BOWL

*Artist unknown. c. 1840. New England. Maple burl. Diameter: 13 in. The Shelburne
Museum, Shelburne, Vermont.*

*The beautiful figure of the burl and the carefully shaped rim of the lid distinguish this early
bowl. Burl, cut from tight-grained tree growths, was favored for bowls because it did not crack.*

▲ BUTTER PRINT

*Artist unknown. c. 1850–1870.
Region unknown. Carved wood.
Height: 5 1/8 in., diameter: 3 1/16 in.
Abby Aldrich Rockefeller Folk Art
Center, Williamsburg, Virginia. Gift of
Mr. and Mrs. Foster McCarl, Jr.*

Flowers, acorns, sheaves of wheat,
cows, and pineapples were the most
common motifs for butter prints. The
anchor is an unusual and seemingly
incongruous image, leading to the spec-
ulation that the dairy where it was used
was possibly located in or near a port.

BUTTER PRINT ▶

*Artist unknown. c. 1870. Probably
Pennsylvania. Carved wood. Length: 3
1/2 in. The Shelburne Museum,
Shelburne, Vermont.*

A number of copies of this image,
known to collectors as the Vigilant
Cow, were apparently crafted by a single shop. All of the virtually identical
prints are carefully carved by hand and
have short lathe-turned handles.

▾ SPOON

Unknown Potawatomi Indian artist. c.
1840–1880. Wisconsin. Maple. Length: 6 1/4
in., width: 4 3/8 in. © The Detroit Institute of
Arts. Museum Purchase with funds from the
state of Michigan, the city of Detroit, and the
Founders Society.

Woodland Indians often carved large serving
spoons with figural handles that represented animals or birds.

◄ BUTTER PRINT

Artist unknown. c. 1840. Pennsylvania. Tulip poplar. Diameter: 7 3/8 in. The Henry Francis du Pont Winterthur Museum, Winterthur, Delaware.

This relief-carved, half-round print is distinguished by its intricate detail and powerful design. Initials identifying the butter maker appear in the print's border. Although the print was hand carved, its handle (which cannot be seen in this photograph) was turned on a lathe.

▼ VESSEL

Rude Osolnick. 1987. Berea, Kentucky. Turned laminated birch plywood. Height: 10 3/4 in., diameter (base): 4 1/4 in., diameter (lip): 9 3/8 in. Museum of Fine Arts, Boston. Gift of Daniel and Jessie Farber Theodora Wilbour Fund in memory of Charlotte Beebe Wilbour.

Osolnick taught at Berea College from 1937 to 1977, where he exerted an important influence on woodworkers and turners throughout the country. He pioneered several new ideas, often working with wood that was ignored or discarded by most other turners to find the possibilities inherent in the most common materials. This vessel is crafted from laminated plywood, the basest imaginable material for a turner, and yet it achieves great beauty of both form and figure.

F U R N I T U R E

The typical country furniture maker was, of necessity, a jack-of-all-trades. Unlike his big city counterpart, the country furniture maker's business was service oriented and nonspecialized, as he generally had to provide a wide range of work to suit a diversity of customer needs. He usually did not keep stock on hand; all his work was done on demand and his furniture made to order. Like his neighbors, he farmed part time and performed a variety of seasonal tasks. In addition, he used his woodworking skills to build coffins, make handles for tools, repair broken chair rails and seats, plane window sashes, and, when asked, offered his own versions of the latest in city furniture fashions. Stylistic changes were often slow to move from the city to the country, and this, combined with the fact that most rural communities were essentially conservative in nature, placed the country cabinetmaker sometimes decades behind the more fashion-conscious city craftsman in the adoption of new techniques.

Most country furniture was made from readily available local woods, and, unlike high-style furniture made from such imported fine woods as mahogany or rosewood, was painted rather than varnished. Paint decoration enlivened the relatively plain surfaces of chests and tables made of pine, poplar, birch, and other common woods, enhancing the visual interest of the pieces. Paint decoration was not reserved solely for furniture; in New England particularly, boxes, household implements, and tools, as well as pine floors and staircases, also sometimes received detailed painted treatments.

The most common painting technique employed by country craftsmen was grain painting, achieved by using special combs or swirling, freehand brush strokes to imitate the naturally patterned grains of fancy or highly figured woods. To achieve a grained surface, the painter first laid down a light-colored coat of paint, which was allowed to dry completely. Then, a second, darker color was laid on top of the first and, while still wet, the comb or brush was drawn through the top coat to create parallel graining lines by revealing the contrasting undercoat. When red and black were used, this technique gave a very convincing imitation of the strong-grained pattern of highly prized and expensive tropical rosewood. Other decorators applied more fanciful patterns that were not based on natural phenomena. Paint could be daubed or spread on with sponges or crumpled paper to give a variegated surface, not unlike children's finger painting, or it could be smoked by passing a candle close enough to blacken the wet paint surface in spots and achieve a muted, scumbled decorative effect. Some decorators mixed vinegar, linseed oil, or other solvents into a second coat of paint, which was then patterned with putty or rags. The addition of the solvent caused the second layer to dry unevenly, producing a mottled, bleeding effect.

Another popular painting technique used to decorate furniture, especially chairs and household walls, was stenciling. The stenciler painted through precut cardboard or metal designs to create pre-

◄ CONOID LOUNGE CHAIR

George Nakashima. Designed c. 1980, production date of this example: 1985. English walnut, hickory. 33 1/4 x 22 1/2 x 26 1/2 in. Collection of Kevin Nakashima.

Nakashima's Conoid Lounge Chair, a variation on his classic Conoid Chair, has shortened legs, which adapt the design to comfortable lounging height.

SLANT-TOP DESK ▸

*Artist unknown. 1834. Schwaben Creek
Valley, Northumberland County, Pennsylvania. Painted tulipwood. 49 1/8 x 39 x
9 3/4 in. The Henry Francis du Pont
Winterthur Museum, Winterthur, Delaware.*

*This desk is inscribed "Jacob Maser 1834"
above the small top drawers; since Maser was
married in that year it was probably a gift to
him. The variety, color, and carefully balanced placement of the stylized motifs distinguish the piece.*

cise and sometimes intricate patterns on the crest rail of the chair
or the top of the trunk he was decorating. Depending on the skill of
the stenciler, the results could
range from extremely simple to
highly complex. Stenciling was a
special boon to amateur decorators
who felt uncomfortable wielding a
freehand brush, but it was also
practiced by a number of talented
professionals. These men often
worked as itinerants, moving from
small town to small town embell-
ishing walls and furniture.
Stenciling also provided such entrepreneurs of manufactured furniture as Lambert Hitchcock with an
inexpensive and consistently attractive means of decorating his mass-produced chairs. Hitchcock's
highly successful rush-seated side chairs, introduced in the 1820s, carried floral stencils on the central
back slat and were also adorned with some freehand gilding and striping.

The most commonly crafted form of seating furniture in America between the mid-1700s and the
1830s, when factory-produced chairs like Hitchcock's began to saturate the marketplace, was the
Windsor. This stick-style furniture derived from English prototypes and subsequently flourished in
America, where a wide range of regional and stylistic variations developed. Unlike other chair forms,
in which the legs and back are contiguous, Windsor furniture is built around a solid plank seat, into
which thin vertical spindles are inserted to form the back, arm supports, and legs. It is an extremely
practical form of furniture, sturdy enough to be used both inside and out, and versatile enough to
appeal to every level of society in early America. Although Windsor furniture's apparent simplicity is
deceptive, it is relatively easy to make and was readily adopted by rural makers in all parts of the country, as well as by sophisticated city furniture craftsmen in the major urban centers of Philadelphia,
Boston, Newport, and New York.

Windsor craftsmen employed several types of wood to make their chairs, choosing species particularly suited to the task at hand. Seats were usually made from pine or poplar, both of which were easy to
carve and shape into comfortable forms. Arm supports, legs, and stretchers, all of which typically were
turned on a lathe, were usually made of hickory or ash because these woods were extremely strong
even when turned quite thin. Windsor craftsmen also often incorporated bent wood in crafting crest
rails and arched or bowed backs. Hickory, white oak, or ash was steamed to soften the wood, which
was then bent and shaped over a form. When dried and taken out of the mold, it retained the new

shape and much of the inherent tensile strength of the natural grain, therefore making a sturdy element in the chair.

One of the most ingenious and sculpturally beautiful Windsor forms was the continuous arm, in which a single piece of bent wood formed the arms and back of the chair. The point at which the arms were bent up into the back created an inherent weak point but, in this case, the aesthetic appeal of the flowing lines of the design was preferred in spite of somewhat reduced strength and practicality. Because Windsor chairs were composites, made from several different types of wood with different grain characteristics and appearances, they were usually painted all over in solid colors such as green, black, yellow, or red, which integrated the surface, bringing the disparate woods together in a unified sculptural statement.

Among the most innovative and original furniture designers of the nineteenth century were members of the many Shaker communities of New York, New England, and Kentucky. Most Shaker settlements included a furniture shop among their craft buildings, where their craftsmen made furniture for the community's use as well as for sale to the "world." The spare, clean, and utterly unadorned lines of their chairs, tables, chests, and other forms are instantly recognizable and quite different from other furniture of the time. Following their strict religious precepts, the Shakers looked back to the furniture they were most familiar with—that of early New England and New York—and reinvented it.

They rejected complex and ornate forms such as the high chest of drawers, as well as any sort of surface decoration, either painted or carved. And they simplified the forms of the pieces that appealed to them, such as traditional ladder-back chairs, stripping them down to bare essentials, thereby revealing the essential beauty and timelessness of the basic form.

The Shakers developed many remarkable designs, among which were large cupboards and chests containing many drawers that were built into dwelling spaces and used communally by Brothers or Sisters to store clothing and bedding.

◄ STAND

Unknown Shaker artist. c. 1825–1850. New Lebanon, New York. Cherry, iron plate at base of post. 25 1/2 x 17 x 17 in. Hancock Shaker Village, Hancock, Massachusetts.

Shakers used portable stands like this to hold a candle or oil lamp. The swelling of the post above the legs perfectly balances the deceptively simple form. A further refinement is achieved by the carefully shaped legs, which are widest and tallest at the top and taper gracefully in both dimensions as they descend to the floor.

These storage units, built into room corners, beside chimneys, and in attics, were beautifully proportioned; the many drawers with their small, single wooden pulls projected an overall feeling of delicacy surprising for such large and bulky objects. Perhaps the most impressive of all such built-in storage units is found in the attic of the Church Family Dwelling at Canterbury, New Hampshire; it consists of six closets, fourteen cupboards, and 101 drawers.

To their contemporaries, Shaker craftsmen were best known for their chairs. The community at New Lebanon, New York, in particular, had a very active mail-order business in chairs, and by the last quarter of the nineteenth century was shipping its products all over the country. The Shakers made both side chairs and armed rocking chairs for sale. Both forms had turned rear posts ending in finials, three or four back slats, graduated in size with the narrowest on the bottom, and a woven seat of rush or cane, wool or cotton tape. Most Shaker chairs slanted backwards to provide the sitter with a more natural and comfortable angle. Many of their side chairs also had "tilts," semicircular wooden ball feet, built into the hollowed rear legs to allow the sitter to lean back in the chair without marking a wooden floor with a sharp corner of the chair's leg.

Shaker chairs were of consistently high quality and, as was the case with many other Shaker products, they sold well in the marketplace. The Shakers continued to produce virtually identical chairs at New Lebanon until 1942. Although many Victorians deplored the stark simplicity of Shaker furniture (Charles Dickens in *American Notes* described "six or eight stiff, high-backed chairs [that] partook so strongly of the general grimness, that one would have much rather sat on the floor"), this very quality has had a profound influence on a number of important designers, including turn-of-the-century American Gustav Stickley and several of the Danish and Swedish craftsmen whose Danish Modern style became nearly ubiquitous in the 1950s. Both Stickley's Mission-style chairs and the Danish Modern pieces borrowed the Shaker aesthetics of simplicity, directness, quality, lack of ornament, and attention to function.

Because storage space was at a premium in the early German homes of southeastern Pennsylvania, free-standing cupboards, wardrobes, and blanket chests were the most commonly crafted forms. One of the most impressive and unusual types of furniture made in Pennsylvania were schranks, massive, standing, communal wardrobe closets that often held the entire family's clothing. Schranks followed a form common in medieval Europe and usually incorporated such architectural features as cornices, dentils, and paneled doors and sides. They were often elaborately paint decorated and could be disassembled so they could be moved easily.

◄ BLANKET CHEST

Decorated and possibly made by Johannes Spitler. c. 1795–1810. Shenandoah County, Virginia. Yellow pine. 28 x 49 1/2 x 22 3/8 in. Collection of the Museum of Early Southern Decorative Arts, Winston-Salem, North Carolina.

Johannes Spitler (1774–1837) is known to have decorated a number of chests as well as two tall clocks. His highly original designs were drawn with a compass.

BUCKET BENCH AND CUPBOARD ▸

Artist unknown. c. 1830. Pennsylvania. Maple and pine with walnut knobs. 77 1/2 x 44 x 15 1/2 in. Private collection.

Waves and swirls of paint undulate under a zebra-striped cornice on this uniquely decorated cupboard. The bench below the shelved cupboard provided space for buckets of water, which had to be carried in from an outside well or pump.

Most Pennsylvania Germans owned a lift-top chest, used to store clothing and other personal belongings. As the most common furniture form of the Pennsylvania Germans, these pieces were crafted with special attention to detail. Typically, they were made from pine or tulipwood with well-crafted, interior wrought iron hinges, sometimes in decorative shapes, and a lock. A rectangular box or "till" for smaller possessions fitted inside the top of the chest. The chests were almost invariably paint decorated with favorite pictorial designs, often based on such familiar Germanic motifs as the heart, tulip, or birds. Pennsylvania German decorators employed a vivid palette of oil-based reds, greens, blues, and oranges contrasted with black, brown, and white, and sometimes combined a variety of painting techniques on a single piece of furniture. A number of German immigrant craftsmen, some of them documented but most anonymous, are known for their distinctive, personal decorative styles. One noteworthy group of chests features intricate decoration that divides the front of the chest into three arched panels with a pair of rearing black unicorns at the center; stylized tulips grow from pots between the panels. Another group of decorated chests, recently linked to the calligraphic designs of a man named Heinrich Otto, carries highly stylized pairs of lions, hearts, and two-petaled tulips.

Not all German craftsmen lived in Pennsylvania. Johannes Spitler (1774–1837), for example, who lived in the Shenandoah Valley of Virginia, is known to have decorated several chests and tall clocks with intricate compass-drawn geometric designs in red, orange, and black on a blue ground. Like many other paint decorators, Spitler was apparently influenced by fraktur, the traditional, illuminated calligraphic art used on family records and other important documents. Although most known paint-decorated Pennsylvania German furniture was made before 1800, several artists in Pennsylvania's Mahantago Valley produced decorated chests and desks as late as the mid-1830s, typically ornamented with small red and yellow birds, flowers, and geometric designs on a dark green background.

Another Germanic community whose furniture reflected European predecessors was that established by followers of the German Separatist leader Joseph Baumler, who brought around three hundred believers to Zoar, Ohio, in 1817. Like the Shakers and other Utopian groups of the period, the Zoarites built a self-sustaining farming community and practiced a number of crafts that both provided essential goods for the settlement and became a source of outside income. Most Zoarite seating furniture followed the extremely basic, unadorned plank-seat style found in German communities throughout Pennsylvania; however, at least one piece from Zoar has turned legs and decorative carving all over the back and seat. Typically, a handhold cut was made in the solid back of these German chairs so they could be carried easily. Often a heart- or tulip-shaped handhold was the only decorative element in an otherwise stark and plain creation.

Craftsmen in the southern Piedmont backcountry of North and South Carolina also produced a variety of paint-decorated furniture. These makers sometimes decorated their furniture with three or four different, solid paint colors, which were used to emphasize the architectural geometry of the piece; for example, the interior panels of the doors might be one color and the frames another.

Inexpensive, mass-produced, factory-made furniture drove most hand furniture craftsmen out of business in the second half of the nineteenth century, when the Victorian era dictated a preference for more ornate designs. After the 1876 Centennial, however, forgotten styles were modified slightly and brought back to the public eye in an outpouring of national pride and interest in early American design and hand craftsmanship. Early in this century Wallace Nutting, the most important early collector, popularizer, and student of American furniture, introduced a commercial line of reproductions of Windsor chairs and other indigenous forms. Indeed, Windsors have been the most tenacious and well-loved of American furniture forms; they have never completely fallen from favor. Dozens of highly skilled craftsmen continue to produce traditional Windsors today.

One of the last handcraft styles to emerge was the bentwood seating furniture that first appeared in Appalachia in the 1870s. These "rustic" chairs and benches had wooden slat seats and backs; the frames and arms were made of hickory saplings bent, using molds, into curved shapes. Rustic furniture was made throughout Appalachia and in such rural resort areas as the Great Lakes region and the Adirondacks. It was especially popular for use in the many camps and lodges found in these areas, where late nineteenth-century Americans were rediscovering the pleasures of living, or at least vacationing, close to nature. Amish craftsmen in the mid-West communities of Ohio and Indiana also adopted the bentwood rocking chair, which they continue to make entirely by hand today.

Many contemporary hand furniture craftspeople came to handwork late in life, learning their craft by teaching themselves rather than serving an apprenticeship. While traditional forms such as Windsor or Shaker chairs continue to serve as models for many of these makers, other craftspeople, such as George Nakashima, an American-born architectural designer, and Sam Maloof, a Californian who first practiced industrial design, have introduced new concepts to the handcraft tradition. Both men began crafting furniture in the 1940s and both, through their work and teaching, have had an enormous impact on hand furniture making. Nakashima traveled widely as a young man, seeking his Japanese roots in Tokyo, living for a time in Paris, and exploring religious and spiritual concepts in India. All of these experiences profoundly influenced his approach to furniture making. Nakashima explained how his vision was linked to the Japanese concept of *kodama*, meaning spirit of a tree: "It is our deepest respect for the tree that impels us to master the difficult art of joinery so that we may offer the tree a second life of dignity and strength."

Sam Maloof's furniture, like that produced by traditional craftsmen, is at once eminently functional and deceptively simple. It is made to be used, and its beauty is integral rather than decorative. Although his basic designs are very straightforward, Maloof pays a great deal of attention to subtle sculptural details, creating chairs, chests, and tables that, although distinctly connected to the handmade traditions of earlier times, are completely original.

▲ DOUBLE ROCKING CHAIR

Sam Maloof. 1988. Alta Loma, California. Hardrock fiddleback maple. 47 x 42 x 47 in. Private collection.

Sam Maloof is best known for his rocking chairs, which combine deceptively simple forms with extraordinary attention to small, sculptural details that invite the sitter's tactile involvement. This wide-seated rocker was made to accommodate two people.

WRITING-ARM WINDSOR CHAIR ▸

Ebenezer Tracy. c. 1765–1790. Lisbon, Connecticut. Oak, hickory, maple, and pine. 45 1/4 x 27 x 18 3/4 in. Memorial Hall Museum, Pocumtuck Valley Memorial Association, Deerfield, Massachusetts. Bequest of Francis J. Kellogg.

Writing-arm chairs served as moveable desks complete with drawers below the arm and seat for papers, books, pens, and ink. Tracy made a number of writing-arm Windsor chairs. He designed the most sculpturally successful version of this inherently awkward form, balancing the heavy writing arm by setting the spindles of the comb-back off center, moving them one step farther to the right than expected. This example was owned by Reverend Theophilus Packard, pastor of the Congregational Church at Shelburne, Massachusetts, from 1799 to 1855. The chair was originally painted red.

◂ FOUR-POSTER BED

Artist unknown. c. 1790–1810. Pennsylvania. Painted poplar. 85 x 74 3/4 x 49 1/2 in. Philadelphia Museum of Art, Philadelphia, Pennsylvania. Titus G. Geesey Collection.

This brightly painted Pennsylvania German bed features an elongated heart shape on its headboard. Four-poster beds allowed the hanging of curtains, which could be drawn around the sleepers for privacy and added warmth.

▲ SCHRANK

Artist unknown. c. 1790. Lancaster County, Pennsylvania. Pine. 85 x 88 in. Henry Ford Museum and Greenfield Village, Dearborn, Michigan.

Schranks were massive, free-standing closets common in the homes of German immigrants. This example features an unusual combination of floral motifs and faux marble paint decoration. The "rat-tail" hinges, wrought by a blacksmith, add another decorative element.

PRESS ▸

Artist unknown. c. 1770–1790. Randolph or Chatham County, North Carolina. Yellow pine. 84 1/4 x 48 3/4 x 21 3/4 in. Collection of the Museum of Early Southern Decorative Arts, Winston-Salem, North Carolina. Gift of the estate of Katherine Hanes.

The press is a German furniture form used as a free-standing storage closet for folded linens and other household fabrics. The top section of this press is "stepped back" above the drawers, meaning that it is shallower than the bottom section. The use of a cornice, arched top upper doors, and large bracket feet are all typical of the work of German-American craftsmen.

▲ BLANKET CHEST

Attributed to Nehemiah Randall. c. 1800–1820. Belchertown, Massachusetts. Pine. Length: 37 1/4 in. The Metropolitan Museum of Art, New York. Gift of Mrs. E. Herrick Low, Nelson Holland, and Hudson Holland, in memory of their mother, Mrs. Nelson Clarke Holland, 1955.

This unusual chest is decorated with Federal-style architectural carving as well as paint. The carving was probably planned with the aid of a compass. Like many rural furniture makers, Randall probably also worked as a house wright and therefore may have brought design concepts from that trade to his furniture.

▲ "BLACK UNICORN" DOWER CHEST

Artist unknown. c. 1794–1803. Bern Township, Berks County, Pennsylvania. Pine. 27 3/4 x 50 3/4 x 23 5/8 in. The Henry Francis du Pont Winterthur Museum, Winterthur, Delaware.

Paint-decorated dower chests were traditionally made for young women (and occasionally young men) living in German settlements. The chests were given to the child between ages eight and ten and used to store the young person's dowery of quilts, blankets, linens, clothes, small furnishings, and other necessaries that were accumulated in anticipation of marriage and the outfitting of a household.

Twenty-seven Pennsylvania Dutch dower chests with painted black unicorn decoration are known. The chests, as well as a related group of smaller storage chests and boxes, are believed to have been produced by a handful of cabinetmakers and decorators working in Berks County in the late eighteenth and early nineteenth centuries.

TALL-CASE CLOCK ▶

*Artist unknown. c. 1810–1835. Probably Connecticut. Painted
and decorated pine case, iron works. 87 x 21 1/2 x 12 3/4 in.
The Museum of American Folk Art, New York. Gift of the Eva
and Morris Feld Folk Art Acquisition Fund.*

*The "paw print" decoration on this clock probably was achieved
by daubing paint with a crumpled piece of paper or a sponge.*

▲ CANDLE STAND

*Artist unknown. c. 1810–1830. New England. Birch. 25 3/8 x
14 11/16 x 14 1/4 in. The Henry Francis du Pont Winterthur
Museum, Winterthur, Delaware.*

*This graceful and well-proportioned candle stand is decorated
with fanciful grain paint.*

▲ SIDEBOARD TABLE

*Artist unknown. c. 1820–1835. New England. Grain-painted and decorated
wood, brass knobs. 34 1/2 x 26 x 20 in. Collection of the Museum of American
Folk Art, New York. Eva and Morris Feld Folk Art Acquisition Fund.*

*This Federal-style table is decorated with sponged and feathered graining intend-
ed to imitate the wide variety of fancy woods used for inlays by city cabinetmakers that were unavailable to this maker.*

▲ TABLE

*Artist unknown. c. 1820–1830. Essex County, Massachusetts.
Pine. Width: 18 1/2 in. National Museum of American
History, Smithsonian Institution, Washington, D.C.*

*The variegated patterns of the paint on this table were created
by working a second coat of paint over a ground color with a
piece of putty or leather. Vinegar mixed into the overcoat
reacted with linseed oil as the different layers dried, causing
them to separate into distinctive swirling patterns.*

CUPBOARD ▶

*Artist unknown. c. 1800–1830. Mount Joy, Lancaster,
Pennsylvania. Painted poplar, pine, glass. Width: 60 in.
Philadelphia Museum of Art, Philadelphia, Pennsylvania.
Titus G. Geesey Collection.*

*The upper shelves of this Pennsylvania German cupboard
have built-in grooves and slots for the storage and display of
tableware. The elaborately decorated ornamental sgraffito-
ware plates made by Pennsylvania potters would have been
displayed proudly in such a cupboard.*

◄ BLANKET CHEST

Artist unknown. c. 1820– 1840. New England. Pine. Width: 39 in. Old Sturbridge Village, Sturbridge, Massachusetts.

Lidded blanket chests, used to store quilts, coverlets, and other warm bedcovers, were a fixture in early New England homes. Because they were made of pine, all such chests were painted, and many examples, like this piece, received much more imaginative treatment than a flat coat of a single color.

◄ WINDSOR FAN-BACK SIDE CHAIR

Artist unknown. c. 1800. Northern New England. Maple, pine, ash. Height: 38 in. The Shelburne Museum, Shelburne, Vermont.

The undulating crest rail of this unusual country Windsor ends in inverted volute-carved ears. The legs and backposts were turned on a lathe, while the spindles, stretchers, and the thick plank seat were carefully shaped by hand.

▼ TRUNK

Artist unknown. c. 1820–1835. New England. White pine. 14 x 33 x 15 in. The Shelburne Museum, Shelburne, Vermont.

Stenciled decoration, created by painting through cut paper or metal patterns, reached its peak popularity between 1820 and 1840. Stenciling was most often used as a wall decoration, providing the middle-class homeowner with an attractive alternative to prohibitively expensive wallpaper.

▾ WINDSOR ROCKING CHAIR

Artist unknown. c. 1830–1860. Franklin County, Massachusetts. Maple and pine. 42 3/4 x 21 x 26 1/4 in. Historic Deerfield, Inc., Deerfield, Massachusetts.

The maker of this rocker added a decoratively shaped crest rail with enormous ears and a pierced front stretcher to a simple Windsor form. The chair was originally painted green.

SUGAR CHEST ▸

Artist unknown. c. 1840. Kentucky. Cherry. 28 1/2 x 38 x 20 3/4 in. Collection of the J. B. Speed Art Museum, Louisville, Kentucky. Gift of Mrs. Hattie Bishop Speed.

Small and simply constructed chests like this were used in the South to store sugar. The form was especially popular in Tennessee, where the chests were often made of locally available cherry. The wood was inherently beautiful, thus eliminating the need for more elaborate decoration.

SAFE ▶

*Attributed to the Rich family shop.
c. 1830–1880. Wytheville, Wythe
County, Virginia. Poplar with pierced
tin panels. 53 1/2 x 53 1/2 x 18 in.
Collection of Wallace and Liza Gusler.*

*Safes were ventilated food and kitchen
storage cupboards that were popular in
the Southeast and Midwest throughout
much of the nineteenth century. Sheet
tin panels punched in decorative
designs were nailed to or recessed into
the doors and sides of the safes.
Cabinetmakers and tinsmiths in
Virginia and Tennessee produced a
large number of notably well-decorated
safes. The Rich family operated a cabi-
netmaking firm in Wytheville from
1830 to 1943. Between 1840 and 1849
the firm, which in early years also
included a tinsmithing shop, produced
no fewer than 280 safes.*

◄ HIGH REVOLVING CHAIR

A member of the South family. c. 1860. New Lebanon, New York. Maple, apple, birch, and oak with cast-iron swiveling mechanism. 39 1/4 x 17 1/8 x 17 1/8 in. Collection of David A. Schorsch, Inc., New York.

The Shakers at New Lebanon offered several different types of "turning" chairs to their customers. All pivoted on a central screw. The long legs of this high revolving chair are thickest where the stretchers attach to provide strength at the stress points.

CASE OF DRAWERS ►

Unknown Shaker artist. c. 1825–1850. New Lebanon, New York. Pine case, red-orange stain, butternut drawer fronts, maple drawer partitions, apple or maple pulls. 21 1/2 x 39 1/2 x 9 7/8 in. The Shaker Museum, Old Chatham, New York.

This case of eighteen graduated drawers was possibly used in a doctor's office. The well-proportioned drawers measure from one to three inches in height, with no two exactly the same from top to bottom on a side. Each drawer has interior partitions running back-to-front and side-to-side.

HANGING CRADLE ▶

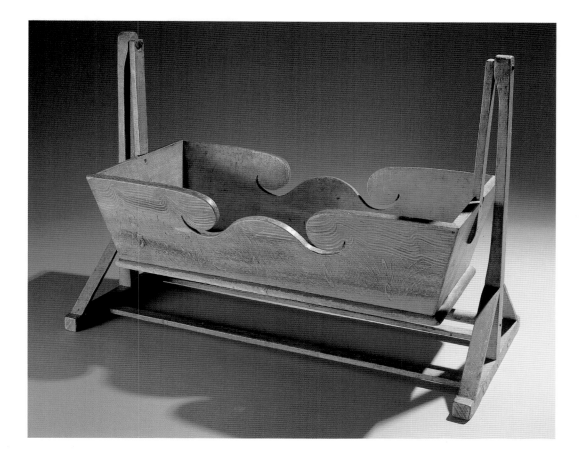

Martin L. Linfield. 1875. Braintree, Vermont. White pine. 26 x 35 3/4 x 14 3/4 in. The Shelburne Museum, Shelburne, Vermont. Bequest of Sarah Rebecca Linfield Brown.

Martin Linfield made this cradle for his infant daughter, Sarah Rebecca, the year she was born. The pine cradle is grain painted to look like oak, the most fashionable of contemporary woods. The dynamic side scrolls are reminiscent of Victorian handlebar mustaches, another fashion of Linfield's time.

BENTWOOD ROCKING CHAIR ▸

*Artist unknown. c. 1910. Michigan. Hickory and ash. Public
Museum of Grand Rapids, Grand Rapids, Michigan.*

*American society became increasingly urban in the late nineteenth
and early twentieth centuries, and many city dwellers traveled to
country resort areas during the summer months to enjoy contact
with the natural world they had forsaken. Rustic furniture, which
often incorporated roughly finished roots, branches, and logs, was a
fixture of the lakeside camps of visitors to the Adirondacks and
Great Lakes. The arms of this purposefully naturalistic rocker are
made from bent saplings.*

◂ ARROW-BACK CHAIR

*Brian Boggs. 1991. Berea, Kentucky. Hickory. 42 3/8 x
18 1/2 x 21 1/8 in. Collection of Owensboro Museum of
Fine Art, Owensboro, Kentucky.*

*Brian Boggs apprenticed with Windsor chair maker David
Sawyer (see p. 164) but decided to specialize in traditional
Appalachian chairs with woven seats. Boggs says of his
chairs, "I do use power tools to rough out the pieces, but
all the shaping and smoothing is done by hand with
drawknife and spokeshave. I also weave the seats myself
from hickory bark or oak splints. And to make the seats
really comfortable and wear well, I add a pillow of wood
shavings between the woven layers."*

WRIGHT RUSTIC CHAIR ▸

*Daniel Mack. Designed: 1987; made: 1988. Warwick,
New York. Red maple, sugar maple, upholstered seat.
62 x 21 x 17 in. Private collection.*

*Mack says of his chairs, "I explore the forms, textures and
deformities of wood and other natural materials. I separate the trees from the forest and, in that displacement,
try to select, refine and represent their elemental energy
and beauty.*

*"At times my work is quite minimal and sculptural,
reflecting an interest in the fewest necessary pieces. I
often interpret traditional furniture styles in sticks. This
clash of history and nature produces both playful and
beautiful hybrids. I try to create work/furniture which is
multidimensional. A chair should reward the viewer each
time it is encountered: textures, symmetries, accidents,
references to the Elements and to History. Secondly, I am
interested in dread, that mixture of awe, reverence and
terror. I want my work to evoke concern about strength,
permanence, seriousness. Though the furniture is truly
strong, its appearance of delicacy, its illusion of animation, is sometimes unsettling."*

CONTINUOUS-ARM WINDSOR CHAIR ▸

*David Sawyer. 1992. East Calais, Vermont. Pine, maple, and ash.
Private collection.*

*Windsor furniture has survived many changes in fashion without
compromise. It has always had broad appeal because of its versatility:
it can be used indoors or outdoors and fits equally well in modest or
elegant surroundings, complementing furniture of many other types.
This contemporary chair could have been made two hundred years
ago, yet its deceptively simple and direct form also speaks to modern
design sensibilities.*

*The continuous arm is a classic and uniquely American Windsor
form. The back and arms are formed from a single piece of steam-
bent wood. The form appears to have originated in New York City
and spread throughout New England in the late 1700s. The inherent
tension of the bent-wood back gives the continuous-arm form a dramatic sense of energy and movement.*

DAVID SAWYER,
WINDSOR CHAIR MAKER

David Sawyer of East Calais, Vermont, makes a variety of Windsor arm and side chairs following (but not duplicating exactly) traditional designs. Sawyer gave up a career as a mechanical engineer to devote himself full time to hand woodworking, crafting traditional multipronged wooden hayforks and ladder-back chairs before deciding to specialize in the traditional Windsor. He says, "My chairs are made like the Windsors of two hundred years ago, using the same materials and most of the same tools. My lathe has a motor instead of foot power, and I use a band saw occasionally, but it's ninety-eight percent handwork, just a lot of careful shaving, carving, turning, fitting, and finishing. Seats are two-inch pine plank, carved deep for real comfort.

Other parts are split from green wood following the grain, then shaved or turned. Maple for turnings, ash for the back. Legs and stretchers are selectively dried so dry tenons go into green holes and everything shrinks together. Legs and posts are fitted to tapered sockets in the seat, then wedged. Glue provides additional insurance."

Like most traditional Windsor craftsmen before him, Sawyer usually finishes his chairs by painting them all over with milk paint. The result is a durable and comfortable seat, designed to provide comfort and beauty for many years. In fact, all of David Sawyer's chairs come with a lifetime guarantee, "to outlast either myself or the original owner."

▲ CONOID CHAIR

George Nakashima. Designed c. 1960, production date of this example: 1972. East Indian rosewood, hickory. 33 1/4 x 20 x 16 in. Collection of Mr. and Mrs. Irving Winter.

Nakashima's Conoid Chair, like much of his earlier work, was clearly influenced in part by Windsor chairs. The design features thick, continuous, backward-slanting stiles and legs that are balanced on heavy sled runners and intersected by an unsupported solid wood seat. Nakashima's use of tapered Windsor-style spindles softens the chair's severely modern architectural geometry.

The Random House dictionary defines conoid as "a geometrical solid formed by the revolution of a conic section [an ellipse, parabola or hyperbola] about one of its axes." The slanting back of this chair thus could be described as conoid.

BOXES

Boxes served a wide array of personal and domestic functions in the early American household. Locked wooden boxes kept money, deeds, and important documents safe in the home. Kitchen and pantry boxes of different sizes and shapes held butter, cheese, herbs and spices, tea, sugar, corn and other meals, dried grains and fruits, candles, and tinder or tapers for lighting fires. Salt was kept dry in small boxes that hung on the wall near the fire. Typically, the saltbox lid slanted down from the vertical back of the box. In modern times, the term "saltbox" identifies the lean-to house form, common throughout early New England, that coincidentally resembles these boxes.

Boxes were also used to hold personal items. Ladies filled boxes with jewelry, combs, hairpieces, and toilet articles, as well as buttons, thimbles, spools of thread, and other sewing accessories, while gentlemen used them to store their shaving equipment, tobacco, and snuff. Boxes made for personal use were often decorated, either with carving or painted designs. Some were grain painted, but more often the designs were based on floral or figural motifs. A woman's boxes for personal items were among her most prized and intimate possessions, so in many cases they were decorated with great care, often personalized with the owner's initials or full name and a date.

Virtually every member of nineteenth-century society wore hats, and most of these hats were protected in boxes. Both men and women carefully matched hats and outfits to suit particular social situations and therefore needed protective cases to store and carry their headgear safely when traveling. Hatboxes were made of either thin bent wood or pasteboard, lined with newspaper, and often covered with swatches of decorative wallpaper. A wide variety of hand-blocked wallpapers were available in the early decades of the nineteenth century, ranging from floral and geometric patterns to elaborate historical and other pictorial designs. The gaily colored and often intricately patterned papers provided hatbox makers with a relatively inexpensive and decorative means of covering their boxes.

Bandboxes (the generic term that includes hatboxes) could vary in size from a few inches to several feet in diameter. They were used not only to store hats but also served as suitcases to carry clothing, collars, ribbons, jewelry, combs, and other personal accessories. Most were circular, although a few small bandboxes were heart shaped. Some hatboxes were shaped specifically to hold the stiff-brimmed, men's beaver top hats fashionable in the mid-1800s. Hatboxes and bandboxes were especially popular among the young "factory girls" who worked in the vast textile mills of such burgeoning

◄ OVAL BOX

Attributed to Daniel Crosman. c. 1844–1870. New Lebanon, New York. Maple with pine bottom and lid, copper tacks. 8 1/4 x 15 1/8 x 11 1/8 in. Hancock Shaker Village, Pittsfield, Massachusetts.

The Shaker community at New Lebanon produced great numbers of distinctive oval storage boxes in a variety of sizes and colors. The boxes produced at New Lebanon and other Shaker communities were eagerly sought by worldly customers, who prized their careful workmanship, practicality, and attractively painted surfaces.

Daniel Crosman (1810–1885) was in charge of the oval-box business at New Lebanon from 1844 until sometime in the 1870s. This large box, big enough to hold a woman's bonnet, is slightly larger than the biggest standard size offered by the New Lebanon workshop and has six "swallowtail" joints, one more than usual.

New England manufacturing centers as Nashua and Manchester, New Hampshire, and Lowell, Massachusetts. In the first half of the nineteenth century, thousands of young girls from all over New England took jobs in the booming textile factories, often working for a year or two to save money before being married. Part of their income typically went to purchase fancy new clothing, and bandboxes provided attractive and affordable travel and storage containers for these delicate new garments.

Among the many New England craftspeople who made hat and bandboxes, the best known was "Aunt" Hannah Davis (1784–1863) of Jaffrey, New Hampshire. She was renowned in her own time for the high quality of her boxes. A fastidious craftsperson, she searched out suitable trees to cut into box material, chopped and steam bent her own wood splints, and covered her boxes with carefully chosen wallpapers. Her boxes, which came in two sizes, were made with spruce splint sides and pine bottoms and sold for twelve or fifty cents each.

Probably the best-known box makers of the nineteenth century were the Shakers, whose fingered oval boxes have become emblematic of Shaker craftsmanship. Usually made of maple, with pine bottoms and lids, the Shaker oval box represented a refinement of box forms and joinery that became traditional in New England. Shaker boxes were joined with delicately cut, pointed fingered joints called "swallowtails." The boxes were finished with copper tacks and painted or stained in a wide range of colors, ranging from earth tones to brilliant blues and yellows. They were made in a variety of sizes, from under four inches in diameter to over fifteen inches, and used to store everything from herbs and spices to dry paint pigments and nails. Unlidded boxes were filled with wood shavings and used as spitoons. Boxes were produced in virtually all the Shaker communities, with commercial production concentrated in the northern communities of New Lebanon, New York, Alfred and Sabbathday Lake, Maine, and Canterbury, New Hampshire. Shaker boxes were popular throughout New England and New York and were produced for sale by some of the communities well into the twentieth century. A number of talented contemporary craftsmen, including Bruce Pyle of Vermont and Charles Harvey of Berea, Kentucky, have revived the art of the Shaker box in recent years. Appreciation of these extraordinarily graceful containers, fostered by both careful preservation of originals and attention to detail in reproductions, has never been higher.

As society's needs and technology's capabilities changed in the later half of the nineteenth century, handmade boxes were gradually replaced by factory-made containers of cardboard or wood. Today, perhaps more than any other objects, the boxes used by our predecessors, which often held the secrets and treasures of their owners, acquaint us with the course of our ancestors' daily lives.

◀ HANGING CANDLE BOX

Artist unknown. c. 1790–1810. Connecticut River Valley. Carved and painted wood. 24 5/8 x 12 3/4 x 5 3/8 in. The Museum of American Folk Art, New York.

Tallow candles, made from animal fat, were stored on a wall near the fireplace in boxes like this decoratively carved and painted example. The circular designs were drawn with the aid of a compass.

▲ Salt Box

Decorated by John Drissell. 1797. Pennsylvania. White pine. Overall height: 11 in., overall width: 7 1/4 in., overall depth: 8 1/2 in. The Henry Francis du Pont Winterthur Museum, Winterthur, Delaware.

Salt was a precious commodity in early homes and was stored near the kitchen fire to keep it dry. This brightly decorated Pennsylvania German salt box is inscribed at the top with its owner's name, "Anne Leterman/Anno Dominni 1797," and at the bottom with the decorator's, "John Drissell/ his hand May/22/1797." The stylized floral decoration is typical of decoration found on chairs, chests, boxes, woodenware, and fraktur drawings in German settlements in Pennsylvania.

▲ DOMED-LID BOX

*Artist unknown. c. 1800–1820. Probably Lancaster County,
Pennsylvania. Tulip poplar, paint, sheet-iron latch and hinges. 12
13/16 x 15 3/4 x 10 11/16 in. The Henry Francis du Pont
Winterthur Museum, Winterthur, Delaware.*

*Several similar boxes, some lined with early Lancaster County news-
papers, have also survived. Some of the designs on this box were
formed with the aid of a compass.*

◄ Birch-Bark Box

Unknown Penobscot Indian artist. Early nineteenth century. Maine. Birch bark. Diameter: 10 in., cover diameter: 10 3/4 in. Peabody & Essex Museum/ Peabody Museum Collection, Salem, Massachusetts.

The bark of paper birches provided eastern Woodland Indians with a flexible but hard-wearing material used for canoes as well as boxes. Birch-bark storage boxes were made with the bark turned inside out so that the dark-colored underside was shown. The decorative accents were scratched through the surface of the reversed bark.

▼ Hatboxes and Bandboxes

Artists unknown. c. 1820–1850. New England. Wood splint, pasteboard, wallpaper. Largest box: 17 1/2 x 15 x 12 in. The Shelburne Museum, Shelburne, Vermont.

Hatboxes and bandboxes were made in a wide assortment of sizes and shapes. They were used by young women of the early nineteenth century who could not afford leather luggage, and provided attractive, portable storage for bonnets as well as for dresses, jewelry, combs, and other accessories. The elegant, men's white beaver top hat dates c. 1840.

◄ SAMPLE BOX CONTAINING TEN PANELS

Moses Eaton. c. 1800–1830. Dublin, New Hampshire. Painted and decorated pine, brass. Box: 8 3/4 x 15 1/16 x 2 5/8 in., panels: 6 7/8 x 14 x 1/8 in. Collection of the Museum of American Folk Art, New York. Anonymous gift and gift of the Richard Coyle Lilly Foundation.

Eaton was a professional paint decorator who is best known for his many surviving stenciled walls. This painted box could be shown to his customers, who would consider the different samples and select an appropriate decoration for their chest or box.

▼ SHAKER PRESENTATION BOX

Elder Henry Clay Blinn. c. 1880. Canterbury, New Hampshire. Bird's-eye maple. Diameter: 7 in. Collection of David A. Schorsch, Inc., New York.

This late Shaker-made box is remarkable for its unique form, possibly influenced by Oriental designs popular in contemporary society, and for its use of figured wood. Henry Clay Blinn (1824–1905) was a stone carver, carpenter, historian, inventor, and master printer as well as a spiritual leader in the Canterbury community.

▴ LUCY FRANCIS'S SEWING BOX

Artist unknown. c. 1850. New England. Mahogany with inlays of whale-bone and various tropical woods. 3 1/2 x 10 1/4 x 6 1/4 in. The Shelburne Museum, Shelburne, Vermont.

Probably made on board ship by a sailor for his sweetheart, this box is decorated with momentos of a whaling journey: pieces of engraved whalebone and inlays of exotic woods gathered during shore leaves in tropical ports.

▲ TABLE CHEST

Artist unknown. c. 1835. New Market, Virginia. Yellow pine. 16 1/2 x 25 x 15 in. Collection of Roddy and Sally Moore.

This large, footed box has a dovetailed case with the top and bottom nailed to the sides. The unusual dome-topped lid is dovetailed at the corners. The decoration is both stencil and freehand work.

Over thirty similar boxes are known. Many have been linked to a Lutheran girl's school in New Market. The boxes were probably made by a craftsman at the school and then decorated by female students. Drawing, stenciling, calligraphy, needlework, and other arts were part of the curriculum at female seminaries throughout the country in the first half of the nineteenth century and were considered essential accomplishments in a young woman's "finishing."

▼ ISAAC CHANDLER'S BOX

*Artist unknown. c. 1825–1845. Region unknown. Carved and painted wood. Height: 3 1/2
in., diameter: 7 1/8 in. Abby Aldrich Rockefeller Folk Art Center, Williamsburg, Virginia.
Bequest of Effie Thixton Arthur.*

*Circular storage boxes like this were used to hold herbs, spices, flour, nuts, seeds, and other dry
goods in early American kitchens and pantries. The name Isaac Chandler, probably the person
for whom the box was made, is lettered in black paint on the top of this box. The splint sides of
the box and lid are nailed together, and the top and bottom are nailed into the sides.*

MUSICAL INSTRUMENTS

Handmade musical instruments have always played an important role in American society. American craftsmen adapted European and African instruments in a variety of inventive ways and, in the process, made music available for everyday use in the home and community. Much of the invention was born of necessity; Native Americans and rural craftsmen often made their own instruments simply because they could not afford to buy an instrument made by someone else. The results ranged from the rudimentary—fiddles made of corn stalks and gourds, and transverse blown flutes and pan pipes of different lengths of hollowed-out sugar cane reeds—to carefully crafted wooden dulcimers, guitars, banjos, and mandolins that could sometimes equal the work of the finest city craftsmen.

The fiddle was the only folk instrument brought to America by early settlers from the British Isles. In both Britain and America, the fiddle was used primarily to play dance music. Most ballad singers sang without accompaniment, although a few played the fiddle in unison with their singing. Before the Civil War, dance music was played by a solo fiddler, but in the later years of the nineteenth century, the fiddler was often accompanied by the driving rhythm of a frailed banjo. American fiddlers, particularly in the North, adapted the traditional Irish dance tunes played by their forefathers. Fiddlers in the southern mountains of the Virginias, Kentucky, Tennessee, North Carolina, and Georgia, however, developed a distinctive style and repertoire of their own. Southern fiddlers often held the fiddle against their bodies rather than under their chins and played two strings at once, using propulsive, sawing bowing rhythms. The familiar tunes "Turkey in the Straw" and "The Arkansas Traveler" (to which children sing "I'm bringing home a baby bumblebee") are typical of southern-style fiddling.

Many of this country's most interesting and fertile musical traditions resulted from the fusion of European and African traditions in the rural American South. The banjo, perhaps the quintessential "American" instrument, is a case in point. Although the instrument is most often associated with the rural musical traditions of Appalachia, such as old-timey and bluegrass, its origins lie not in Europe, but in Africa. Thomas Jefferson noted as early as 1781 that the "banjar" was something "which they brought hither from Africa," and Stephen Foster's pre–Civil War minstrel who "come (*sic*) from Alabama with a banjo on my knee" was a white man impersonating a slave.

The prototype of the banjo can be found in a number of similar west African instruments with gourd or calabash bodies, fretless necks, and gut strings. American craftsmen adapted these instruments to a circular wooden frame with the skin of an animal tightly stretched over it, like a drum. As a result, the banjo is the most percussive of all stringed instruments, both in sound and playing technique. Early

◄ VIOLIN

Artist unknown. c. 1840–1870. New England. Wood, whalebone. Kendall Whaling Museum, Sharon, Massachusetts.

This inexpensive, European-made violin was refitted with tuning pegs, fingerboard, and a bridge made of whalebone and incised with elaborate scrimshaw decoration. Singing and dancing helped sailors pass the long hours of inactivity and boredom between encounters with whales.

*Joe Henry Hunley of Axton,
Virginia, is known to have made
sixty to seventy stringed instruments, many of them unique in
design and some completely of his
own invention. In this c. 1940
photograph, Hunley is surrounded
by some of his creations, including
fiddles, guitars, banjos, and a couple of mysteries.*

*Blue Ridge Heritage Archive,
Ferrum College, Ferrum, Virginia.*

minstrel-show banjos, which presumably were modeled after African-American prototypes, had four
strings. Sometime before the Civil War, the addition of a short fifth string, tuned much higher than the
other four and struck by the thumb as a ringing drone, transformed the instrument into something
uniquely American. Early banjos were fretless, allowing the player rather than the maker to choose the
intervals playable on the instrument. Although the fretted five-string banjo is preferred among today's
bluegrass and country musicians, old-time fretless, gut-strung mountain banjos are still made and
played in Appalachia.

Fretless instruments were favored in the rural South because they allowed the player to bypass easily
the well-tempered tuning system that was defined by frets and favored by European art music. Ballad
singers and instrumentalists in the isolated southern mountains preserved the archaic modal scales, odd
meters, and microtonal intervals of the ancient rural ballads and dance tunes brought to America by
their forefathers. Early twentieth-century folk song collectors were astonished to discover that variants
of centuries-old British tunes, many presumed lost to oral tradition, were still being sung and played in
the southern mountains.

The origins of the old-time music of the Appalachian mountains predate the adoption of the well-
tempered system, which did not become widely used even by classical musicians until the early 1700s.
Old-time music was linear and melodic rather than chordal. It was made to be sung or played by a single musician and did not lend itself readily to the limitations imposed by chordal accompaniment and
ensemble playing. Even the region's dominant early church music—so-called sacred harp or shape-
note music—put more emphasis on melody and rhythm than harmony. Although sacred harp music
was written for four parts, the voices often moved independently, and the widely spaced harmonies
avoided sweet-sounding thirds, more frequently moving in parallel fifths, a technique rejected by the
European classical tradition.

Another well-known American folk instrument is the mountain, or lap, dulcimer. This relatively simple instrument was developed and popularized by the rural people of Appalachia, who used it to
accompany their singing. The lap dulcimer, so-called because it is played with the back of the instrument flat against the lap and the fretboard facing up, is a fretted instrument with three or sometimes
four strings. Strummed with a goose-feather quill, the dulcimer was a small-voiced and personal
instrument, perfectly suited for intimate gatherings in the log cabins of Appalachia. Although modern
players have greatly expanded and exploited its harmonic potential, the lap dulcimer was traditionally
played only as a melodic instrument, with the lower strings droning rhythmically against a melody fretted with a finger or stick on the top string.

FRETLESS BANJO ▸

Stanley Hicks. 1988. Vilas, North Carolina. Cherry, inset groundhog hide head. Length: 37 in. International Folk Art Foundation Collection at the Museum of International Folk Art, a unit of the Museum of New Mexico, Santa Fe.

Stanley Hicks, who died in 1990, learned to make traditional fretless banjos and Appalachian dulcimers from his father. In addition to his instrument building, Hicks was also a talented "flat-foot" dancer and a fine singer of the ancient ballads brought to Appalachia from England and Scotland by early settlers. He was honored as a National Heritage Fellow by the Folk Arts Program of the National Endowment for the Arts in 1983.

Stanley Hicks of Vilas, North Carolina, playing one of his homemade, fretless banjos.

North Carolina Arts Council, Raleigh, North Carolina.

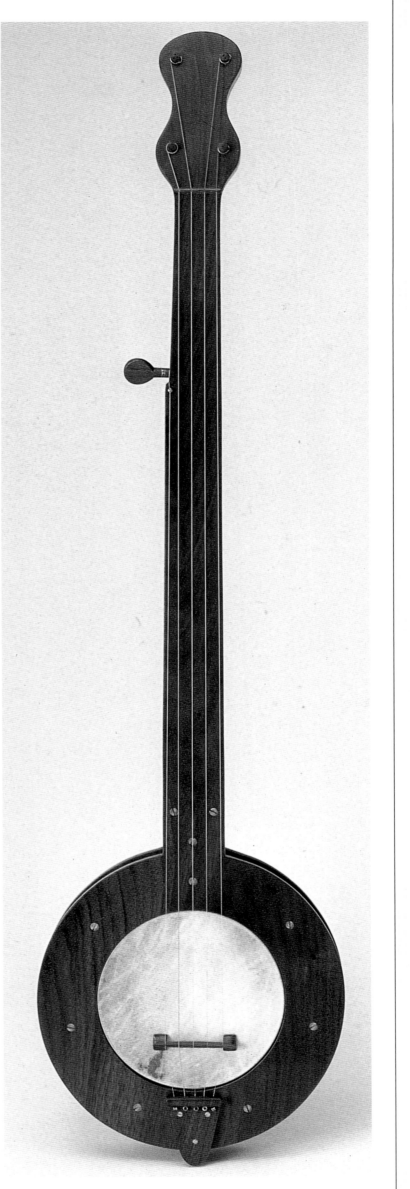

CELLO ▶

George Jewett. 1795. Lebanon, Maine. Wood. National Museum of American History, Smithsonian Institution, Washington, D.C.

The tailpiece of this extraordinary homemade instrument is heart shaped and marked "Pamela/ 1794, J. Jewett Fecit" on one side and "George Jewett, AD 1795" on the other. The peg box is carved in what may be a portrait of said Pamela. Fecit is a Latin term meaning "he made it." In Scotland, cellos often accompanied fiddles playing dance and parlor music, a tradition that was brought to the Northeast by early settlers.

▾ SNARE DRUM

*Artist unknown. Mid-nineteenth century. Region unknown. Wood, calfskin, rope, leather.
Diameter: 17 in. The Metropolitan Museum of Art, New York.*

*This brightly painted, two-headed regimental drum is typical of those used by military bands
throughout the country during the nineteenth century.*

▾ MINSTREL-SHOW BANJO

*Thomas Rhoades. 1865. Rockingham County, Virginia. Cedar neck,
curly maple tailpiece, bird's-eye maple rim, hide head, silver
escutcheon, bone inlays. Length: 36 in. Collection of Roddy and Sally
Moore.*

This type of elaborately decorated banjo was used by minstrel-show
entertainers made up in "blackface." The acorn-shaped escutcheon at
the top of this banjo's head is made of silver taken from a Kentucky
rifle. According to family tradition, the bone inlays on the fingerboard
and tailpiece were taken from a comb owned by Rhoades's sweetheart,
although they may also have been part of a rifle. A miniature
Kentucky rifle form is inlaid on the back of the neck. Like a drum,
this banjo has double heads, a construction preferred by many early
players. The decoratively shaped neck beneath the unfretted fifth
string balances the elongated curved head.

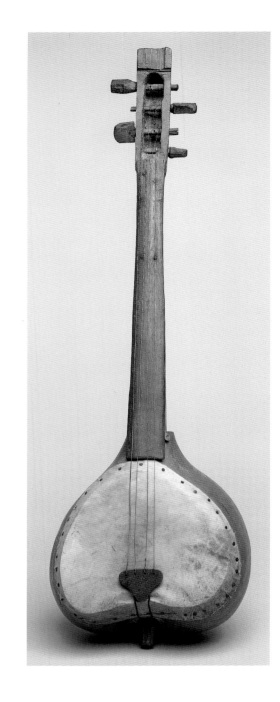

◄ GOURD FIDDLE

Artist unknown. Nineteenth century. Hillsville, Carol County, Virginia. Gourd body, hide head, hickory neck. Length: 23 1/2 in. Collection of Roddy and Sally Moore.

Fewer than ten gourd-bodied fiddles are known to survive. While a number were undoubtedly made by African-Americans who recalled African calabash-bodied instruments, this and another known example were made by an unidentified Anglo-American craftsman. The unusual hide head suggests that the maker was influenced by banjo construction.

▼ ZITHER

A member of the King family. c. 1850–1875. Speedwell section, Wythe County, Virginia. Walnut. Length: 35 in. Collection of Roddy and Sally Moore.

This early type of dulcimer was brought to America by German immigrants in the late 1700s. Examples made in this country have been traced to German communities throughout Pennsylvania and the South and as far west as Ohio and Indiana. Like the lap dulcimer, the zither usually has three strings, but the fretboard is not raised off the body of the instrument as it is on the dulcimer. Zithers like this example undoubtedly influenced the development of the American lap dulcimer, but the evolutionary lines are unclear since both instruments were being made simultaneously in the early nineteenth century. The lap dulcimer, with its centrally placed raised fretboard, became the dominant form in the nineteenth century and continues to be widely made and played today.

▾ Hand Drum

Eddie Little Chief. c. 1900. Pine Ridge Indian Reservation, South Dakota. Wood, pigskin, pigment. Diameter: 15 1/2 in., width: 2 in. Buffalo Bill Historical Center, Cody, Wyoming.

Northern Plains Indians often accompanied ceremonial dancing with hand drums that typically were painted with images received in visions. Eddie Little Chief was a Sioux Indian; his drum is decorated with a painting of a spirit horse.

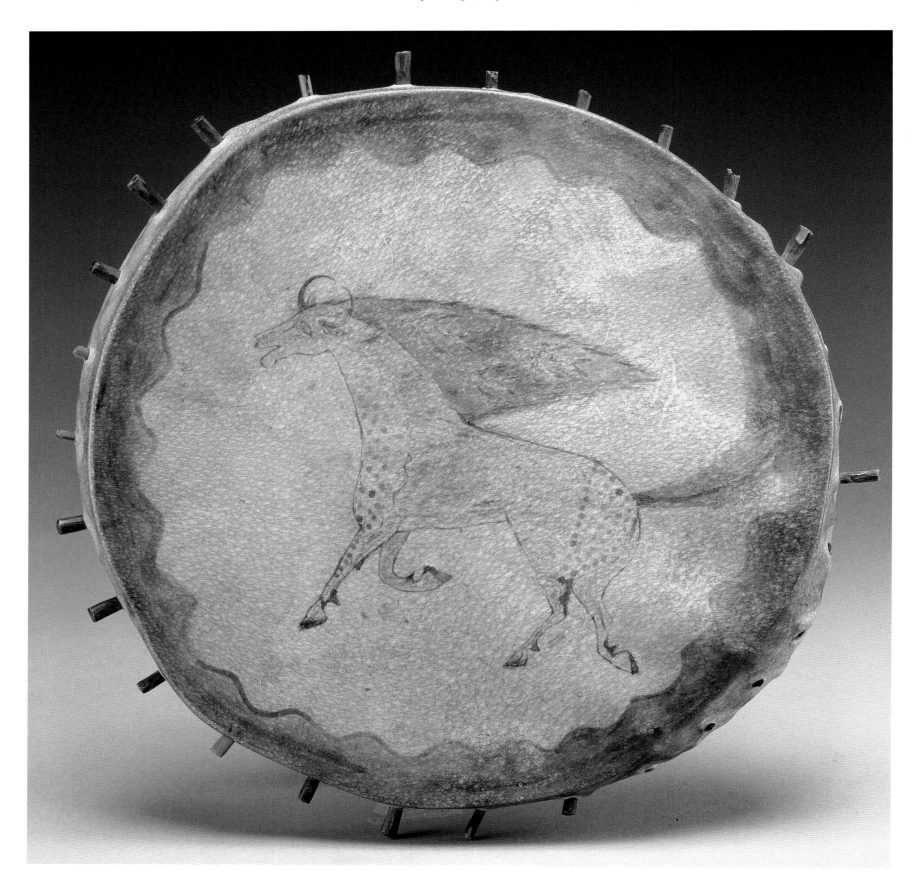

◄ OCTAGONAL-BODIED
BANJO

*Artist unknown. c. 1880–1920. Rural
Retreat, Wythe County, Virginia. Walnut
top, hickory or oak neck, inset hide head.
Length: 34 in. Collection of Roddy and
Sally Moore.*

*This rare, octagonal form was made only in
a few German and Ulster-Scots communities
in Virginia. Round-bodied banjos, often
built around a commercially made metal
rim, were preferred in the Blue Ridge area
of Virginia and throughout many other parts
of the South.*

ABSTRACT DESIGN FIDDLE ▶

*Joe Henry Hunley. c. 1925. Axton, Henry County, Virginia.
Yellow pine body, maple neck. Length: 25 in. Collection of Roddy
and Sally Moore.*

*Joe Henry Hunley played in a family band on a local radio station in
the 1920s and 1930s. The forms of the instruments he made often
appear to have been dictated by the materials he had close at hand.
This fiddle has an extremely thin body.*

◀ DOG-HEAD FIDDLE

*Joe Henry Hunley. c. 1925. Axton, Henry County, Virginia.
Walnut fingerboard, maple neck, aluminum tailpiece. Length: 22 in.
Collection of Roddy and Sally Moore.*

*The dog and neck on this extraordinary fiddle are carved from a sin-
gle piece of maple. The dog looks down over the fingerboard as the
instrument is played.*

▼ DULCIMER

*A member of the Pilleaux family. c. 1850.
Knox County, Tennessee. Figured walnut.
Length: 39 1/2 in. Collection of Wilson and
Lynn Beamer.*

This extremely sophisticated and well-made
dulcimer has a heart-shaped cutout at the tailpiece and a carved scroll as well as heart-shaped
wrought iron tuning pegs made by a blacksmith. The instrument came from an area of
German settlements and may have been made
by a cabinetmaker since the back is dovetailed
expertly into place.

C A R V I N G S :
D E C O Y S   A N D
C A N E S

D E C O Y S

Bird and fish decoys, made to lure prey within the reach of hunters' weapons, are both inventions of Native Americans, their precise origins lost in prehistory. Bone fish decoys are known to date back to 2000 B.C., while the earliest documented bird decoys extant are a group of lures discovered in Colorado's Lovelock Cave in 1923 and carbon dated to at least A.D. 1000. The best-crafted of the Lovelock Cave decoys are made from reeds and feathers and are instantly recognizable representations of the canvasback duck, the king of American game ducks. The sophistication of the Lovelock lures suggests that they represent an already long-established tradition.

Observations of Indian bird decoys and hunting methods are preserved in the journals and letters of early explorers. In 1687 the French explorer Baron Lahontan wrote about Indian hunting a continent away from Lovelock Cave on Lake Champlain: "For a decoy they have the skins of geese...and ducks, dried and stuffed with hay. The two feet being made fast with two nails to a small piece of light plank, which float....The place being frequented by wonderfull (*sic*) numbers of...waterfowls—see the stuffed skins swimming with their heads erected as if they were alive. They repair to the same place and so give the savages an opportunity of shooting them either flying or upon the water, after which the savages get into their canows (*sic*) and gather them up." Europeans took the Indian idea of the bird decoy and, sometime around the Revolution, applied their own woodworking traditions to the form, and began fashioning sturdy, long-lasting wooden lures. These early decoys were simple and made no attempt to depict the quarry realistically. In truth, decoys did not need to be realistic but rather suggestive, since they were made to be seen at great distances. The best and most effective gunning "birds" fooled wildfowl not because they looked exactly like their living counterparts, but rather because they captured something of the essence of their prey—a gesture, an attitude, a sense of motion, restfulness, or even exhaustion. These traits caused the wild observer to remain confident long enough to prove fatal.

◄ PIKE DECOYS

Oscar Peterson. c. 1930–1940. Cadillac, Michigan. Wood, tack eyes, metal fins. Lengths: 6 to 11 in. Top to bottom: Private collection, Collection of Steven J. Michaan, private collection, Collection of Steven J. Michaan, Collection of Leonard Gottlieb.

Oscar Peterson (1887–1951), who carved professionally, was the most prolific of all fish decoy makers. He may have carved more than ten thousand decoys from 1907 on. His flat-bottomed, elongated, thin, and brightly painted fish always had slightly curved tails so they would turn in the water as they were being jigged through the ice. In addition to decoys, Peterson carved a number of decorative vases, bowls, plaques, and signs for the tourist trade, all decorated with fish. Young pike were often eaten by their voracious, cannibalistic elders and are among the species most commonly represented by fish decoys.

Wood

―――

*America's
Traditional
Crafts*

•

192

The history of decoy making in America is inseparably linked to the commercial exploitation of the country's great numbers of wildfowl. Indeed, the largest wildfowl hunt in the history of the world took place in North America between 1865 and 1918. Following the Civil War, the combination of improved railroad transportation systems and new technologically advanced weapons, especially the breech loading shotgun, impacted with devastating results upon the seemingly limitless supplies of wild game. Professional market gunners worked the prime hunting grounds of all the principal flyways, supplying birds to city restaurants and game markets to meet the intense public demand. Well-made decoys were among the tools most vital to their trade. In addition to table birds such as canvasback and redhead ducks, geese, and brant, professional gunners hunted plumage species such as terns, gulls, and heron, whose showy feathers were in great demand by the millinery trade for use in fashionable women's hats. An early conservation report, issued in 1886, asserted that five million birds a year were being killed for the millinery trade alone.

Scores of craftsmen turned to decoy making full time to meet the needs of the commercial market, feather gunners, and the many well-to-do sportsmen who traveled from the cities to shoot wild birds. Master craftsmen in every part of the country produced decoys specifically designed to use in a particular area's waters, to match local hunting methods, and to attract a region's most common species. Illinois' Robert (1849–1915) and Catherine (d. 1953) Elliston, for example, created two-piece, hollow-bodied lures with bold and highly detailed combed feather paint. Their duck decoys, imitating mallards and pintails—the dominant mid-West species—as well as lures representing the less common

▲ CANADA GOOSE DECOY

A. Elmer Crowell. c. 1917. East Harwich, Massachusetts. Wood with glass eyes. Length: 22 1/2 in. Collection of James M. McCleery, M.D.

Throughout his long professional career as a birdcarver, Crowell (1861–1951) crafted miniature and decorative birds as well as working decoys. This goose, although in decoy form, was made as a special order presentation piece for a wealthy client and was never intended for use in the field. The goose epitomizes Crowell's unmatched combined talents as carver and painter.

Elmer Crowell posed for this photograph in his East Harwich, Massachusetts workshop, c. 1930. He is shown surrounded by his work and tools, including a carved fish and some decorative shorebirds.

The Shelburne Museum, Shelburne, Vermont.

bluebills, redheads, canvasbacks, black ducks, and blue-winged teal of the area, had V-shaped hulls designed to ride well in the swift waters of the Illinois River. A thin strip of lead that ran the length of the center of the hull served as weight and ballast. By contrast, the decoys of Nathan Cobb, Jr. (1825–1905) of Virginia, made for use in corrosive salt water, were painted in solid blocks of color that only suggested the broad outline of the species' plumage pattern. The bodies of Cobb's decoys, while hollow, were often plump with simple, carved split tails. In addition to the geese, brant, and black ducks common to his region, Cobb carved decoys for bluebills, redheads, and buffleheads as well as stickup shorebird decoys for Hudsonian curlew, red knot, and black-bellied plover. Like many decoy makers, Cobb often made use of readily available materials; the necks and heads of his geese and brant were often represented by the suggestively gnarled shapes of seaside locust branches, while all of his shorebirds have hardwood oak bills splined through the back of the head for strength.

Not all carvers were professionals like Elliston and Cobb, who sold their decoys to hunters. A number of other early and influential craftsmen carved exclusively for their own use. Among the earliest documented of these sportsmen carvers was Albert Davids Laing (1811–1886), who was born in New Jersey and lived for many years in New York. Laing's hollow, two-piece decoys, some of them believed to have been crafted as early as the 1840s, apparently grew out of an already existing New Jersey coastal tradition. A fastidious craftsman, Laing refined the concept of the hollow bird by compressing and streamlining his forms, and introduced the use of nonrusting copper nails to hold the body together. He also popularized the use of varied head positions, carving birds with heads turned and tucked in addition to the conventional straight-head form. When he moved to Stratford, Connecticut, in 1865, he brought his masterful decoys with him, where they exerted such a profound influence on local carvers that they became the regional norm within a generation.

In the late 1800s, decoy making became a cottage industry. Several "factories" produced thousands of decoys and began to market their wares by mail order. The Mason Decoy Factory of Detroit (active 1896 to 1924) was the largest and most successful of these enterprises. The Mason company's decoys had lathe-turned bodies, but all the finish and head carving, as well as the painting, was done by hand. In addition to a standard line of ducks, geese, and shorebirds, the company also made doves for upland shooting and apparently welcomed special orders, as evidenced by the more than a few aberrant Masons that have been found over the years.

The last decades of the nineteenth century and early years of the twentieth witnessed an increase in public awareness concerning the ongoing slaughter of wild birds. The budding conservation movement, the press, and thousands of outraged citizens put increasing pressure on Washington for the protection of dwindling wildfowl populations. Federal conservation legislation, which outlawed interstate sale of wildfowl and imposed bag limits throughout migratory routes, finally brought the market gunning era to an end just after World War I and thus substantially reduced the demand for decoys. With the market gunners essentially out of business, decoy makers turned their attentions to sport gunners, who often demanded and could pay for the finest in handmade decoys. Master craftsmen such as Cape Cod's A. Elmer and Cleon Crowell, Illinois' Charles and Edna Perdew, and Maryland's Lem and

Steve Ward created decoys of such sculptural and painterly intricacy that more than a few owners put them on mantelpieces rather than into hunting rigs. As interest in the aesthetics of these pieces grew, all three teams not coincidentally also created purely decorative decoys, miniatures, and life-size bird models, intended solely for display. These decorative carvings, particularly those of Lem Ward, who lived until 1984, have exerted an enormous influence on today's carvers, who sometimes spend thousands of hours on a single decorative bird sculpture, carving and inserting individual wooden feathers and fashioning intricate feather patterns with sophisticated wood-burning tools.

Although many craftsmen continued to make decoys during the Depression years, by the end of World War II the traditional wooden bird faced increasingly strong competition from the cheap, sturdy, and effective new lures made of plastic and other new synthetics. These mass-produced, low-cost, and comparatively indestructible decoys eventually dominated the market and drove the handmade wooden decoy and its makers into history.

Another type of lure, fish decoys, was used by ice fishermen. Winter spearing for pike, muskellunge, salmon, lake trout, sturgeon, and other large lake-dwelling species was a common practice on ice-bound northern lakes. As was the case with bird decoys, the idea of using fish decoys was introduced to Europeans by Native Americans. Indians often crafted fish decoys from bone, a durable and readily available material which would sink quickly. The Europeans preferred to use wood, which was also readily available and could be easily carved and painted to create a realistic looking lure.

Typically, fish decoys had metal fins and tails and an attachment for a lead line. The decoy was usually weighted with an inset of lead to sink it and balance it in the water, and was attached to a line held by a short jigging stick. Fish decoys were usually made to represent minnows, such as chubs or shiners, or fingerling trout, pike, perch, bass, or suckers. Far less common models were "critters," which included such tantalizing fishy delectables as frogs, crayfish, turtles, butterflies, mice, and even baby muskrats and ducklings.

The spear fisherman watched carefully for signs of prey as he sat or crouched in a dark ice shanty while jigging his lure through a hole cut in the ice. When a large fish appeared beneath the ice (an event that might occur perhaps once in several hours of waiting), the fisherman attempted to spear it with a quick, strong jab of his multipronged fork. Even if the blow was successful, he still often faced a mighty struggle, because wrestling a fifteen- or twenty-pound pike or musky through the ice and into a small shanty on the end of a spear was no easy task. It was not a sport for either the impatient or the faint-of-heart.

New York's Lake Chautauqua, a large body of water near the Ohio border, was the earliest center for intensive commercial spearing and the place where many of the finest fish decoys have been found. Unlike midwestern decoys, Lake

Decoy carvers Lem and Steve Ward in their Crisfield, Maryland, workshop, c. 1935.

The Shelburne Museum, Shelburne, Vermont.

PAIR OF PINTAIL DECOYS ▲

Lemuel and Stephen Ward. c. 1932. Crisfield, Maryland. Wood with glass eyes. Length of each: 18 in. Collection of William Purnell.

Lem and Steve Ward worked all their lives as barbers and decoy makers in Crisfield, a small town on the "Eastern Shore" of Chesapeake Bay. Billing themselves as "Wildfowl Counterfeiters in Wood," the Ward brothers produced an extensive and diverse body of work that has profoundly influenced generations of subsequent carvers. Lem, who was honored as a National Heritage Fellow shortly before his death in 1984, was particularly influential, pioneering in the art of decorative bird carving. Today, the Ward Museum of Wildfowl Art in Salisbury, Maryland, perpetuates the legacy of these two master craftsmen.

Chautauqua lures usually had leather tails. Spearing activity on Lake Chautauqua was so intense that it had to be outlawed in 1905 to prevent depletion of the lake's game fish. Michigan, Minnesota, and Wisconsin were the other primary sites of spearing and fish decoy making, with the peak years being between 1920 and 1950. Mt. Clemens, Michigan, located just north of Detroit on Lake St. Clair, was home to several of the most highly regarded fish decoy carvers, including Hans Janner, Sr. and his son-in-law, Andrew Trombley. Janner's large and highly stylized interpretations of bass and trout represent the form in one of its finest expressions, while the realism of Trombley's scale painting, achieved by brushing glittery gold or silver paint through a fine mesh fishnet, is extraordinary. The best known of all fish carvers is Oscar Peterson of Cadillac, Michigan, a prolific commercial fish carver who turned out thousands of stylized fish for spearers, as well as decorative fish plaques and other sculptures for the local tourist trade. Peterson's instantly recognizable fish have long, thin bodies with slightly curved tails embellished with detailed, brightly hued paint.

C A N E S

Canes or, as they were more commonly called, walking sticks, were widely "worn" by men of all classes throughout the eighteenth and nineteenth centuries. Many walking sticks were commercially manufactured and ranged from simple, unadorned wooden canes to elegant sticks made of the finest materials. For a city gentleman of means, few accessories made such a statement as a carefully crafted, gold-handled, ebony cane.

Handcrafted sticks were the work of carvers throughout the country and particularly in the rural South. Locally available woods were the craftsman's raw materials, and creativity one of the tools with which he produced a distinctly personal body of work wrought within the severe limitations of the form of a three-foot-long stick. The majority of handcarved sticks are unique examples either made by the men who used them or crafted for a specific individual. Canes acted as extensions of the hand and arm and thus often bore a close physical relationship to their owners. Handles could be shaped to fit a particular hand, and the length of the cane was often decided by the owner's height and angle of use.

Walking sticks often also carried a symbolic or even emotional relationship to their owners. Carvers employed images that held special meaning to them. On many canes, animals of power such as snakes, lizards, or alligators encircled or crawled up the shafts, often seemingly in pursuit of, or even eating, frogs, turtles, fish, or birds. Other sticks carried images of dogs, lions, monkeys, or eagles, or human heads, torsos, hands, or legs. Since they were used in public, canes could also be employed to communicate to others aspects of the owner's personality, interests, profession, and affiliations. For example, a number of canes bear symbols of the approximately three hundred fraternal organizations in existence in the late nineteenth century, including such well-known groups as the Masons, the Improved Order of Redmen, and the Elks. A carpenter might wear a stick with a handle shaped like a hammer, or a railroad worker might carry a cane with trains carved on the shaft.

Walking sticks were also made in the nineteenth century by American Indians and African-Americans. Both groups adopted the European-American cane-making tradition, adding features derived from their own iconographic customs.

◄ DEER-HEAD CANE

Unknown Indian artist. c. 1880. Probably Maine. Painted hardwood, metal eyes, glass beads, brass ferrule. Height: 42 3/4 in. Collection of George H. Meyer.

American Indians carved canes for their own use as well as for sale to the tourist trade. The deer head recalls carved stylized animal images found on eastern Woodland Indian bowls, ladles, and crooked knives dating as early as the 1600s. The five-inch-long ears of this example are applied separately.

Iroquois canes, for example, typically have smooth shafts topped with carved handles that clearly represent animals, animal heads, or human faces. Although evidence indicates that a few False Face canes might have been used in tribal rituals, most Iroquois walking sticks seem to carry personal rather than tribal meaning.

In west and central Africa, walking sticks brought to the region by European traders were highly coveted and considered status symbols. In America, African-Americans, particularly in Georgia and Mississippi, established rich cane-carving traditions that combined elements of African iconography with New World influences. These canes, crafted by early African-American carvers, many of whom had been brought to this country as slaves, proudly displayed ancient African traditions and can be counted among the most powerfully expressive of American folk arts.

CAGES CANES ▶

Left, by Amos Fisher; center, by Zaunheiser; right, artist unknown. Late nineteenth century. Left: Lancaster County, Pennsylvania; center: Mercer, Pennsylvania; right: region unknown. Painted or varnished wood; left: button and brass tacks; right: lithographs, glass, mirrors, hair, or straw. Heights: 34 1/2 to 36 1/2 in. Collection of George H. Meyer.

These elaborately worked examples, the wooden counterparts of embroidered, silk crazy quilts, are representative of the prevailing late Victorian taste for detailed and often totally unrelated ornamentation.

▲ GULL DECOY

*Captain Ketchum. c. 1860. Copiague, Long
Island, New York. Wood. Length: 18 5/8 in. The
Shelburne Museum, Shelburne, Vermont. Joel
Barber Collection.*

This early gull was used as a "confidence" decoy,
representing a species not hunted. When added to
a gunning rig of brant decoys, it helped present a
reassuring picture to passing birds, inspiring their
mistaken confidence that all was well below.

Captain Ketchum's son gave this old gull to Joel
Barber, the first important collector of decoys. In
his seminal 1934 book Wild Fowl Decoys, Barber
recounts that Ketchum told him about hunting
with his father and grandfather as a boy. "When
first allowed to accompany the older men, it was
[his] duty to 'load the guns' and 'keep the box
bailed out.'" For Barber, the gull decoy was
"always reminiscent of a shivering boy, crouching
at the feet of his father and grandfather, in the bottom of a hazy 'box'; alternately bailing and loading
guns to stop the tide of birds. Every time I see that
gull I hear again the end of his story. 'Why some
nights Mr. Barber I couldn't hear at all, from the
shooting over my head all day.'"

TERN DECOY ▶

*Daniel DeMott. c. 1880. Rockaway, Long Island,
New York. Wood. Length: 12 3/4 in. Collection
of James M. McCleery, M.D.*

Terns were sought by "plume" hunters, who sold
their feathers to the millinery trade for use in decorating fashionable ladies' hats. The Audubon
Society was founded primarily in response to the
millions of birds killed annually in the late nineteenth century by feather hunters.

◀ GOLDENEYE DRAKE DECOY

Albert Davids Laing. c. 1850. Stratford, Connecticut. Wood with glass eyes. Length: 13 in. The Shelburne Museum, Shelburne, Vermont. Joel Barber Collection.

Laing innovated by carving duck decoys in differing head positions to give his hunting rigs a more natural appearance. This bird's head is tucked down into its breast, a pose which is often assumed by tired wildfowl.

◄ SWAN

Attributed to Samuel Barnes. c. 1890. Havre de Grace, Maryland. Wood. Length: 36 3/8 in., height: 19 1/4 in. The Shelburne Museum, Shelburne, Vermont. Joel Barber Collection.

Swans were gunned for food until the practice was outlawed in 1908. Many southern gunners in the Chesapeake Bay, Virginia, and North Carolina regions continued to add swans to their rigs as "confidence" decoys.

◀ BRANT AND CANADA GOOSE DECOYS

Nathan Cobb, Jr. c. 1870. Cobb Island, Virginia. Wood with glass eyes. Length of goose: 31 in. Collection of James M. McCleery, M.D.

Both of these animated and expressive decoys, stretching forward in belligerent attitudes, have necks fashioned from the naturally twisted roots of seaside trees. Cobb was a master at incorporating the suggestive natural forms he found around him into his work. All of his decoys capture a strong sense of birds in motion. Tight-grained root heads had the extra advantage of being extremely strong and resistant to breakage.

▼ MALLARD DRAKE DECOY

Attributed to Hucks Caines. c. 1890. Georgetown, South Carolina. Wood. Length: 18 in. Collection of James M. McCleery, M.D.

The Caines brothers lived on land purchased by the financier and statesman Bernard Baruch for his Hobcaw Barony. "Hucks" Caines and his brothers "Pluty," "Ball," "Sawney," and Bob worked as guides for Baruch and his many guests and apparently crafted decoys for Baruch as well. A number of the Caines decoys have wildly exaggerated, elongated "swan" necks that resembled those of no other makers.

Harry Vinucksen Shourds. c. 1890. Barnegat, New Jersey. Wood. Length of largest bird: 12 in. The Shelburne Museum, Shelburne, Vermont.

Shourds (1861–1920), a prolific professional carver, made duck and goose decoys as well as shorebirds. This "rig" includes a Hudsonian curlew, a red knot, a pair of yellowlegs, and four black-bellied plovers, painted in varying seasonal plumage phases.

▲ (LEFT TO RIGHT) BLACK-BELLIED PLOVER, HUDSONIAN CURLEW, YELLOWLEGS, LONG-BILLED CURLEW DECOYS

William Bowman. c. 1890. Lawrence, Long Island, New York. Painted wood with glass eyes. Length of long-billed curlew: 17 in. Collection of James M. McCleery, M.D.

Bowman's remarkably lifelike shorebird decoys capture nuances of bird anatomy and behavior not attempted by most other carvers. More than those of any other carver, Bowman's decoys appear to be alive, seemingly caught in suspended animation and ready to fly off at the slightest provocation. They must have been deadly effective lures for the hunters who were lucky enough to gun over them.

GREAT BLUE HERON DECOY ▼

*Artist unknown. c. 1890. Barnegat, New Jersey. Wood. Length: 30 1/8 in. The Shelburne
Museum, Shelburne, Vermont.*

*Heron were sought by feather hunters for their beautiful long plume feathers, which were used
to decorate women's hats in the late nineteenth century. This deceptively simple decoy is made
in four pieces: a triangular beak, a neck, and joined body halves. The beak and neck are shaped
from tight-grained and virtually unbreakable roots or tree branches, while the body is crafted
from found and flawed pieces of gnarled and knotted wood.*

▾ RUDDY DUCK DECOY

Lee Dudley. c. 1890. Knott's Island, North Carolina. Wood. Length: 9 3/4 in. The Shelburne Museum, Shelburne, Vermont. Joel Barber Collection.

Lee Dudley (1861–1942) carved a number of graceful duck decoys for gunning clubs on Knott's Island, located on the Virginia–North Carolina border. Ruddy ducks, a small and vivacious species, were common in North Carolina waters. They were called "dollar ducks" by late nineteenth-century gunners for the price a pair brought at market.

◄ MALLARD DECOYS

*Robert and Catherine Elliston. c. 1890. Bureau, Illinois. Wood with glass eyes. Length of
each: 16 in. Collection of Jim Cook.*

*The Ellistons worked as a team; Robert did the carving, and wife Catherine applied the highly
detailed paint. Like a few other talented and fastidious decoy painters, including Elmer
Crowell, Catherine Elliston kept a study collection of bird skins to guide her efforts. "The
Elliston Decoy," as the birds were labeled on their weights, set a standard to which all subsequent Illinois River area carvers aspired.*

▲ EIDER DECOYS

*Artist unknown. c. 1900. Monhegan Island area, Maine. Wood. Length of each: 18 in.
Private collection.*

*The bird on the right has a wooden oval carved into his open mouth to represent a mussel,
the favored food of the eider, a large sea-going duck common in Downeast waters. The plug
at the front of the bird's mouth was inserted to prevent the bill from breaking.*

▼ PEEP DECOYS (LEAST SANDPIPERS)

*Attributed to Thomas Hewlett. c. 1900. Long Island, New York. Cork. Collection of
James M. McCleery, M.D.*

*Cork was widely used to make life preservers, which often washed up on Long Island
beaches, where resourceful decoy makers salvaged them. Cork provided an easily
worked material for decoy bodies and was used to make ducks as well as shorebirds.
Peeps were shot for food and cooked into "peep pie," which was considered a delicacy
by some hunters.*

▲ SNOW GOOSE DECOYS

John Tax. 1917. Wisconsin. Wood. Length of each: 23 1/2 in. Collection of James M. McCleery, M.D.

John Tax, who died in 1967, was a harness maker by trade who carved decoys for his own use. These two decoys are part of a large rig of standing snow and Canada goose decoys he crafted for use in field shooting. The decoys, made of laminated sections of wood, were carved in a number of different attitudes, including feeders, nestled heads, and sentinels. All of them stood on iron poles which were pushed into the ground.

HAROLD HAERTEL,
DECOY AND BIRD CARVER

Harold Haertel of Dundee, Illinois, now in his eighties, is the dean of American decoy and decorative bird carvers. In 1965, William Mackey, who assembled the finest documented collection of bird decoys, wrote, "Many so-called decoy makers of the present lose sight of the fact that a decoy is first of all a working tool and not a decoration or an ornament. When the objective is beauty and fussy detail rather than practicability, the product must be classified as an ornamental....In the case of a man like Harold Haertel..., who has made decoys for three or four decades, an exception should be made. His perfection of detail and adherence to species conformation and plumage pattern are second to none, and his present work is incomparable." (*American Bird Decoys*, p. 193.)

Haertel came to carving naturally, cutting gravestones as a boy in his father's monument shop. His involvement with birds took many forms: he hunted avidly, often with live decoys, was fascinated with the masterfully realistic paintings of Louis Aggasiz Fuertes, practiced taxidermy, and studied wildfowl photographs. He became a trendsetter in decoy competitions, pushing the limits of what was considered acceptable for working lures. In the 1960s and 1970s, Haertel also broke new ground by making many decoys of shorebirds, including such unusual species as phalaropes, intended as lures to facilitate conservation banding rather than gunning.

As William Mackey recognized, it is Haertel's experience as a decoy maker that gives his decorative carvings their air of authenticity. Like old masters such as Elmer Crowell and Lem Ward, Haertel has been able to successfully bridge the enormous gap between the practical and the merely beautiful, producing carvings that skillfully embody the essence of the living bird.

◄ PAIR OF GADWALL DECOYS

Harold Haertel. 1965. Dundee, Illinois. Wood with glass eyes. Length of each: 15 in. Private collection.

This gracefully carved and painted pair of decorative decoys demonstrate Haertel's subtle artistry. The hen is reaching forward to feed, while the drake cocks his head watchfully.

▼ RED-BREASTED MERGANSER DRAKE DECOY

Nathan Rowley Horner. c. 1930. West Creek, New Jersey. Wood with glass eyes. Length: 15 1/2 in. The Shelburne Museum, Shelburne, Vermont.

Horner brought the hollow-bodied coastal New Jersey decoy-making tradition, epitomized by the work of Harry V. Shourds (1861–1920), to its highest level of refinement. Horner took the forms learned from his master's decoys and reduced them to their essences, at the same time imparting an elegance of line that only the finest of Shourds's birds approach.

▼ Bass "Ghost Fish" Decoy

Hans Janner, Sr. c. 1939. Mount Clemens, Michigan. Walnut, brass fins, glass eyes. Length: 12 in. Collection of Alastair B. Martin.

Hans Janner, Sr. created utterly distinctive fish with powerfully sculpted body forms and stylized fins cut from pieces of brass or used tin cans. The light yellow paint on this decoy outlines a smaller "ghost fish," superimposed on and echoing the carved form of the red-painted body.

▲ FISH DECOYS

Artists unknown. c. 1900. Lake Chautauqua, New York. Wood with metal fins and leather tails. Lengths: 7 3/4 to 13 1/2 in. Collection of Steven J. Michaan.

Fish decoys, jigged through holes cut in winter ice, were used to lure pike, muskellunge, walleye, trout, bass, and other gamefish within striking distance of a fisherman's spear. Lake Chautauqua was the site of active winter commercial fishing in the last quarter of the nineteenth century. Spearing so seriously depleted the lake's population of gamefish that it was outlawed in 1904. Lake Chautauqua fish decoys are small, simply carved, and realistically painted. Their leather tails are unique to the region.

HUMAN-HEAD CANES ▸

Unknown African-American artists, except, left, by Fred Wilson. c. 1850–1920. Southern United States (left: Florida). Painted wood, metal. Heights: 36 1/2 to 45 in. Collection of George H. Meyer.

African-American cane carvers sometimes created shafts topped with strangely expressive, stylized human visages. Like those found on stoneware "face jugs," their purpose and meaning may have been ritualistic, but is now impenetrable. The abstract head at left was probably influenced by remembered west African sculptural traditions.

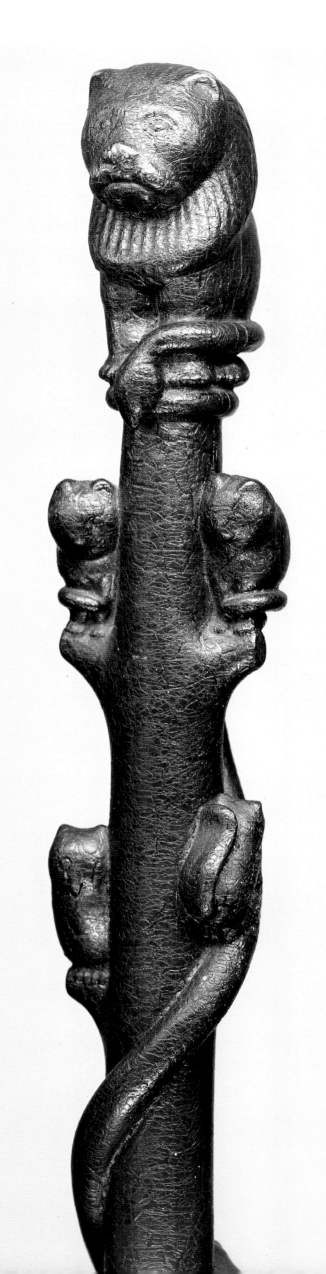

◄ LION AND CATS CANE

Artist unknown. c. 1900. Possibly New Jersey. Varnished, painted wood, probably cherry, metal ferrule. Height: 36 in. Collection of George H. Meyer.

The king of beasts sits atop this cane, presiding over a kingdom that includes two domestic cats, a pair of squirrels, a bear, an owl, and a mouse. The animals are perched on trimmed twig stubs along the shaft as well as on the carved vine that winds from top to bottom.

SNAKE CANES ►

Artists unknown. c. 1900. Regions unknown, except right: probably southern Ohio. Painted wood with nail or bead eyes. Heights: 31 to 35 in. Collection of George H. Meyer.

Snakes were a common motif of cane carvers, who often worked from serpentine forms found in naturally twisted roots, branches, or saplings.

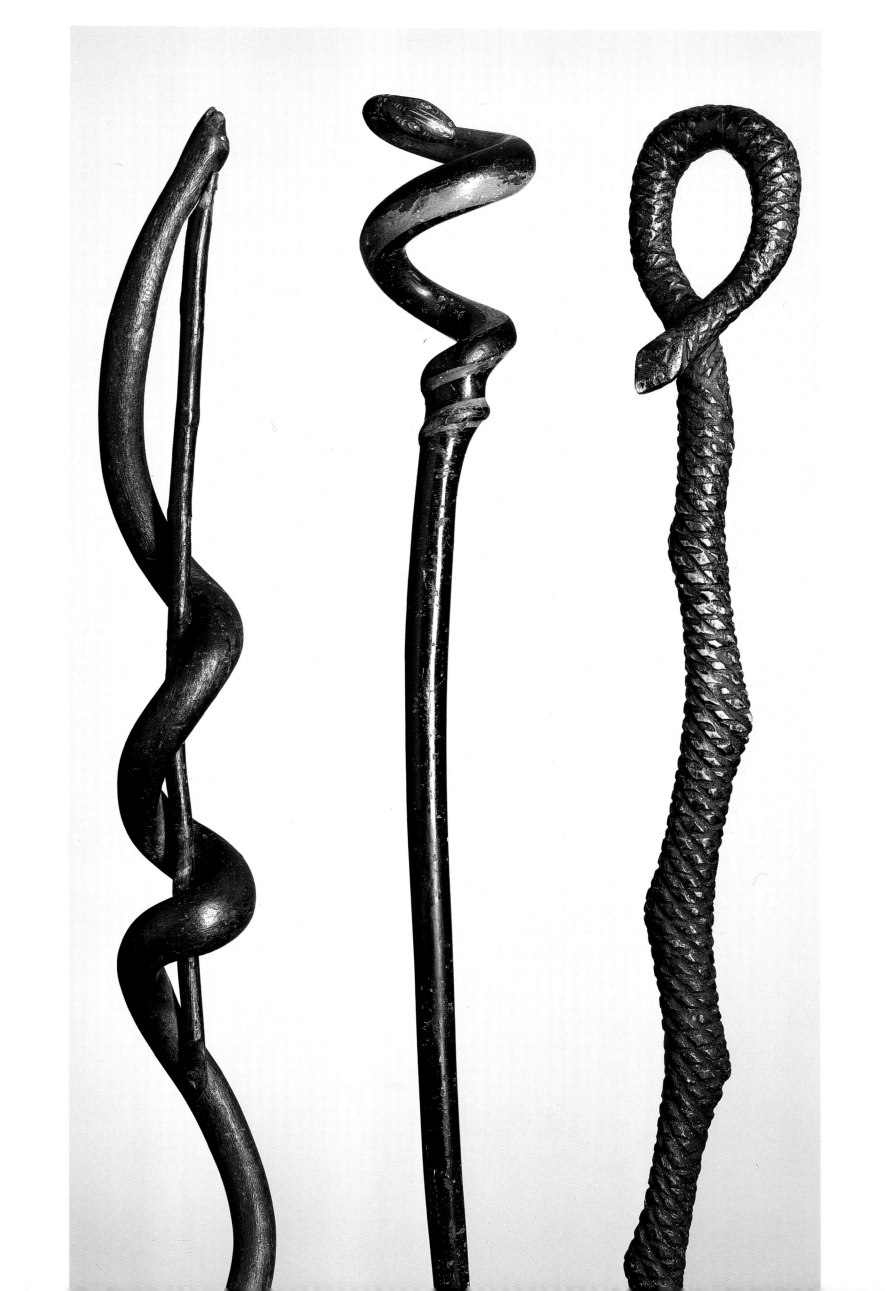

◄ DOG-HEAD CANES

*Artists unknown, except center two by Mr.
Simmons. c. 1880–1920. Left three:
Pennsylvania, right: possibly Ohio. Shellacked or
painted wood. Heights: 34 to 38 1/2 in.
Collection of George H. Meyer.*

*Simmons was an itinerant German immigrant cane
carver who peddled his wares door to door, traveling by foot with a pack of carved canes on his
back. He was known locally only as "der
Schtockschnitzler"—the cane carver.*

INTERLOCKING PIECES CANE ►

*Artist unknown. c. 1900–1920. Possibly Georgia.
Stained walnut. Height: 35 3/4 in. Collection of
George H. Meyer.*

*The interlocking, twisting turnings of the upper
shaft resemble the blade of a spiral auger. The
maker may have been a carpenter or woodworker
by trade. George Meyer has speculated that the
maker may also have drawn inspiration from similar knob handles and swirl patterns that he found
in contemporary blown glass canes.*

N A T I V E
A M E R I C A N
P O T T E R Y

The oldest and most enduring of all continuing American craft traditions is found in the Indian pottery of the Southwest, particularly that of the Pueblo people of New Mexico. As early as 300 B.C., Pueblo predecessors formed pottery that is remarkably similar to some still being made today. The native cultures of the Southwest were primarily agricultural and nonmigratory, so pottery vessels served as practical containers for storage of corn, their primary crop, as well as cornmeal and water.

Southwestern pottery was formed by hand rather than at a wheel. The wheel was a European invention unknown to the Americas until the sixteenth century and never was adopted by Indian potters. After forming a base for the bowl or jar, the Pueblo potter set it into a form for stability and built up the walls of the piece by adding thin coils of clay one at a time. When the desired height or width was achieved, the potter smoothed the wet clay with a dried gourd, curving and shaping it into its final form, eliminating seam lines and tightening the coils into a strong, unified whole. The resulting pottery had extremely thin walls, far thinner than would have been possible from working the piece at a wheel. After the clay form had dried, it was covered with colored liquid slip and decorated with stylized painted designs that were sometimes geometric but often symbolic and abstract. The pottery was fired in simple, open kilns, which were fueled with dried sheep manure because wood was reasonably scarce in the predominately desert climate of the region. Although men occasionally decorated the vessels, the making of pottery was considered primarily a woman's craft, and traditional methods, forms, and designs were passed down from mother to daughter for generations. Particularly among the Zuni, however, male transvestites, who from an early age dressed and considered themselves as women, also made pottery. These men-women potters were allowed access to sacred clay gathering sites ordinarily restricted to females.

Traditional pottery making declined in the late nineteenth century as many older potters stopped working. Around 1900, many native potters of the Southwest turned their skills from making pottery for their own use to selling it to the tourists who had begun to inundate the Santa Fe region. The motivation for creating pottery was then derived from commercial considerations, and, as a result, the connection with the older traditions loosened, and quality began to deteriorate. Larger traditional forms, especially the olla or storage jar and the dough bowl, introduced when the Spanish brought wheat and bread making to the area, were abandoned in favor of such tourist-oriented trinkets as ashtrays, candlesticks, and figurines. In the early years of this century, however, anthropologists and native peoples

◂ WATER JAR

Unknown Zuni Indian artist. c. 1825–1840. Zuni, New Mexico. Earthenware. Height: 12 3/4 in., diameter: 12 3/4 in. The Brooklyn Museum, New York.

This rare survivor from the early nineteenth century is decorated with stylized butterfly motifs.

worked together to revive the integrity of the craft. Museums and other cultural institutions sponsored digs, collecting and displaying examples of the older pottery. Native people assisted in the digs and, encouraged by the new scholarly respect for traditional pottery, began making pots again following the old forms and designs.

Among the most talented of these revival potters were Maria and Julian Martinez, who studied shards of ancient black pottery recovered in digs at the San Ildefonso Pueblo. Traditional black pottery, named for its sooty black surface, was fired at a very high temperature to assure a hard and durable product. The characteristic black appearance was achieved by smothering the fire when it had reached its maximum heat, forcing discoloring smoke into the walls of the pottery. The Martinezes experimented with the firing and finishing processes and came up with an innovative method of making black pottery with a shimmering polished surface covered with painted, matte black designs. Julian Martinez, who painted their pottery, died in 1943; Maria continued to practice for many years, working with several other decorators, most notably her son, Popovi.

There are many other southwestern potters who have continued the tradition of decorated ceramics, producing bowls, ollas, and other forms that retain strong links to the ancient pottery of their ancestors. Young, contemporary Pueblo potters such as Lillian Salvadore (b. 1944), who learned much of her craft from her clan (but not blood) grandmother, Pablito Concho, carry on the tradition, expanding its potential by incorporating subtle refinements and expressions of their own twentieth-century experiences into their work.

Potters Maria and Julian Martinez of San Ildefonso, New Mexico, were demonstrating their craft at the Palace of Governors in Santa Fe when this photograph was taken in 1912.

Museum of New Mexico, Santa Fe.

▲ OLLA

Lillian Salvadore. 1984. Acoma, New Mexico. Slip-decorated earthenware. Height: 9 in., width: 11 1/4 in. Museum of Fine Arts, Boston. Gift of a friend of the Department of American Decorative Arts and Sculpture.

This decorative water jar, modeled in an ancient traditional form, carries symbolic images representing the rain, clouds, and sky of the Southwest. Repeating designs encircle the body and neck of the vessel, while solid red slip covers the base and inner lip.

▲ STEW BOWL

*Unknown Zuni Indian artist. c. 1850–1890.
Cibola, New Mexico. Earthenware.
Diameter: 14 1/2 in. School of American
Research Collections in Museum of New
Mexico, Santa Fe.*

Earthenware pottery made by southwestern
Indians represents North America's oldest
native craft tradition, a tradition uninterrupt-
ed for over two thousand years. This bowl is
decorated with the stylized geometric patterns
common to the region's wares from approximately A.D. 500 on to the present day.

◄ BOWL

*Hohokam culture. A.D. 700–900. Gila or Salt
Rivers, Arizona. Red-on-buff earthenware.
Height: 3 3/4 in., diameter: 10 1/2 in.
Museum of Fine Arts, Boston. Gift of Mr. and
Mrs. Peter S. Lynch, Anne and Joseph
Pellegrino, anonymous gift, and Frank B.
Bennis Fund.*

The desert farming culture of the Hohokam
lasted from approximately 350 B.C. to A.D.
1450. Although the culture died out over five
hundred years ago, it has exerted a profound
influence on all subsequent Indian peoples
in the region.

Like present-day Pueblo Indians, the
Hohokam employed expressive stylized symbols to decorate their earthenware pottery.
This early and miraculously undamaged medi-
um-sized bowl demonstrates the ancient continuity of southwestern ceramic traditions. It is
decorated with swirling images of birds in
flight, a dominant motif of Hohokam culture
and southwestern mythology.

▼ BOWL

*Attributed to Nampeyo. c. 1890. Hano, New Mexico. Earthenware. Height: 4 in., diameter: 13 in.
Museum of Fine Arts, Boston. Gift of Laura F. Anderson.*

Nampeyo, who was part Hopi, studied ancient Hopi pottery shards excavated by traders and anthropologists in the late nineteenth century and revitalized the largely forgotten decorative tradition by copying the long-lost designs. After mastering the elements of ancient Hopi design, she began creating her own imaginative interpretations. As she once said, "I used to go to the ancient village...and copy the designs. But now I just close my eyes and see designs and I paint them."

▲ WATER JAR

Unknown Pueblo Indian artist. Before 1750. Acoma, New Mexico. Earthenware. Field Museum of Natural History, Chicago, Illinois.

Water jars, or ollas, were often made with a depression in the base so they could be carried on the head. The squat, flared base provided the jars with a low, easily balanced center of gravity.

◄ JAR

*Unknown Pueblo Indian artist. c. 1900. Aco-
ma, New Mexico. Polychromed earthenware.
Height: 12 3/16 in., maximum diameter: 13
5/16 in. California Academy of the Sciences,
Elkus Collection, San Francisco, California.*

*Turn-of-the-century potters at Acoma decorated
their jars with geometric designs that extended
from the lip to the red-painted base.*

JAR ►

*Unknown Pueblo Indian artist. c.
1920–1930. Zia, New Mexico.
Polychromed earthenware. Height: 10
7/8 in., maximum diameter: 12 in.
California Academy of the Sciences,
Elkus Collection, San Francisco,
California.*

*The Zia potter who made this jug broke
the decoration into three segments, separated by black bands: simple geometric
designs on the shoulders, large floral
and bird motifs in the center, and a
solid red base.*

▲ TALL VASE

Maria Martinez. c. 1927. San Ildefonso, New Mexico. Polished earthenware. Height: 14 1/2 in. Private collection.

Maria Martinez and her husband Julian revolutionized polished blackware pottery, bringing an old tradition to new heights of refinement. Blackware, fired in banked cow dung, is created by smothering the fire to produce sooty black smoke. Martinez's wares have stylized matte black designs that are placed against a shiny black background.

◄ BOWL

Margaret Tafoya. c. 1984. Santa Clara Pueblo, New Mexico. Carved and polished earthenware. Height: 7 1/2 in., diameter: 14 in. Museum of International Folk Art, a unit of the Museum of New Mexico, Santa Fe.

Margaret Tafoya learned to make pottery from her mother. This polished blackware bowl carries one of her signature motifs: an impressed bear paw, a symbol for water also learned from her mother.

MARGARET TAFOYA,
PUEBLO INDIAN POTTER

Margaret Tafoya, now in her late eighties, has been making traditional polished blackware and redware pottery for more than sixty years. Her pottery is made by coiling strips of clay on top of each other in the traditional Pueblo manner. The resulting vessels are decorated either with a single bear-paw design impressed into the side of the vessel while the clay is still wet or with carved, matte-painted, geometric designs. Both decorative methods are unique to Santa Clara pottery. Before baking her pottery in an open cedar-wood fire, Margaret Tafoya rubs the pieces for hours with special smoothing stones she inherited from her mother, Sarafina Tafoya.

Sarafina Tafoya, who taught Margaret the craft, is thought to have originated the idea of carving designs into the highly polished surface of traditional Santa Clara pottery. Margaret Tafoya, in turn, has taught her seven daughters and many grandchildren how to make pottery. Four generations of the family now carry on the tradition, gathering clay from the same hills as their ancestors did. They will carry the Santa Clara Pueblo's traditions into yet another century.

Margaret Tafoya was honored as a National Heritage Fellow by the National Endowment for the Arts Folk Arts Program in 1984.

R E D W A R E

Redware was the most common utilitarian pottery of early America. Redware, more accurately called earthenware since not all such pottery was made of red-colored clay, was made from widely available alluvial earthenware clays, which were easily fired at relatively low temperatures ranging from 1500 to 1800 degrees Fahrenheit. However, because the material could not withstand heat high enough to vit- rify or fuse the silica in the clay, redware products, unlike stoneware, were brittle and porous. They were used primarily for serving and storing nonacidic foods, and were particularly useful for cooking because they expanded and contracted when heated.

Redware potters created a wide array of simple, functional forms including plates, mugs, bottles, pitchers, jugs, bowls, inkwells, chamber pots, and teapots. Redware was usually glazed with lead, which, like the pottery itself, was widely available, inexpensive, and easy to work with. A thin lead glaze, often applied only inside the pot, sealed the vessel, making it watertight. Unfortunately, lead is poisonous and soluble in even a weak acidic solution, so redware could be fatally unsuited to the stor- age of such staples of the early American diet as vinegar, wine, apple cider, pickles, and sauerkraut.

The typical redware potter was a farmer who worked alone or, with the help of one or two assistants in a small shed, made pots as a sideline to his main occupation. For these men, potting was one of the farm's many seasonal activities. Clay was dug in the fall, when the ground was driest, and firewood was gathered during the winter months. The pottery was made during the warm months, in between other farm chores, and fired when enough "greenware" had been crafted to fill the kiln.

Most redware was formed by hand on a wheel. The potter placed a lump of wet clay on the wheel and drew it into the desired shape as he turned the foot-powered apparatus. After the greenware had been formed, the potter allowed it to dry and, before firing, applied any glazes and decorative touches. By adding metallic oxides to the basic lead glaze, the potter could produce distinctive color effects. The most commonly added agent was manganese dioxide, which, when fired, produced an elegant all- over black surface. Manganese was also often used as an accent, especially by Connecticut and Pennsylvania redware makers who added drips or blotches of manganese slip to the red-glazed lead body of their wares. Other frequently used oxides included copper, which produced green, iron, which gave yellow to reddish brown, and antimony, which produced a bright yellow. Tin produced white, as did the pure white kaolin clay also used to make porcelain.

After being glazed, the greenware was ready to be fired in a kiln. Early kilns were invariably fired with wood. The kiln, often built into a hillside to provide support and insulation, had a firebox or

◄ BOWL

Peter Bell. c. 1805–1810. Hagerstown, Maryland. Red earthenware. Depth: 4 7/8 in., diameter: 22 3/8 in. Museum of Early Southern Decorative Arts, Winston-Salem, North Carolina. Gift of Titus G. Geesey.

Peter Bell, the son of a German immigrant, was the patriarch of a long line of Shenandoah Valley potters. Three of his sons, includ- ing the well-known John Bell, and a number of his grandsons also were traditional potters in the area. This slip-decorated bowl reflects Bell's Germanic heritage.

Possibly by Peter Clark. c. 1800. Lyndeborough, New Hampshire. Earthen redware. Height: 8 in., diameter: 6 1/4 in. Bennington Museum, Bennington, Vermont. Gift of Mrs. William Whitman, Jr.

Peter Clark was the first of three generations of potters who worked in New Hampshire. His pots typically carry the distinctive glaze and combination of straight and wavy incised bandings that are seen here.

boxes where fuel was loaded and burnt, a "firing chamber" where the greenware was stacked, and some form of venting apparatus to allow the heat to escape. Many potters, particularly those who worked at the trade part time, did their firing during the winter, when the tremendous heat generated by the kiln was welcome. A typical kiln could be brought to firing temperature in a day to a day and a half. Potters called the final period of the firing process "blast off" for good reason. As maximum temperature was reached, long tongues of flame reached from the firebox into the firing chamber, the kiln's contents glowed red and then yellow hot, and tall plumes of blue flame shot from the venting chimneys. Wood was fed into the firebox as quickly as possible to keep the temperature rising. Potters drew test shards out of the kiln to check the firing and glaze, and if these test pieces proved satisfactory, the kiln's orifices were sealed and it was allowed to cool. A wait of at least two to three days was required before the vessels within were cool enough to handle and the kiln could be opened. Potters waited with considerable apprehension because the process was imperfect at best, and many unpredictable variables of wood firing could affect the results and spoil some or even all of the wares in the kiln. Uneven heat could leave some pots underfired and others overheated, destroying forms and glazes. If the kiln had been brought up to temperature or cooled too quickly, pots might crack. And flying ash in the kiln could ruin the appearance of glazes.

Although most redware was undecorated, some pieces were embellished. The most elaborately decorated form of redware pottery was sgraffito ware, a European tradition brought by German immigrants to Pennsylvania. Although jugs and pitchers were sometimes sgraffito decorated (*sgraffito* is Italian for scratched), by far the most common sgraffito form was a plate or platter. After applying a thin cream-colored glaze to the redware form, the decorator scratched portions of it away while the piece was still wet to reveal the red clay underneath. The resulting relief designs could be extremely complex. Many were pictorial, depicting horses, deer, fish, birds, or human figures. More abstract pieces drew upon favorite design motifs of the Pennsylvania Dutch, such as tulips, hearts, urns, and twining vines. Finally, calligraphic inscriptions, usually bits of folk wisdom or humor, could be added around the rim of the plate. After completing the design, the potter could add touches of colored green, black, or yellow slip to accent the piece and then cover the entire plate with a protective glaze before firing. Sgraffito ware was expensive and time-consuming to produce. Most sgraffito wares were therefore made as decorative presentation pieces, and recipients were proud to display the highly prized pottery prominently in their homes.

Another distinctive decorative redware tradition with European roots was practiced by Moravian potters in North Carolina. The immigrant master potter Gottfried Aust, who had trained in Germany, first introduced this form of the craft to the region in 1756. The Moravian potteries of North Carolina became extremely prolific. Like the Pennsylvania Germans, Moravian potters produced a wide variety of functional wares as well as purely decorative presentation pieces. The presentation pieces, usually plates, were slip decorated with abstract graphic and floral designs.

Redware was made throughout the South, and many southern potters continued to produce redware long after northern craftsmen had switched over to stoneware. Among the most notable southern redware potters were Peter Bell and his sons, Solomon and John, who worked in various locations in the Shenandoah Valley. The Bells created both redware and stoneware for more than one hundred years and are perhaps best known for their whimsical redware lions, made as decorative doorstops and widely coveted today as icons of American folk art. Some of the most impressive earthenware pieces made in the South were massive jugs with molded handles and black manganese glazes fashioned in southwestern Virginia and northeastern Tennessee.

In New England, redware potteries flourished from the mid-1600s through the first decades of the nineteenth century. A host of glazing and decorating traditions were developed that were widely disseminated throughout the region, often making firm identification of the source of a particular piece extremely difficult. New England potters experimented with many complex glaze combinations; nowhere else did glazing techniques reach such sophisticated levels. Calligraphic slip-trailed decoration, which is the decorative technique best known today, was widely practiced in Pennsylvania and epitomized by Norwalk, Connecticut makers such as Absalom Day and Henry Chicester. Using a liquid-clay slip, usually yellow, which stood out vividly against the red body of the ware, the potter drew names, dates, or sayings in script. The slip was held in a cup and trailed through a narrow opening onto the surface of the pottery.

Although redware continued to be made throughout the nineteenth century, the concern over lead poisoning and the increasing availability of more durable and versatile stoneware drove the majority of redware potters out of business in the first half of the twentieth century. In recent years, a number of highly skilled potters such as C. Ned Foltz of Pennsylvania and Stephen Nutt of New York have taken up redware production, creating detailed reproductions and adaptations of traditional decorative sgraffito ware and calligraphic slipware.

CHARGER ▶

Absalom Day. c. 1794–1800. Norwalk, Connecticut. Red earthenware. Diameter: 15 1/2 in., depth: 3 in. High Museum of Art, Atlanta, Georgia. Purchase with funds from the Decorative Arts Endowment.

The Reverend Absalom Day (1770–1843) was a Methodist minister and also, like many redware potters, a farmer. This charger, decorated with typical Norwalk calligraphic slip reading "Day's Pottery," may have been made as a sample to advertise his wares. Norwalk potteries specialized in molded plates decorated with calligraphic slip, a style that may have originated in Absalom Day's shop.

▲ COVERED JAR
_____

*Artist unknown. c. 1790–1830. Bristol County, Massachusetts. Lead-glazed earthenware. Height:
10 in., diameter: 7 3/4 in. Collection of Hilary and Paulette Nolan.*

*Green was created by adding copper oxide, a relatively expensive and therefore normally sparingly used
ingredient, to the glaze mixture. Bristol County potters achieved an unmatched complexity of color in
their glazes and, as seen in this example, were sometimes extravagant in their use of copper oxide.*

▼ DISH

*Friedrich Rothrock. c. 1795. Southern Wachovia, North Carolina. Earthenware. Old Salem,
Inc., Winston-Salem, North Carolina.*

*The Moravian potters of North Carolina created a distinctive and sophisticated body of work.
Unlike most American potters of the period, highly skilled Moravian masters such as Gottfried
Aust (1722– 1788) and his successor Rudolph Christ (1750–1833) were well versed in the most
current European styles and techniques. These techniques were passed on to apprentices who
worked with the masters in a strictly ordered European guild system. This dish combines a
bold, central floral design with a wave and dot border set between solid bands of dark brown.*

▼ COVERED JAR

Unknown Moravian artist. c. 1785–1830. North Carolina. Red earthenware. Height: 12 3/4 in. The Metropolitan Museum of Art, New York. Rogers Fund.

This jar is simply but effectively decorated with brightly colored stripes of slip clay. Double-handled, covered "sugar" jars, as they were called locally, were one of the most common forms crafted by the Moravians.

▲ DISH

*Artist unknown. c. 1810–1840. Region
unknown. Red earthenware. Length:
13 5/8 in. The Henry Francis du Pont
Winterthur Museum, Winterthur,
Delaware.*

*The artist achieved the marbled glaze of
this serving dish by swirling different
colored slip clays together.*

DOME-TOP PRESERVE JAR ▶

*Artist unknown. c. 1820–1850.
Probably Norwalk, Connecticut. Red
earthenware. Height: 13 1/2 in.
Collection of Samuel Herrup.*

*Connecticut redware potters often
daubed their ware with manganese
oxide to produce black accents on the
deep reddish-brown overall glaze typical
of the region.*

▲ STORAGE JAR

Artist unknown. c. 1800-1840. Probably eastern Tennessee. Lead-glazed earthenware. Height: 8 5/8 in., diameter: 8 1/2 in. Collection of the Museum of Early Southern Decorative Arts, Winston-Salem, North Carolina. Gift of G. Wilson Douglas, Jr.

A number of redware potters worked along the so-called Great Road, which ran from Roanoke through southwestern Virginia and northeastern Tennessee and into Kentucky. Great Road potters appear to have been influenced by Moravian pottery from Salem, North Carolina; some evidence exists of Moravian potters working in Tennessee prior to 1800.

This lead-glazed jar was colored with black iron oxide, probably obtained from a local blacksmith. The thick handles of the jar were formed in a mold and applied to the wheel-thrown form. Incised lines at the shoulder add a subtle, decorative element to the classic form.

▼ LIDDED STORAGE JAR

Artist unknown. c. 1800–1825. Sugar Grove, Wythe County, Virginia. Kaolin with clear lead glaze over manganese and copper slip decoration. Height: 15 in., base diameter: 6 in. Collection of Roddy and Sally Moore.

This early jar's decoration and form closely resemble Moravian earthenware from Pennsylvania and North Carolina, suggesting that the piece was made by a German-American potter. The jar is made from kaolin, a fine clay that fires to pure white and is used to make porcelain. An overall, clear lead glaze gives the jar its slightly yellow color.

PRESERVE JAR ▶

Michael Cline. c. 1847–1860. Hartford City, Indiana. Red earthenware. Height: 5 3/4 in. Private collection.

This is one of three known pieces by Cline, an Ohio potter who moved to Indiana in 1834. It is distinguished by its deep purple, manganese oxide glaze and simple classical form.

◀ VASE

Solomon Bell. c. 1860. Strasburg, Virginia. Earthenware with clear lead glaze over copper and manganese slip decoration. Height: 7 1/2 in., base diameter: 4 in. Collection of Roddy and Sally Moore.

Solomon Bell (1817–1882) was the son of Peter Bell (see p. 231). His brothers Samuel and John also were potters. Like other Shenandoah Valley redware potters, Solomon Bell produced a variety of forms that, after an initial firing, were covered with an overall cream-colored slip and decorated with liberal splashes of green, brown, blue, or black. The pieces were finally covered with a clear lead glaze and fired a second time.

▾ APPLE CIDER COOLER

Artist unknown. c. 1860–1880. ·Probably New York State. Red earthenware. Height: 16 1/2 in. Private collection.

Fermented "hard" cider, or applejack, was a popular drink wherever apples were grown in the nineteenth century. This whimsical representational cooler may have been placed on a bar to advertise its contents. At least one other similar but smaller jug, undoubtedly by the same hand, is known. Coolers held drinking liquids; a tap fit into the plug at the bottom.

▼ STORAGE JAR

A member of the Huan family. c. 1850-1875. Greene County, Tennessee. Lead-glazed earthenware with manganese-slip decoration. Height: 13 in., base diameter: 5 1/2 in. Collection of Roddy and Sally Moore.

This jar's deep reddish-orange color, thick, mold-formed handles, and manganese decoration are typical of Great Road pottery. Coggle wheel and stamp decoration was applied at the shoulder.

PLATE ▶

Possibly by Henry Roudebuth. c. 1793. Montgomery County, Pennsylvania. Red earthenware. Diameter: 12 1/4 in. The Metropolitan Museum of Art, New York. Gift of Mrs. Robert W. de Forest.

Pennsylvania German sgraffito pottery, featuring designs created by scratching through an overall application of cream-colored slip to reveal the contrasting red clay surface, was a decorative ware usually given to mark a special occasion. The incised designs were generally accented with splashes of brightly colored slip glaze.

S T O N E W A R E

Stoneware is an extremely dense and durable pottery that, unlike porous earthenware such as redware, will hold water even without a glaze. It is fired at a much higher temperature than earthenware (typically 2300 degrees Fahrenheit) and therefore demands clay that can withstand the intense firing heat. Stoneware lends itself to a wide variety of forms, and stoneware potters explored its versatility in many utilitarian wares, from spitoons, chamber pots, and washbasins to butter churns, milk pans, and poultry fountains. The most common stoneware forms were storage jugs, jars, and crocks, used in virtually every nineteenth-century American home before the age of refrigeration to store and preserve foods. Narrow-mouthed jugs, stopped with a cork or wood plug, were used to store liquids such as water, hard liquors, beer, wine, vinegar, maple or corn syrup, ink, turpentine, and mineral oil. Small-mouthed jars and wide-mouthed crocks held such necessaries as salted meats, pickles, sauerkraut, fruit butters, lard, butter, cream, and soft soap.

The first European stoneware was made along the Rhine River in the 1400s. By the late 1600s, the Rhenish tradition had migrated to Great Britain, where a number of stoneware potteries were established. The earliest American stoneware was apparently made by German immigrants from the Rhineland, two of the earliest and most influential American stoneware potters being William Crolius and John Remney, both of whom emigrated from Germany and established potteries in New York City in the early decades of the eighteenth century. Both craftsmen produced sophisticated wares featuring graceful forms and often elaborate decoration that appealed to their well-to-do city clientele.

Unlike redware potteries, which were usually small shops run by independent craftsmen who sold their wares locally, some stoneware potteries produced massive amounts of pottery, which were shipped by rail to markets throughout the country. In the northern states particularly, potteries were sometimes backed by investors, enabling them to grow into large concerns that employed a number of skilled handcraftsmen. The best known of these large, northern stoneware potteries was founded by the Norton family at Bennington, Vermont, in 1785. The original Norton pottery employed six men, but by 1860, a staff of eighteen men produced $35,000 worth of wares each year. The consistently high quality of Norton wares earned the pottery a wide reputation, and orders were received from as far away as Texas. The pottery continued in operation until 1894, when the sudden death of twenty-nine-year-old Edward L. Norton, who had taken over management of the firm on his father's death in 1885, forced it to cease production. Throughout its 109-year history, the Norton pottery was known as a superbly managed business that marketed excellent products.

Like redware, most early stoneware was formed by hand on a potter's wheel. After drying, the brittle wares were stacked in a kiln for firing. The firing process drove any residual moisture from the clay

---

◄ PITCHER

Henry Remney. c. 1810–1820. Philadelphia, Pennsylvania. Salt-glazed stoneware. Height: 9 3/4 in. Abby Aldrich Rockefeller Folk Art Center, Williamsburg, Virginia.

Henry Remney was the grandson of John Remney, Sr., one of the most prominent early New York City potters. Henry Remney's descendants operated the family pottery in Philadelphia until 1895. This delicately decorated pitcher is inscribed below the handle "to Muvy P. Hall from her frendd [sic] Henry Remney."

and strengthened the body of the vessel through vitrification, a fusing process in which the silica in the clay melted to form the final, hard, durable stoneware product. Firing also melted the glaze, causing it to spread over the body of the vessel.

Most American stoneware was salt glazed. Salt was poured in through the top of the kiln when firing temperature was reached; it vaporized on contact with the heat of the fire, producing bursts of chlorine gas and covering the wares within with a hard, glasslike, light gray glaze. Another commonly used stoneware glaze was the so-called Albany slip, a dark brown glaze created by dipping the piece into a soupy liquid mixture of clay and water that then melted in the kiln. Albany slip was named for the vicinity (Albany, New York) where clay with these special properties was first discovered in quantity.

Many American salt-glazed stonewares were decorated with cobalt. The brilliant dark, metallic blue of the cobalt contrasted perfectly with the light gray of the overall salt glaze. Cobalt was applied freehand as a liquid slip after the clay had dried, but before it was fired. Any decoration was usually applied to the front face of the pot, although occasionally the decoration did cover more than one side of the piece. Common decorative motifs included a wide range of floral and animal forms, although many creative cobalt decorators painted human portraits and caricatures, landscapes, houses, circus scenes, and a host of other designs. A few potters, particularly in the early days, employed incised or impressed decoration, sometimes in combination with cobalt designs. A number of the finest Crolius family pieces, including an extraordinary presentation punch bowl with elaborate floral designs, are fine examples of this technique. Incising was most frequently used on early New York and New Jersey pots. Many of the most spectacular overall cobalt decorations extant cover water-storage kegs, since the large size of these vessels afforded decorators broad expanses of space on which to display their designs.

Because both salt and Albany clay were sometimes hard to come by or relatively expensive to import, a number of southern potters, especially in Georgia and the Carolinas, used a dipped alkaline glaze made of mixtures of readily available wood ashes or lime that were mixed with local slip clays. This technique apparently originated early in the nineteenth century around Edgefield, South Carolina, a major pottery center, and, by the beginning of the Civil War, had spread throughout the southern states, including Texas, where several highly productive potteries were founded. Southern alkaline glazes produced a hard, durable surface, usually with considerable variations in texture such as mottling, pebbling, or agglutinized streaking that has been graphically

◄ FIVE-GALLON JAR

Burlon Craig. c. 1987. Vale, North Carolina. Stoneware with alkaline glaze runs. Height: 19 in. International Folk Art Foundation Collection at the Museum of International Folk Art, a unit of the Museum of New Mexico, Santa Fe.

Craig's full-bodied, four-handled jar is decorated with the running alkaline glaze that is typical of the North Carolina pottery tradition he perpetuates.

Burlon Craig, southern alkaline glaze potter, at work in his studio in Vale, Lincoln County, North Carolina.

described as "tobacco spit." Colors also vary greatly, from blacks and browns to greens, yellows, blues, reds, and combinations of these hues.

The southern alkaline glaze tradition reached its highest development where it began, in the Edgefield District of South Carolina, northeast of Augusta. Here, European, Asian, and African influences came together in the early 1800s to create an entirely new type of stoneware pottery. Edgefield potters were primarily of Irish and Scottish descent, and the dominant forms of their wares can be traced to European antecedents. Edgefield's distinctive glazes, however, are another matter entirely. Glazes made from slip clay mixed with wood ash or lime had been used in Japan, China, and Korea as early as the tenth century. How this Oriental technique came to backwoods South Carolina is unclear, although there is some indirect evidence that written accounts describing the glazes were available to British potters who settled in the Carolinas. In any case, the technique was quickly adopted, primarily because it was inexpensive and relatively easy to master.

The third element contributing to the development of Edgefield pottery was the use of slave labor. Most potteries in the area employed slaves, who chopped firewood, loaded and unloaded kilns, mixed clays and glazes, and performed other relatively unskilled work. A few learned to make pottery, with fascinating results. The best known of these innovators was "Dave," who worked for the prominent potter Lewis Miles in the 1850s and 1860s. Dave made the largest storage pots attributed to the area, some holding up to forty gallons. His pots are beautifully crafted, with powerful ovoid forms, and are further distinguished by verses composed and inscribed by the literate slave potter. Edgefield slave potters also created a number of perplexing, nonfunctional face jugs, using bits of clay applied to the jug to depict facial features, and then adding white porcelain teeth and eyes. These face jugs, some of which were less than three inches tall, have direct antecedents in figural sculptures of the Congo, where most of the area's slaves originated. The purpose of these pieces is unknown, but they probably had ceremonial significance.

Both northern and southern stoneware potteries flourished in the last decades of the nineteenth century. However, a number of innovations and changes in society foreshadowed the rapid demise of the industry in the early decades of the twentieth century. The proliferation of inexpensive, industrially produced glass, metal, and ceramic containers ultimately forced many hand stoneware potters out of business. In addition, improved methods for storing food, particularly the introduction of refrigeration, in the late nineteenth century, largely eliminated the need for large stoneware containers. Although some traditional hand potters continued to produce utilitarian wares, only a few, mostly southern potters working with alkaline glazes, survived the Great Depression. Most of these surviving craftsmen had stopped production by the 1950s or switched their focus to the creation of decorative ware, since by that time the demand for functional pieces had completely disappeared. Today, while a number of potters do produce traditional hand-thrown stoneware that is functional, most of their wares are primarily intended and appreciated as decorative objects.

▼ STORAGE JAR

*Probably by Thomas Commeraw or David Morgan. c. 1797–1819. New York City. Salt-glazed
stoneware. Height: 9 1/2 in. The Metropolitan Museum of Art, New York. Rogers Fund.*

*Commeraw and Morgan both worked at a pottery at Corlear's Hook on the East River in Manhattan.
This storage jar is inscribed "COERLEARS HOOK N. YORK" under the rim. The large, incised flower
decorated with cobalt is typical of early New York stoneware.*

◄ THREE-GALLON JUG

Unknown German-American artist. c. 1810–1840. Possibly mid-Atlantic region. Salt-glazed stoneware. Height: 17 3/8 in. The Henry Francis du Pont Winterthur Museum, Winterthur, Delaware.

This jug carries three elaborate, incised scenes that must have held special meaning to their creator. On opposite sides of the handle are groups of large and small buildings, some of them labeled with incised lettering reading, "Smoke/ haus. Head haus," etc. The sloop seen here holds a cargo of strange animals.

▼ CASK

Attributed to the Clark Pottery. c. 1825. Athens, New York. Salt-glazed stoneware. Height: 12 in. National Museum of American History, Smithsonian Institution, Washington, D.C.

This small cask is inscribed "Mr. Oliver Gridley/ Newburgh, July 7," and dated 1825. It is beautifully, if inexplicably, decorated with an incised, cobalt-colored swordfish or sail fish.

▲ SANDER

B. C. Miller. 1830. Probably Pennsylvania. Salt-glazed stoneware. Height: 3 in. The Henry Francis du Pont Winterthur Museum, Winterthur, Delaware.

Extremely fine sand was used to blot and dry the India ink used with quill pens. This sander is inscribed on its bottom, "B.C. Miler/ Maker/ Sept. 1st, 1830/ W. H. Amos." Amos probably received the sander as a gift from the maker.

◄ WATER COOLER

Artist unknown. Israel Seymour Factory. c. 1830. Troy, New York. Salt-glazed stoneware. Height: 16 in. The Shelburne Museum, Shelburne, Vermont.

This simply decorated cooler is distinguished by its extraordinary form. Several master potters have commented that the voluptuous shape would be virtually impossible to hold together on the wheel. The tap hole at the bottom is slightly out of line with the spout.

▲ TWO-GALLON JAR

Artist unknown. c. 1800–1810. New York or Pennsylvania. Salt-glazed stoneware. Height: 12 1/2 in. Collection of Chris Machmer.

The following poem is incised on the reverse side of this amusingly decorated jug, opposite the incised, cobalt-decorated portrait of the proverbial town drunk: "There is a man in our town/ Upon his feet he cannot stand/ The reason why you all must know/ He drinks too much before he'll go."

WATER KEG ▸

J. and E. Norton Company, probably decorated by John Haflinger. c. 1855–1859. Bennington, Vermont. Salt-glazed stoneware. Height: 33 1/2 in., diameter: 17 in. Bennington Museum, Bennington, Vermont. Gift of John Spargo.

This elaborately decorated fifteen-gallon keg was probably made for the Stark House in Bennington, a resort hotel owned at one time by pottery owner Julius Norton. The decoration completely encircles the cooler, which apparently was displayed prominently in the hotel lobby, where it probably could be admired from all sides.

▾ JAR

Artist unknown. c. 1850–1875. Probably New England. Salt-glazed stoneware. Height: 13 in. Henry Ford Museum and Greenfield Village, Dearborn, Michigan.

This unique piece, which captures an equestrian in mid-flip, must have been inspired by the visit of an early traveling circus. The name James Alexander appears in script just below the combed band.

◄ STORAGE JAR

Dave. 1860. Lewis Miles Pottery, Horse Creek, Edgefield District, South Carolina. Alkaline-glazed stoneware. Height: 21 5/8 in., circumference: 58 in. Collection of Tony and Marie Shank.

Dave was a literate slave potter who worked for Lewis Miles. A number of his massive storage jars carry his incised poems. This jar is incised "LM November 9, 1860" on one side and "A noble jar, for pork or beef—/ then carry it around to the Indian chief" on the other. Dave was an accomplished potter who threw the largest pots known to have been made from the Edgefield District; the biggest of his "noble jars" held over forty gallons.

PITCHER ►

Attributed to Benjamin Franklin Landrum, Sr. c. 1850–1880. B. F. Landrum Pottery, Horse Creek, Edgefield District, South Carolina. Alkaline-glazed stoneware. Height: 9 7/8 in., circumference: 22 5/8 in. The Charleston Museum, Charleston, South Carolina.

The Landrum family was actively involved in the Edgefield stoneware industry throughout the nineteenth century as potters and owners of pottery-making concerns. One member of the family went so far as to name three of his sons Manises, Palissey, and Wedgwood after famous European potters. This pitcher is decorated with a dripped "rattlesnake" glaze.

◄ JUG

Possibly by Thomas Chandler. The Phoenix Factory. c. 1840–1842. Edgefield District, South Carolina. Alkaline-glazed stoneware. Height: 2 1/2 in., diameter: 13 1/2 in. Collection of the Museum of Early Southern Decorative Arts, Winston-Salem, North Carolina.

The Phoenix Factory was established by Collin Rhodes and Robert W. Mathis in 1840. Rhodes employed some of the region's finest potters, including Thomas Chandler, who pioneered in the use of slip decoration applied over alkaline glazes.

Daniel Seagle. c. 1840. Lincoln County, North Carolina. Alkaline-glazed stoneware. Height: 18 1/2 in., circumference: 55 1/2 in. Mint Museum of History, Charlotte, North Carolina.

Seagle was one of the earliest potters working in the Catawba Valley. He crafted many voluminous storage jars like the one shown here, marking them under opposite handles with his initials and a number indicating their capacities in gallons.

Thomas Crafts and Co. c. 1837–1840. Whately, Massachusetts. Salt-glazed stoneware. Height: 15 1/8 in., width: 10 in. Historic Deerfield, Inc., Deerfield, Massachusetts. Gift of Mr. and Mrs. William W. Newton.

The incised decoration on this jug depicts "the Caroline affair," an infamous border conflict between the United States and Canada. In December 1837, the Caroline, a steamship which had supplied a number of U.S. mounted border raids, was set on fire in retaliation by Canadian volunteers on the Niagara River.

FIVE-GALLON HOME-BREW JAR ▶

*Artist unknown. c. 1880.
Alabama. Alkaline-glazed
stoneware. 16 3/4 x 14 x
12 1/8 in. National Museum
of American Art, Smithsonian
Institution, Washington, D.C.
Gift of Herbert Waide
Hemphill and museum pur-
chase made possible by Ralph
Cross Johnson.*

*This unusual jar combines
incised straight and wavy
lines, the latter formed by
holding a wooden comb
against the turning pot, with a
typical southern alkaline glaze.
The wide-mouthed jar was
probably used to make, as
well as store, home-brewed
whiskey.*

◀ FACE JUG

*Attributed to African-Americans working at Col. Thomas J. Davies Pottery. c.
1856–1862. Bath, Edgefield District, South Carolina. Stoneware with brown sand and
ash glaze, eyes and teeth of unglazed porous white clay. Height: 7 1/2 in. Philadelphia
Museum of Art, Philadelphia, Pennsylvania. Gift of Frank Samuel.*

*Face jugs, probably made by African-American potters for ceremonial purposes,
required considerable skill in the making. The jugs were usually small, with complex,
and therefore hard-to-craft facial features. Furthermore, the use of stoneware and
porcelain (from which the unglazed eyes and teeth were fashioned) in one pot was
unprecedented in ceramic history, and demanded careful fitting and firing to achieve
structural unity.*

DOUBLE-HANDLED WHISKEY JUG ▶

*Franklin Lafayette ("Fate") Beecham. Before 1918. Crawford County, Georgia.
Alkaline-glazed stoneware. Height: 17 5/8 in., diameter: 13 1/8 in. National Museum
of American Art, Smithsonian Institution, Washington, D.C. Gift of Herbert Waide
Hemphill and museum purchase made possible by Ralph Cross Johnson.*

*This jug, covered with running drips of dark glaze, epitomizes the distinctive and total-
ly unpredictable results of the alkaline-glaze process first developed in the Edgefield
District of South Carolina in the early nineteenth century.*

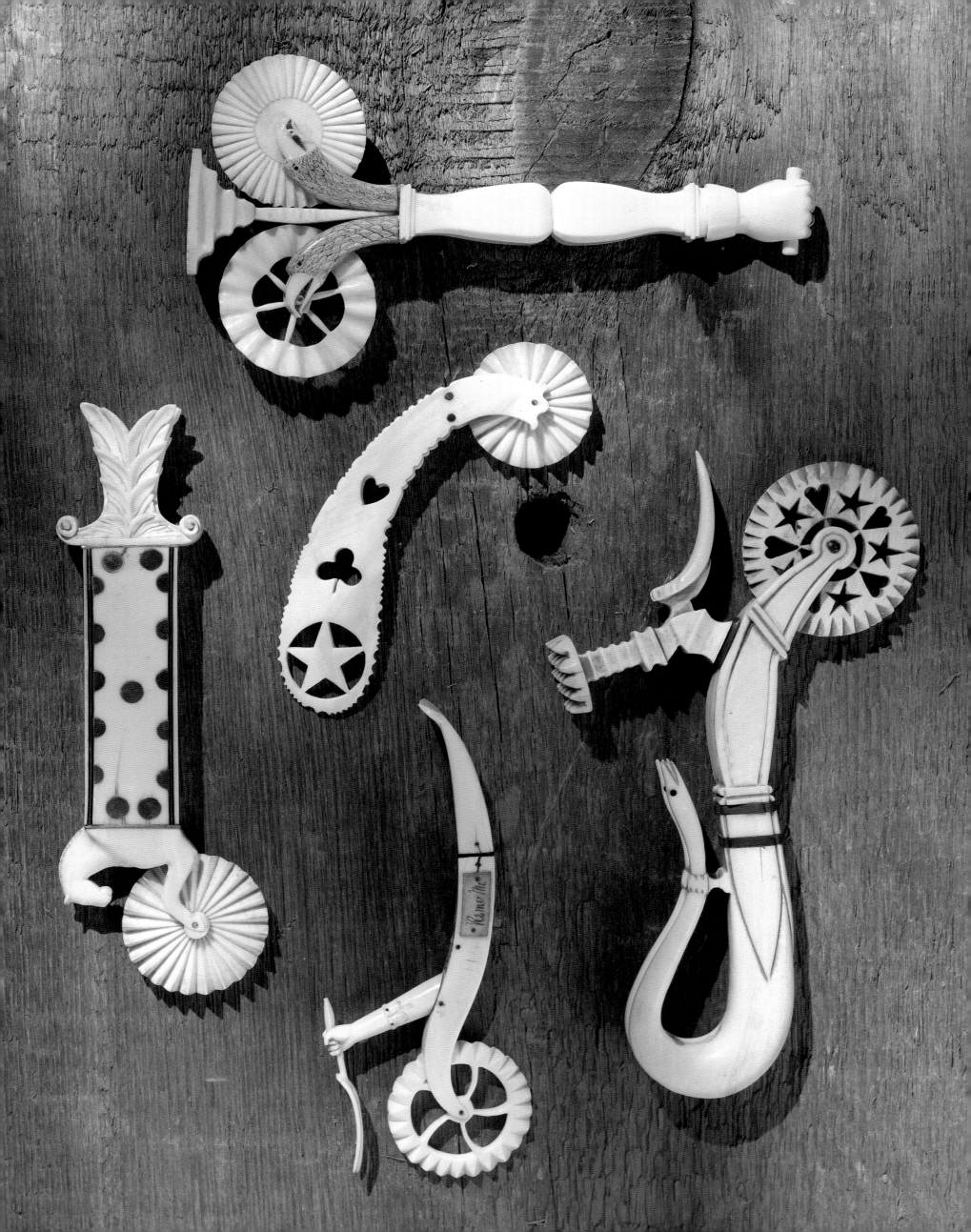

S C R I M S H A W

The craft of scrimshaw was literally a by-product of whaling, a peculiarly American industry that flourished between the Revolution and the Civil War. During these years, the pure, rich oil rendered from whale blubber was highly prized as the most reliable fuel available for lamps, and also proved to be a fine lubricating oil for many types of machinery. Yankee whalers, sailing from such ports as Salem, New Bedford, and Nantucket, Massachusetts, and Mystic and New London, Connecticut, traveled the oceans of the world in search of the leviathan.

A typical whaling voyage could last from two to four years and bring sailors who had never traveled so far from home as Boston or Hartford to such exotic destinations as Tierra del Fuego, the Hawaiian Islands, and the shores of Alaska, all prime whaling grounds at different seasons of the year. However, although the itinerary might seem romantic, the work and living conditions were far from desirable. Whaling was boring at best; terrifying, arduous, and gruesome at worst. Whaleships were small and typically overmanned, food consisted of a steady diet of salted meat and hardtack, and captains were all too often tyrannical and cruel. Rendering the whale was a ghastly, nauseating process and the thrill, danger, and horror of chasing and killing a sperm whale from a small wooden boat was almost unimaginable. As Herman Melville, who knew from personal experience, put it in his 1851 novel *Moby Dick*, "Not the raw recruit, marching from the bosom of his wife into the fever heat of his first battle; not the dead man's ghost encountering the first unknown phantom in the other world;—neither of these can feel stranger and stronger emotions than that man does, who, for the first time finds himself pulling into the charmed churned circle of the hunted sperm whale."

The two most frequently hunted species were the sperm whale, immortalized by Melville, and the right whale, so-called because, unlike most other species, it floated after being killed, making retrieval of the weighty corpse easier. The sperm whale is toothed, while the right whale is a baleen whale, named for the somewhat flexible, keratinous filtering strands found in the mouths of those whales through which tiny krill shrimp, their primary food, is passed. Scrimshaw was crafted from the remnants of the oil-rendering process: mottled, flecked, grayish-white whalebone, pure white ivory from the teeth of the sperm whales, and dark gray baleen, all totemic symbols of man's triumph over beast.

Although a variety of etymologies—many of them fanciful at best—have been suggested, the origin of the word *scrimshaw* may never be firmly established. Perhaps the most plausible explanation was brought forward by scrimshaw researcher Norman Fleyderman, who hypothesized a verbal fusion of

◄ PIE CRIMPERS

Artists unknown. c. 1840–1870. New England. Whale ivory with additions of rosewood, silver, ebony, tortoise shell, horn, bronze, brass, mother-of-pearl, red wax, lamp black, message on paper. Lengths: 5 3/4 to 7 7/8 in. The Shelburne Museum, Shelburne, Vermont. Gift of George Frelinghuysen.

Also called jagging wheels, these small kitchen tools were used to cut a fluted edge in pastry dough, and mark the crust. Crimpers were a favorite with scrimshanders, who produced hundreds of imaginative modifications of the tool's basic form, a fluted wheel with a handle. The crimper with the hand and fork has a small, horn-covered paper message attached to its side, poignantly reading, "Remer [sic] Me."

*Bone and
Leather*

---

*America's
Traditional
Crafts*

•

262

the quintessentially Yankee word *scrimp,* describing the humble and frugal nature of the material used, and the words *shave* and/or *saw,* referring to the act of putting the material to practical use.

Melville described the making of scrimshaw in typically evocative fashion in *Moby Dick*:

> *Throughout the Pacific and also in Nantucket and New Bedford and Sag Harbor, you will come across lively sketches of whales and whaling scenes, graven by the fishermen themselves on Sperm-Whale teeth, or ladies busks wrought out of the Right-Whale bone and other like skrimshander articles, as the whalemen call the numerous little ingenious contrivances they elaborately carve out of the rough material in their hours of ocean leisure. Some of them have little boxes of dentistical looking implements, specially intended for the skrimshandering business. But, in general, they toil with their jack-knives alone; and, with that almost omnipotent tool of the sailor, they will turn you out anything you please in the way of a mariner's fancy.*

Although by far the best-known product of the scrimshander is the engraved sperm whale tooth, elaborately decorated with whaling scenes, portraits, and the like, scrimshanders also produced many practical shipboard tools, boxes, and sewing and kitchen implements. Every sailor wanted attractive and useful gifts to bring home to his wife or sweetheart at the end of his long voyage, and the scrimshanders obliged their wishes, offering everything from pie crimpers and rolling pins to yarn-winding swifts and knitting needles.

Among the most common and popular of the scrimshanders' creations was the pie crimper or jagging wheel, a small-handled device usually attached to a single wheel of about two inches in diameter. The fluted (or "jagged") wheel of the crimper was used to cut a rilled edge in pastry dough for the top of a pie crust; the wheel could cut either strips or a full round top. Many jagging wheels also included a fork, which could be used to tamp and mark the edge of the pie. A few crimpers had two parallel wheels to save time in cutting strips. Despite its limited size, the handle of the crimper provided the scrimshander with an opportunity to express himself, which he often did by carving the handles into the shapes of eagle heads, clenched fists, intertwined snakes, open pierced hearts, unicorns, whale flukes, and hundreds of other contours. At least one carver went far beyond the kitchen and set a naked woman on top of his wheel. Most jagging wheels were made of whalebone and/or ivory; some included tiny inlays of such exotic tropical woods as ebony and mahogany, and such decorative shells as the iridescent abalone.

All functional scrimshaw copied forms that were originally made in wood, but because wood was in short supply on board ship, the scrimshander employed the more readily available whale ivory or bone in its place. In fact, whalebone was favored over wood for many hand tools because it retained its own natural lubricants for some time and thus felt better in hand and required less maintenance than dry wood. Virtually every tool used on ship was fashioned from whalebone at one time or another. Ship's carpenters, for example, made rules, bit braces, mallets, squares, and other hand tools from bone; sail-makers smoothed seams with bone rubbers and kept their needles in bone cases; sailors separated rope for splicing with whalebone fids and hoisted sail with bone double blocks; and mates marked their log-books with whale-shaped stamps to record the species that had been killed. And, more than one sailor, who had lost a leg in an encounter with a sperm whale grimly replaced his missing limb with a peg leg fashioned from the bones of a later conquest.

The whaling industry declined after the Civil War, as petroleum-based fuels were introduced into the marketplace. The war itself had a grave effect on whaling. Many of the Yankee whaleships were destroyed during the war by both sides. In an attempt to disrupt southern shipping, nearly forty whalers were purposely sunk in Charleston Harbor, and dozens more, most notably the legendary *Alabama,* were lost in attacks by southern privateers. A further blow to an already devastated industry came when a number of the remaining whalers were lost in disastrous encounters with arctic pack ice in the early 1870s. Although a few vessels continued whaling, especially in search of baleen, which, due to its combination of flexibility and strength was in great demand for everything from umbrella ribs to corset stays, the American whaling industry, as well as its allied art of scrimshaw, was a thing of the past by the turn of the century. The sole remaining American whaleship, the *Charles W. Morgan,* is preserved today at Mystic Seaport in Connecticut; scrimshaw, the practical, make-do art of the whalers, also may be seen there and in a number of other New England museums.

*Bone and
Leather*

───

*America's
Traditional
Crafts*

•

263

CANES ▸

*Artists unknown. c. 1840–1880.
New England. Whalebone, whale
ivory, wood. Average length: 33
in. Kendall Whaling Museum,
Sharon, Massachusetts.*

*Canes were carried by virtually all
gentlemen in the nineteenth century, and many scrimshanders crafted
canes for their own use on shore.
In addition to finishing off a gentleman's outfit, a whalebone or
ivory cane served as a proud
emblem of the wearer's occupation.*

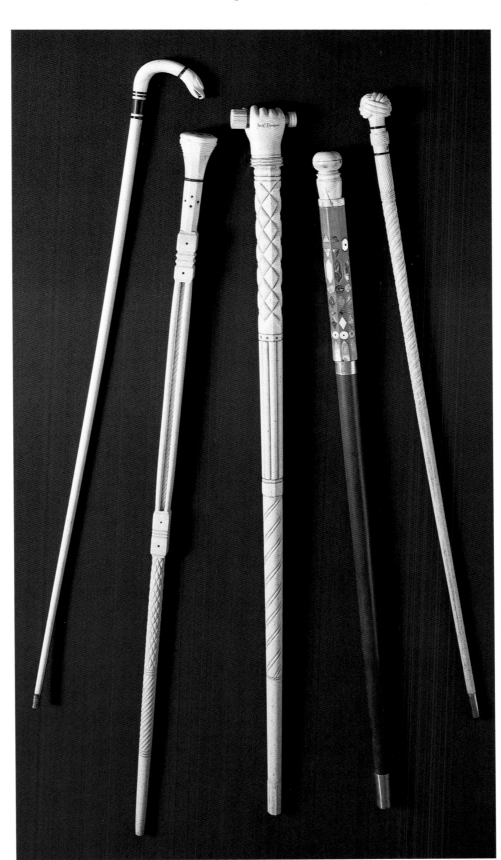

◄ CARPENTER'S TOOLS

Artists unknown. c. 1840–1870. New England. Whalebone. Kendall Whaling Museum, Sharon, Massachusetts.

This grouping of whalebone tools used by a ship's carpenter includes a try square, a T-square, a marking gauge, a chisel, dividers, a cross-cut saw, and an auger. All these tools substitute whalebone for parts normally made of wood.

SEAM RUBBERS ▶

Artists unknown. c. 1840–1870. New England. Whalebone, whale ivory, wood inlay. Average length: 5 in. Kendall Whaling Museum, Sharon, Massachusetts.

Seam rubbers were sailmakers' tools, used to smooth and crease the edge of a canvas sail before sewing the seam. The handles and shafts of seam rubbers were often carved or incised.

▼ DOUBLE BLOCKS

Artist unknown. c. 1840-1870. New England. Whalebone, rope, wrought iron. Height of blocks: 3 1/4 in. The Shelburne Museum, Shelburne, Vermont.

Whalebone was even stronger and more durable than wood and was thus often used to make such heavy-duty ship's tools as blocks, used to haul sail up and down the masts and to lower and raise anchors, chase-boats, supplies, and captured whales.

*Bone and
Leather*

———

*America's
Traditional
Crafts*

•

267

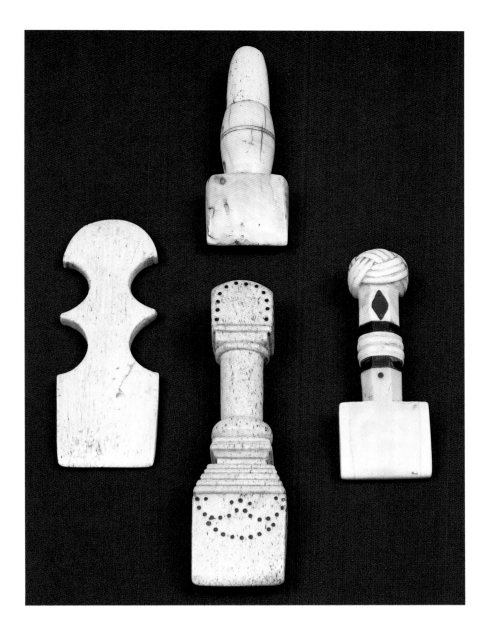

FIDS ▸

*Artists unknown. c. 1840–1870. New England.
Whalebone. Average length: 14 in. Kendall Whaling
Museum, Sharon, Massachusetts.*

*Fids were used to separate strands of thick "hawsers"
and other shipboard rope; other strands of rope could
then be spliced in.*

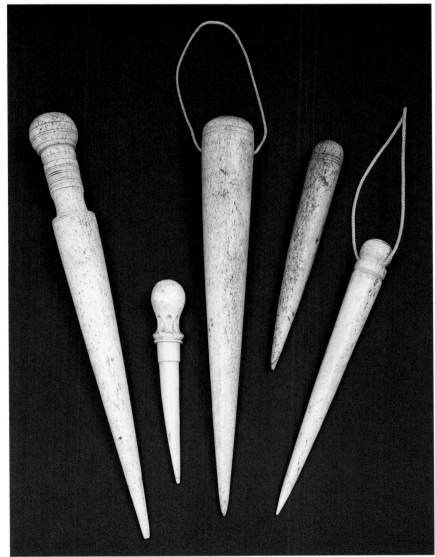

Bone and
Leather

America's
Traditional
Crafts

•

268

CANDLE LANTERN ▶

Artist unknown. c. 1840–1870. New England. Whalebone. Height: 11 in. The Whaling Museum, New Bedford, Massachusetts.

This rare whalebone lantern is footed to stand on a table. By running a rope or chain through the piece of whale vertebrae attached to the top of the lantern, it could also be hung from the ceiling.

▼ BED WRENCH

Artist unknown. c. 1840–1870. New England. Whalebone, ebony. Length: 17 in. Collection of Paul and Diane Madden.

Bed wrenches, usually made of wood, were a common tool in eighteenth- and nineteenth-century American homes, used to tighten the ropes that supported the mattresses in early beds. The powerful form of this unique wrench is suggestively human.

*Bone and
Leather*

———

*America's
Traditional
Crafts*

•

270

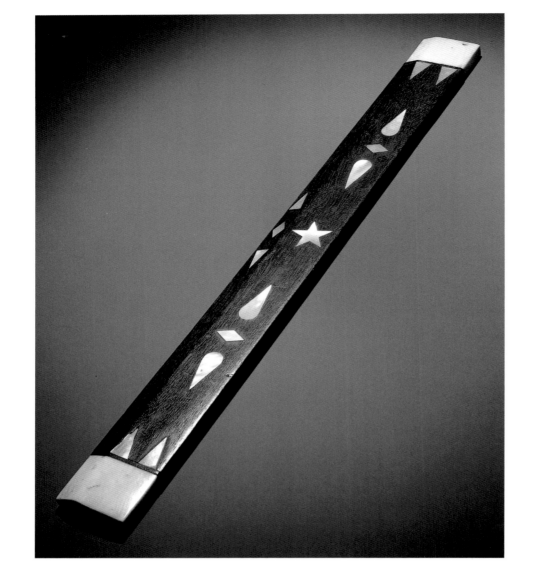

◄ LOGBOOK RULE

*Charles Henry Wilbur. c. 1865. Cranbury,
New Jersey. African ironwood with whale
ivory ends and mother-of-pearl inlay.
Length: 12 1/4 in. The Shelburne Museum,
Shelburne, Vermont.*

*Charles Henry Wilbur (1842–1877) sailed
out of New Bedford on the whaling ship*
Young Phoenix *three times between 1864
and 1869, retired from the sea for three
years, and then sailed again on three different ships in the 1870s. He was reported
drowned in 1877 after leaving the* Abraham
Barker *in Chile, apparently after a dispute
with the captain, whom he considered
incompetent. A subsequent investigation of
his death hinted strongly at the possibility of
foul play.*

*Many of Wilbur's possessions, including two
of his journals, more than one hundred
pieces of correspondence, and several pieces
of scrimshaw, were eventually returned to
the United States. This rule is one of two
such pieces extant that were made and used
by Wilbur as straightedges to mark his journal entries.*

*The ship's journal, usually kept by the first
mate, recorded navigational information,
weather conditions, and whales sighted, pur-
sued, and killed. Many journals, including
Wilbur's, recorded kills with whale-shaped
ink stamps carved from whalebone; stamped
flukes sometimes recorded whales that had
escaped after pursuit.*

▼ CORSET BUSK

*Artist unknown. c. 1840–1870. New England. Whalebone. Length: 13 3/4 in. Nantucket Historical Association, Nantucket,
Massachusetts.*

*The corset, a tight-fitting undergarment designed to restrain and shape the bust, was a common piece of feminine apparel in the nineteenth
century. A busk was inserted into an open slit at the front of the corset to "firm up" the bodice. A busk was thus an intimate gift, given by
a sailor to his wife or sweetheart as a love token and intended, literally, to be taken to heart. Most were made of solid pieces of whalebone
or baleen, engraved with hearts, flowers, birds, and other emblems of the sailor's love. This unusual example is fully pierced, with a heart
at one end and a cross at the other.*

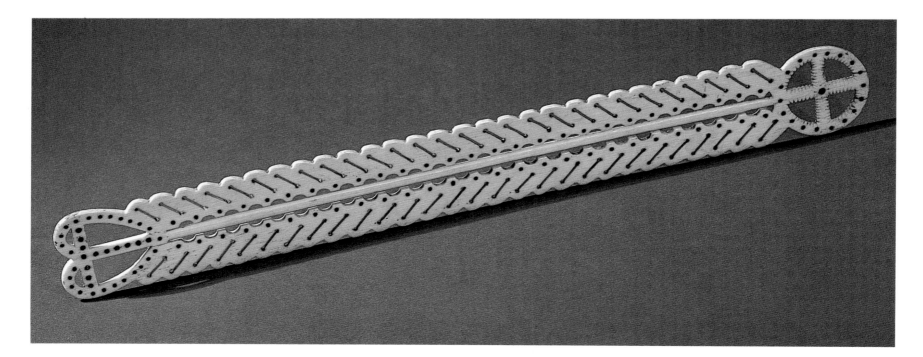

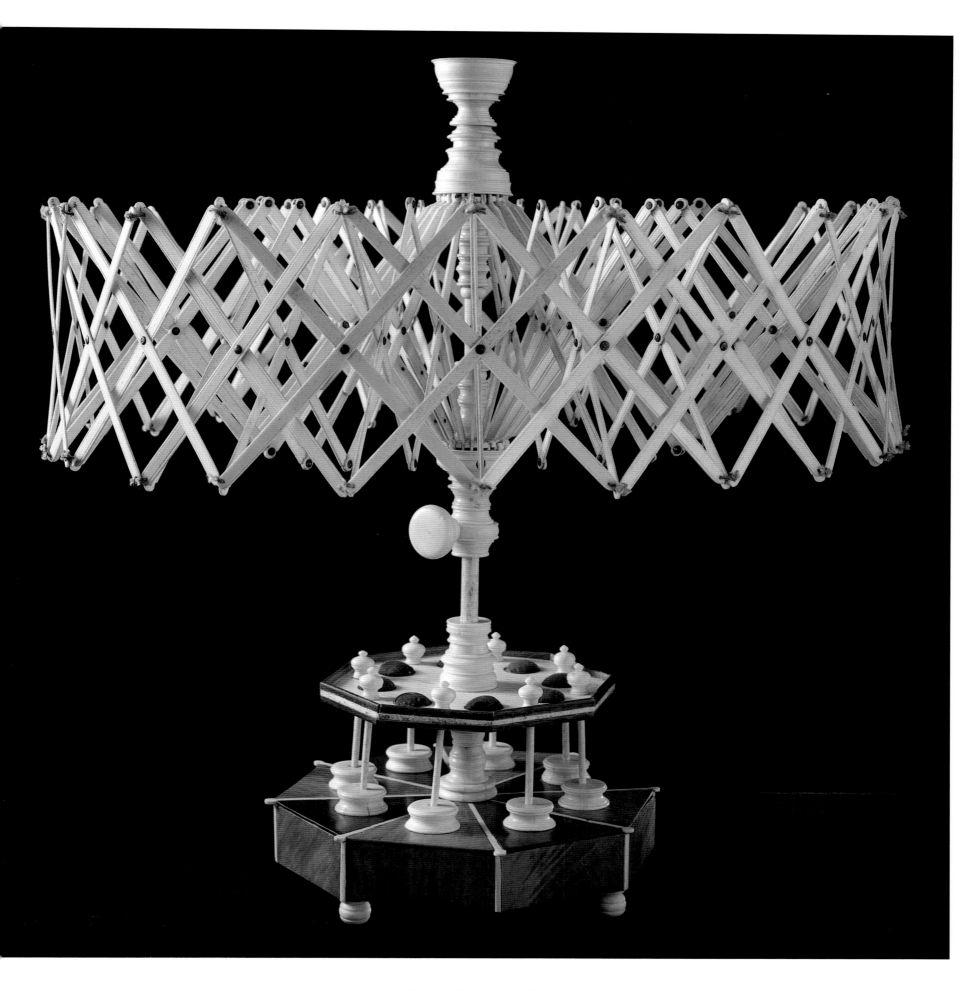

▲ YARN-WINDING SWIFT

Artist unknown. c. 1840–1870. New England. Turned and incised whale ivory and bone, wood. 19 1/2 x 8 1/16 x 8 in. The Shelburne Museum, Shelburne, Vermont. Gift of George Frelinghuysen.

Swifts were folding reels that opened and closed like umbrellas. The reel swiveled on a vertical shaft and was used to hold yarn while it was being wound into a ball. A swift's construction was complex, requiring the careful fitting of dozens of small pieces of carved whalebone, held together with tiny metal rivets. This example is mounted on a base made of exotic tropical woods.

▼ CLOTHES PINS

Artists unknown. c. 1840–1870. New England. Whalebone. Average length: 4 in. Kendall Whaling Museum, Sharon, Massachusetts.

Scrimshanders produced many imaginative variations on this simple theme, carving sets of pins to give to a sweetheart or wife.

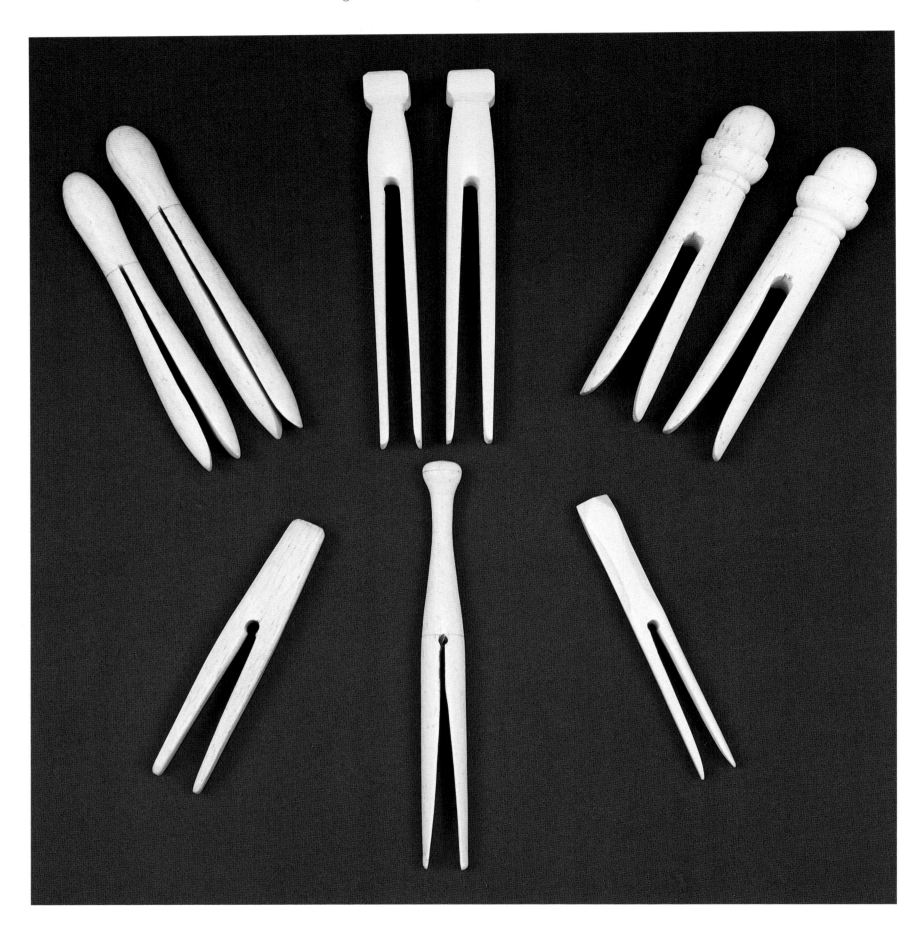

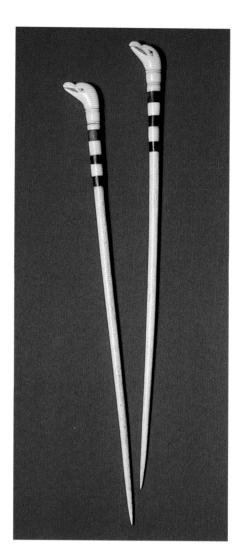

Bone and
Leather
—
America's
Traditional
Crafts
·
273

◄ KNITTING NEEDLES

Artist unknown. c. 1840–1870. New England. Walrus ivory heads and whalebone shafts, carved and incised, colored with red wax, rosewood inlays. Length: 12 3/4 in. The Shelburne Museum, Shelburne, Vermont. Gift of George Frelinghuysen.

This elegant pair of knitting needles has handles tipped with what seem to represent the heads of bottle-nosed dolphins.

▼ BODKINS AND BODKIN HOLDER

Artists unknown. c. 1840–1870. New England. Whalebone, whale ivory, wood inlay. Lengths: 3 to 6 in. Kendall Whaling Museum, Sharon, Massachusetts.

Bodkins were small, pointed, needle-like tools, two to six inches long. Sharp-tipped bodkins were used to punch holes in cloth, while those with blunt ends served as oversized needles to pull ribbon or other material through a loop or hem. Both types were used by sailmakers on board ship as well as by women waiting in port. Women's bodkins could also double as hairpins. Bodkin handles, like those of the canes that scrimshanders also made, were often cleverly decorated with hearts, clenched fists, human or animal faces, and a wide variety of other images and forms.

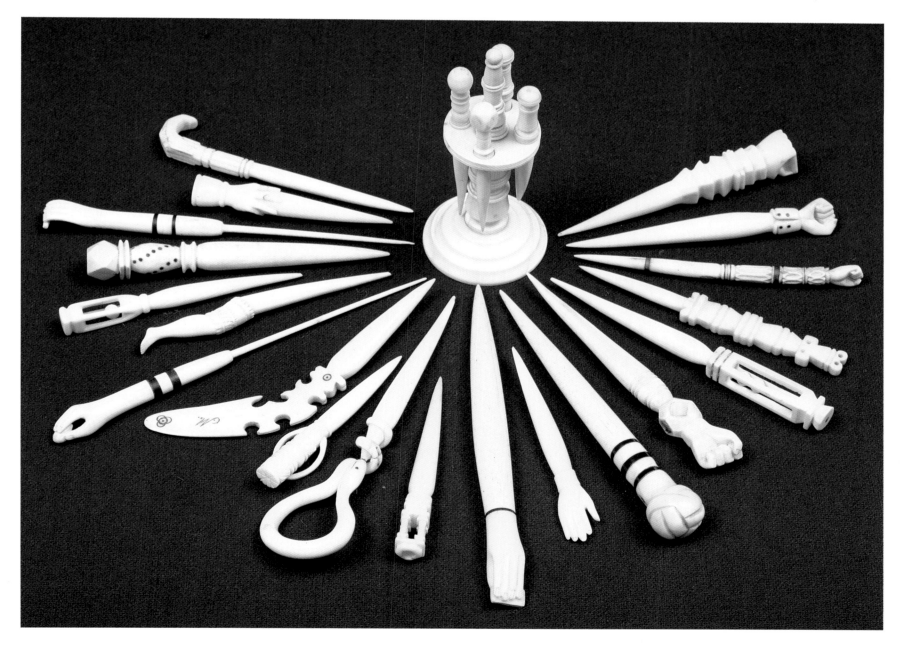

Bone and
Leather

———

America's
Traditional
Crafts

•

274

ROLLING PINS, PESTLE, TABLEWARE, AND KNIFEBOX ▶

Artists unknown. c. 1840–1870. New England. Whalebone, whale ivory, wood. Kendall Whaling Museum, Sharon, Massachusetts.

Rolling pins made a practical, if somewhat unromantic, gift. They were usually made of wood with whalebone handles or inlays; much more rarely they were carved completely of bone, as is the pestle at upper right. The knifebox shown here has a whalebone handle and holds several whalebone utensils.

▼ BUTTER PRINT

Artist unknown. c. 1840–1870. New England. Whale ivory. Height: 3 in., diameter: 2 3/8 in. The Shelburne Museum, Shelburne, Vermont.

When pressed into a tub of butter, this print would leave its incised pattern of a floral wreath surrounding an American shield in relief. The attached handle is made from lathe-turned whale ivory.

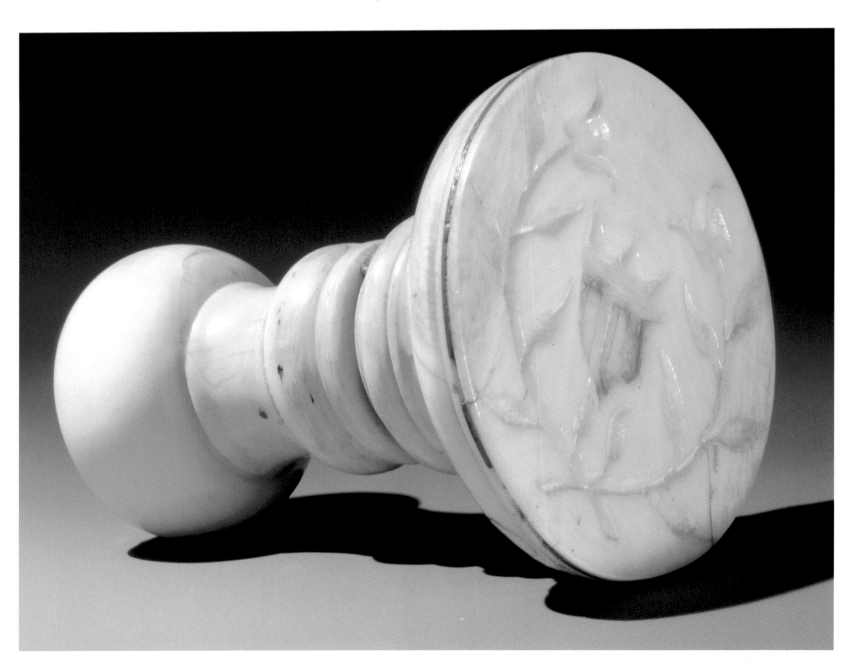

W R O U G H T I R O N

American craftsmen worked with iron from the earliest colonial days, producing a wide variety of useful and decorative objects. Working by hand at his forge, the blacksmith was a central figure in every small town since his work was depended upon by every member of the community. Although a nostalgic view of early America often sees the smith as someone who only shod horses, this was but a small part of his wide-ranging work; he made virtually every sort of metal object needed for daily life. He forged nails essential to home builders, shipbuilders, and furniture makers (manufactured cut nails were not generally available until the mid-1800s); crafted trivets, cranes, peels, pokers, shovels, toasters, and other hearth implements; wrought household utensils such as forks, candle and rush-light holders, food choppers, and flax hetchels; made hand and farm tools including rakes, hayforks and knives, hammers, plows, hoes, ax heads, and saw blades; shaped hardware such as door hinges and latches, and made his own pincers, tongs, swages, and other shop tools. The smith's work was especially critical to the horse-drawn age. He made runners for sleighs (as well as sleds and skates); crafted wheel rims, structural underpinnings, frames, and hardware for wagons and carriages; and forged connecting chains, rings, and bits for harnesses. And, because wrought iron tools and implements usually could be reforged, he could repair most of the items he made when necessary.

The first successful ironworks in America was established in Saugus, Massachusetts, in 1643. By 1750 the industry was firmly established, with ironworks operating throughout the colonies. Early ironworks centered around massive blast furnaces that provided the intense heat needed to melt iron ore. The furnaces were fired with charcoal; limestone or oyster shells provided lime "flux," which, in the heat of the furnace, combined with the nonmetallic parts of the ore to form a glassy slag residue. Two and one-half tons of ore, a ton and one-half of flux, and 180 bushels of charcoal yielded one ton of unrefined pig iron.

Fanned by a constant blast of air, ironworks' furnace fires raged day and night for thirty to forty weeks a year. Molten iron poured from the base of the furnace into trenches that had been dug in sand. When cool, the iron was broken into portable pieces and sold by weight for remelting and casting, or for refining into the wrought iron used by blacksmiths. Most early ironworks also cast simple items such as hearth firebacks, stove plates, trivets, and pots and pans by pressing wooden patterns into sand to form a mold for the object. The pig or cast iron produced by ironworks was hard and brittle because it contained carbon. Fineries purified the metal by removing much of the carbon, thereby converting the raw material into bars of malleable wrought iron for blacksmiths.

The anvil is the blacksmith's essential tool, the equivalent of the woodworker's workbench. Made of a heavy mass of forged iron, the anvil has maintained its basic form for two thousand years. It has a rec-

◂ THUMB LATCH

Artist unknown. c. 1780. Middletown, Connecticut area. Wrought iron. Height: 15 in. Private collection.

This powerfully sculptural "swordfish" latch may have been made by a member of the Warner family, who produced some of the most remarkable door hardware ever made in America. Outstanding examples of Warner family work may be seen on doors at the Congregational Church in East Haddam, Connecticut, and at the Wadsworth Atheneum in Hartford. The sharp points at either end of the latch helped anchor it to the door.

tangular "face" for flattening, set over a spreading base with a tapered beak at one end over which iron can be bent, a one-half to one-inch square "hardie hole" at the "heel," or rear, where various cutting and shaping tools can be set, and a one-half-inch diameter round "pritchel hole" near the hardie hole where a metal rod can be inserted, around which hot iron can be bent. The anvil, which typically weighed between 150 and 200 pounds, was stabilized by being placed in the butt of a log that had been set deeply into the dirt floor of the smithy's shop. A charcoal or, in later years, coal-burning brick forge provided the heat required to soften the wrought iron, and an enormous, hand-operated bellows, which employed an entire ox hide for its lung, fanned the fire. The smith cooled the hot iron by dipping it in a large tub of water that was placed near the forge. He preferred brine or oil, sometimes held in a smaller tub suspended over the large "slack" tub, for tempering edge tools because these liquids cooled the iron somewhat more slowly than fresh water, allowing the smith to achieve a finer temper.

In addition to the anvil, other tools important to the blacksmith's trade included the appropriately named "witches' hat," or mandrel, a three- or four-foot-tall, cone-shaped cast metal form over which larger rings could be formed; the swage block, a massive, square cast form with serrated sides for shaping rods; and a variety of holes of differing sizes and shapes used in making hollow or curved items. Iron was cut over hardies, which look like inverted chisels, and thinned over round-edged fullers. Small rings could be formed over small mandrels that had been made to set into the hardie hole. Items such as kitchen implements were shaped over a smaller, thinner, double-horned anvil called a bickern, which was mounted in its own log butt. The similarly shaped stake was an even smaller device that could be mounted in the main anvil's hardie hole. The smith used a diverse array of hand tools, including hammers, tongs, chisels, punches, and swages. Hammers, which generally weighed between two and five pounds, were the principal tools used to shape the hot iron. They were forged in many different sizes and shapes, each specific to the task at hand. Swages shaped the curved surfaces of bolts and other round bars.

After the pieces of wrought iron were heated to the appropriate temperature in the forge (usually judged only by the experienced eye of the smith), they were lifted from the fire with tongs and held over the anvil to be worked. The iron could be worked in a variety of ways. The most common was drawing out, or fullering, in which the hot iron was thinned and spread out by being repeatedly hammered. "Upsetting" reversed the process by bulging hot iron, usually at one end of a piece of metal, and later reshaping it. Two pieces of iron could be welded together by bringing them to a white heat and then fusing them with a few swift hammer blows on the anvil. Before welding, the smith upset both pieces, anticipating his need for a bit of extra iron to form the weld. The hot iron could also be bent into angles or curved shapes around the side or horn of either the anvil or the bickern.

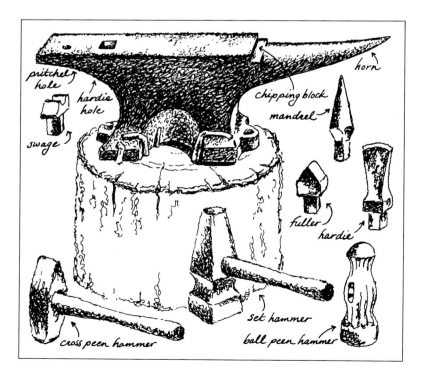

Beginning in the mid-1800s, the advent of factory-made goods, including such staples as nails, edge tools, and horseshoes, gradually changed the nature of the blacksmith's business from production to service. The dependable uniformity and low price of factory products forced the blacksmith to focus on installing and repairing the factory goods rather than forging these particular objects. Farmers brought their broken tools to be welded back together and their worn axes and plows to

be tempered and sharpened. The blacksmith's business then centered primarily on horses. He shoed horses as he had always done, sometimes using cast shoes he had purchased from a factory, but more often matching the special needs of his clients' animals with hand-forged shoes. And he continued to make and repair iron-rimmed wheels for carriages and wagons. In the early decades of the twentieth century, however, the burgeoning popularity of the internal combustion engine spelled the end of the traditional blacksmithing trade. The passing of the era of the horse and horse-drawn transportation left the smith, once the most important craftsman in the community, with almost nothing substantive to do. A few particularly skillful smiths, such as Philip Simmons of Charleston, South Carolina, were able to concentrate on the production of ornamental work such as gates, fences, railings, and hardware, but most of these craftsmen simply went out of business or continued doing repair work only on a part-time basis.

In recent decades, interest in traditional blacksmithing has been fostered by the many historic village and museum re-creations of early American life, and a number of craftsmen have taken up forge work. With the renewed interest in traditional American crafts, wrought iron implements and hardware have come back into fashion. Wrought andirons, hearth tools, and the like are considerably more expensive than cast versions, but contemporary blacksmiths often find that the public appreciates their skills and is willing to support the cost of fine handwork. Contemporary smiths such as Nol Putnam of Virginia use traditional methodology to create artistic works that combine modern design with more venerable customs. Putnam works almost entirely on commission, often working with architects to design site-specific pieces. One of his current projects is for the memorial gates of the Washington (D.C.) Cathedral. On the unique nature of his craft, Putnam says, "Hot forging increases the range of shapes available to the architect/designer. The basic form of a gate, balcony, or railing, for example, may follow a movement in the building, changes in the direction being as gradual or sudden as desired; the frame of the gate may be part of a flower or an abstract design. We think of steel as cold, hard, and unyielding—and so it is. But after being worked, there is a smoothness and often a delicacy to the work which belies the true nature of the medium." Putnam's work, like that of generations of master smiths before him, stands as a tribute to the skill and imagination needed to work this most intractable of traditional craft mediums.

Charles Wesley Allen of Berea, Kentucky, was a mountain blacksmith who specialized in ornamental work in his later years. He was photographed by Doris Ulmann c. 1930.

Photograph, Berea College, Berea, Kentucky.

▾ DOUBLE CALIPER

Artist unknown. c. 1840–1880. Region unknown. Wrought iron. Length: 17 1/4 in. Collection of Paul Kebabian.

The double caliper was used by furniture makers to gauge the diameter of lathe turnings. The two measures could be set to the diameters desired at different points on a chair leg, for example. The leg was then checked periodically until a precise match was achieved.

REVOLVING TRIVET ▸

Artist unknown. Late eighteenth century. Kentucky. Wrought iron. 4 1/2 x 11 3/8 x 24 3/4 in. Collection of the Museum of Early Southern Decorative Arts, Winston-Salem, North Carolina. Gift of Robert B. Hicks III.

A revolving trivet could be placed over hot coals and was easily turned to assure that the pot it held was heated evenly.

SHEARS ▶

*Artists unknown. Late eighteenth century. Eastern United States.
Wrought iron. Private collection.*

*Many different types of shears were developed for specialized tasks.
These are all made by blacksmiths.*

▼ FOOD CHOPPERS

*Artists unknown. Nineteenth century. Region unknown. Wrought
iron and wood. Private collection.*

*Here are six variations on a simple theme, used to chop meat or root
vegetables such as cabbage, carrots, potatoes, beets, and turnips.
The curved bottoms of several of the blades facilitated their use in a
wooden bowl.*

SPATULA ▸

A member of the Long family. c. 1850. Rockingham County, Virginia. Wrought iron. Length: 18 1/2 in. Collection of Roddy and Sally Moore.

Hearts, symbols of love and affection as well as simple and attractive designs, were a favorite decorative motif of many traditional craftspeople.

▴ TRIVET

Attributed to James Sellers. 1837. Philadelphia. Wrought iron. Length: 24 in., diameter: 12 in. The Henry Francis du Pont Winterthur Museum, Winterthur, Delaware.

Trivets, which held hot pots in and out of the fireplace, were an essential tool in early America, and blacksmiths crafted many decorative variations; hearts and floral shapes were especially popular.

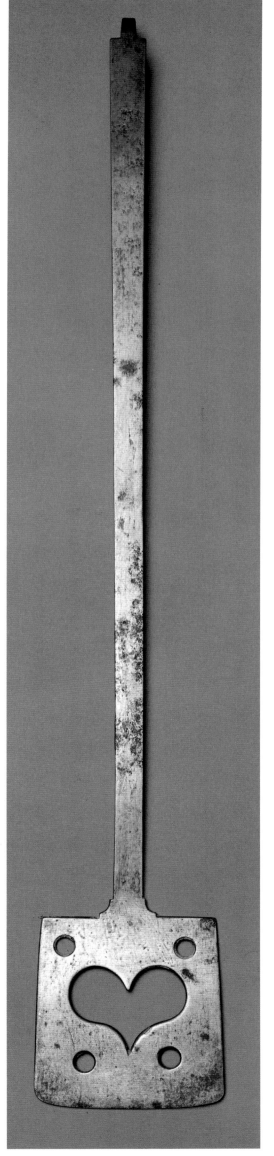

◄ THE PHILIP SIMMONS GATE

*Philip Simmons. 1987. Charleston, South Carolina. Wrought iron. 9 x 9 ft.
South Carolina State Museum, Columbia, South Carolina.*

*This masterful, fancy, driveway gate was commissioned by the South Carolina
State Museum and is exhibited in a specially constructed area in the museum.
The triangle formed by the pair of egrets and the palmetto tree, both state symbols, is perfectly balanced with the intricate symmetrical rhythms built from the
two basic motifs of the diamond and the spiral, while the large pieces of iron
used in the gate's construction give it a sense of depth rare in decorative wrought
iron work.*

◄ WINDOW GRILLE

Philip Simmons. 1988. Charleston, South Carolina. Painted wrought iron. Height: 29 in. International Folk Art Foundation Collection, Museum of International Folk Art, unit of the Museum of New Mexico, Santa Fe.

In addition to more than two hundred gates, Philip Simmons has also made many decorative fences, stair and balcony railings, and window grilles for buildings in Charleston. The central design of this window grille is shaped like a star.

PHILIP SIMMONS, DECORATIVE IRONWORKER

Many of Charleston, South Carolina's buildings are graced with ornamental iron gates, fences, and window grilles wrought by the city's blacksmiths in a tradition that dates back to the 1700s. Charleston's early ornamental iron, like the decorative ironwork found in New Orleans and other southern cities, was designed by architects and follows high-style European models. Many of the smiths who executed the work, however, were African-Americans, who inevitably added creative elements of their own and unwittingly effected a change in the tradition away from its adherence to European fine art design.

One of the city's African-American smiths, a former slave named Peter Simmons, built a business in the 1890s repairing wrought ironwork for people who preferred the look of wrought work to the readily available, foundry-made cast iron that was dominant in the last decades of the nineteenth century. One of Peter Simmons's apprentices, the unrelated Philip Simmons, has continued and expanded the local African-American smithing tradition. Philip Simmons's work can be seen all over Charleston as well as in a number of museums around the country. He is best known for his introduction of animal forms, such as fish, snakes, and birds, into his innovative designs. Philip Simmons was honored by the National Endowment for the Arts as a National Heritage Fellow in 1982, the year the program was started.

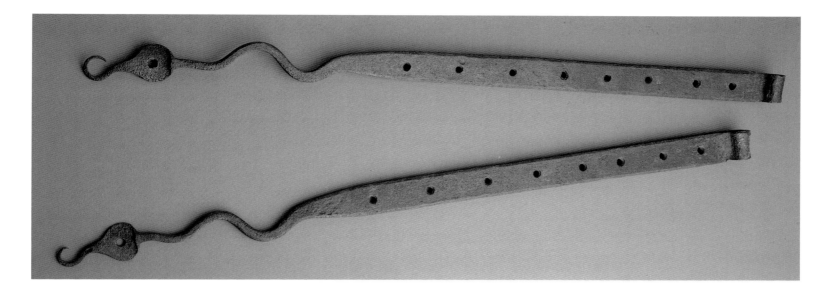

▲ PAIR OF RAT-TAIL HINGES

Artist unknown. c. 1800. New England. Wrought iron. Length: 29 1/2 in. The Shelburne Museum, Shelburne, Vermont.

The snaking ends of these barn-door hinges add a decorative element to an otherwise simple, straightforward form.

TRAVELER ▶

Artist unknown. c. 1870. Northern Vermont. Wrought iron. Length: 7 1/2 in. Collection of Paul Kebabian.

Travelers were used by blacksmiths and wheelwrights to measure the circumference of a horse-drawn vehicle's wheel. The measurement, taken in rotations of the traveler's wheel, could be transferred to iron stock used to make a tire for a wooden wheel.

EEL SPEAR ▸

Artist unknown. c. 1830–1850. New England or New York. Wrought iron. Length: 16 1/2 in. The Shelburne Museum, Shelburne, Vermont.

Eels were considered a delicacy in early America and were avidly sought in the ponds and streams of New England and New York where they spent their adult lives. Eels sometimes fathered in clusters or "balls"; spearing was the most effective method of hunting them.

▾ CRADLE

A member of the Richardson family. c. 1800. Brandon, Vermont. Wrought iron. 29 x 35 x 16 3/4 in. The Shelburne Museum, Shelburne, Vermont.

This unique, Windsor-style cradle, complete with mortise-and-tenon joinery, was made of wrought iron rather than wood. Several members of the Richardson family were blacksmiths in Brandon, Vermont, in the eighteenth and early nineteenth centuries.

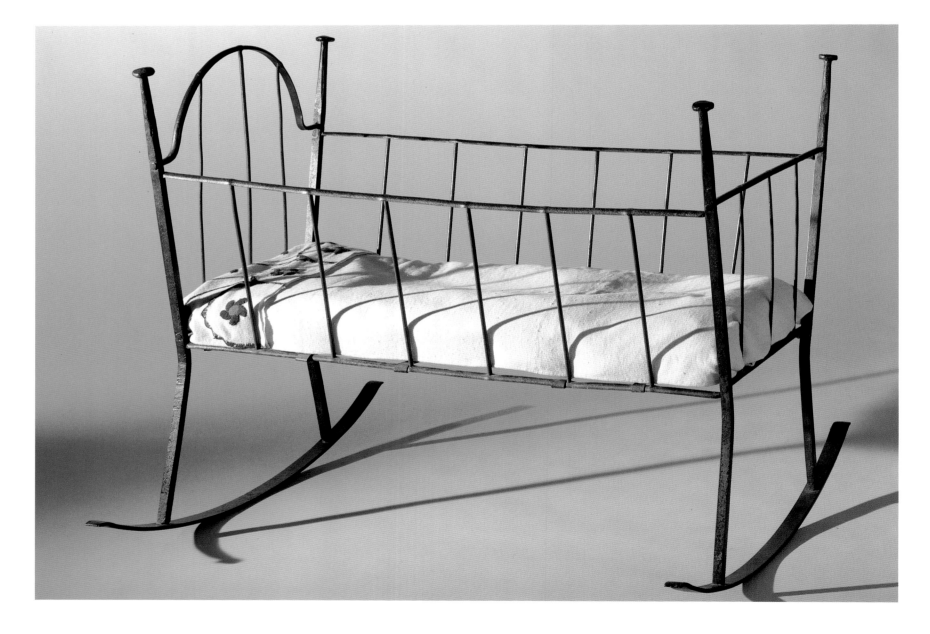

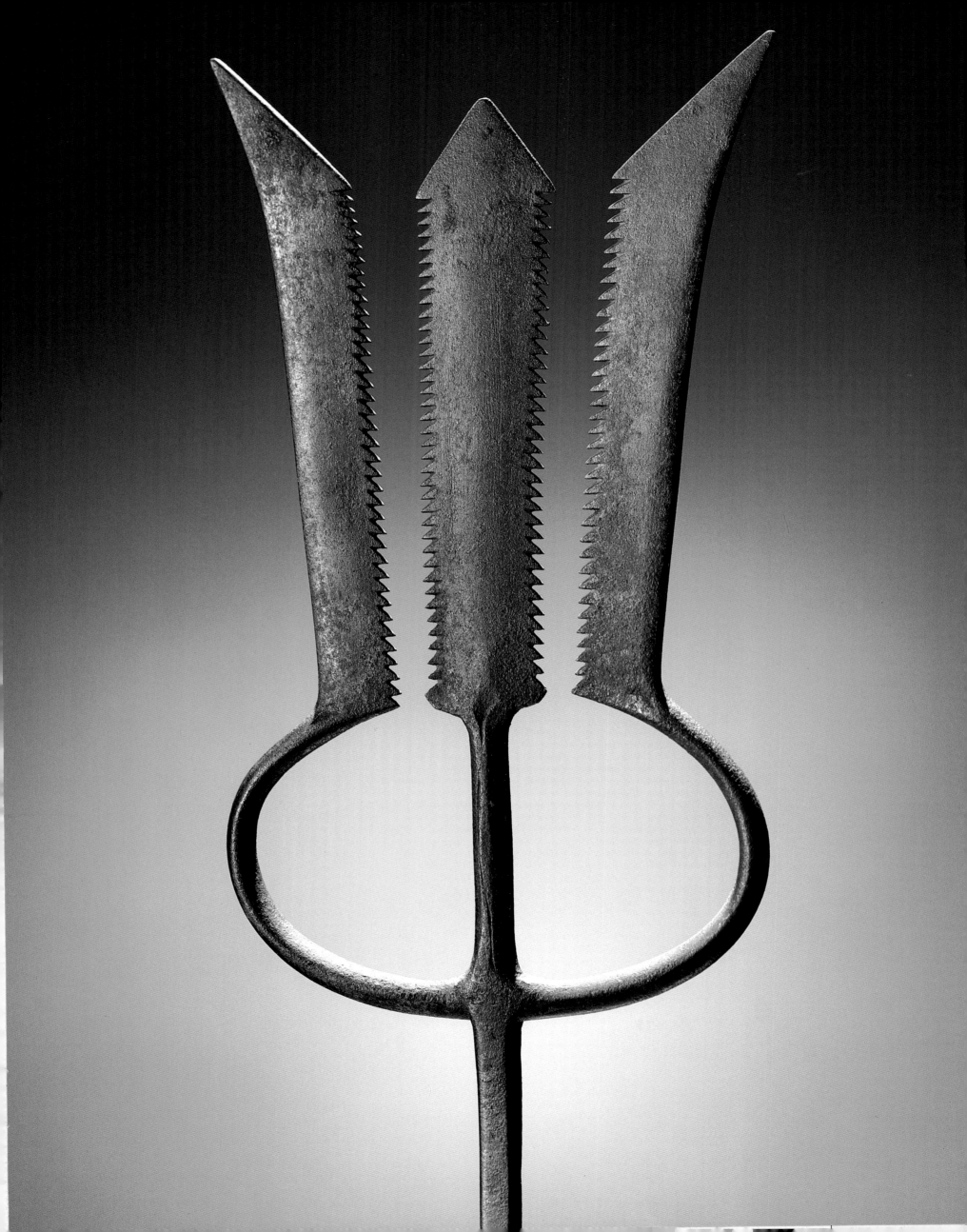

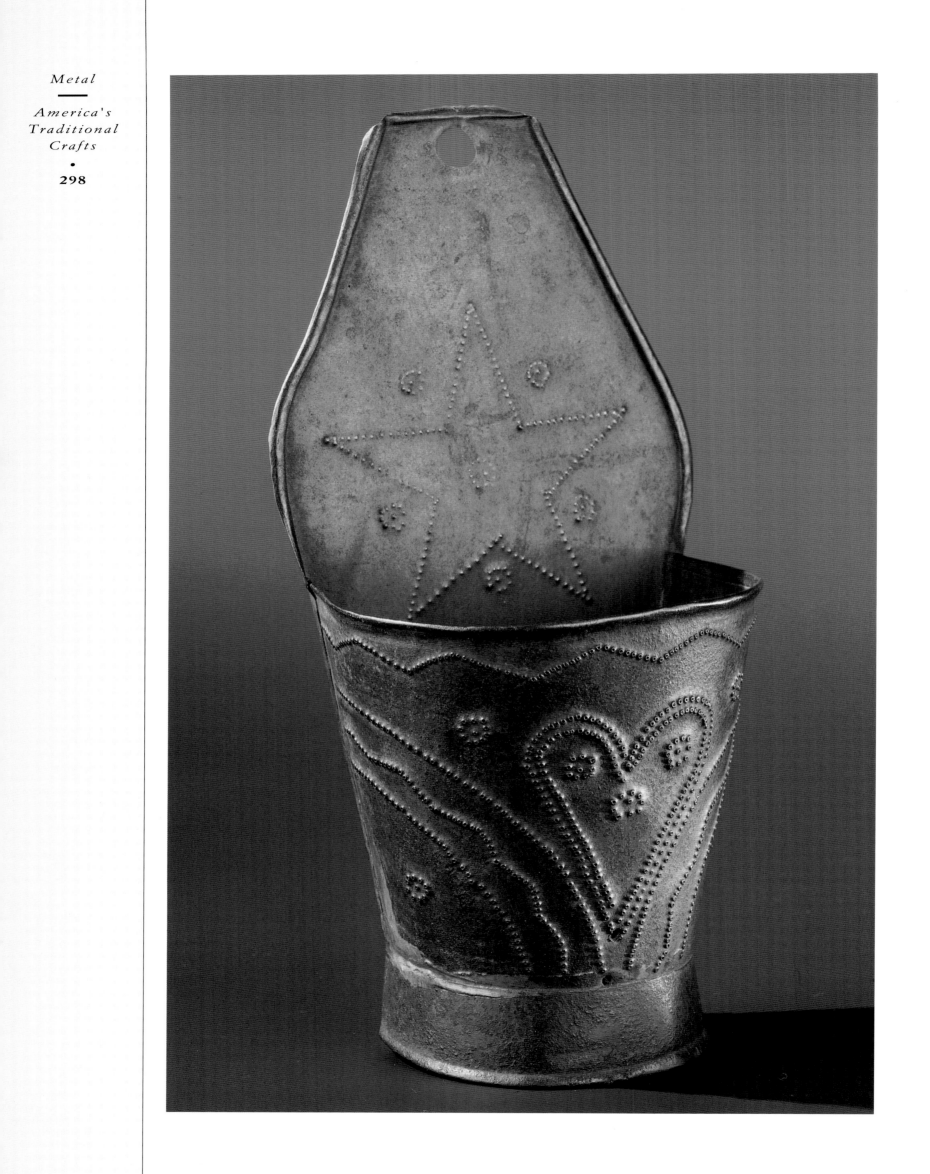

This gigantic coffeepot was made in 1858 as an advertising sign by tin-smiths Samuel and Julius Mickey of Old Salem, North Carolina. The pot, which still hangs in Old Salem, is seven feet, three inches tall; it has been estimated that it would hold 740 1/2 gallons of liquid.

Old Salem, Inc., Winston-Salem, North Carolina.

The tinsmith's principal tools, like the blacksmith's, were an anvil and a hammer. The tinsmith's anvils, called bickhorns, blowhorns, and stakes, were much smaller and thinner than the blacksmith's. To achieve curved shapes, the malleable sheets of thin, unheated tin plate were bent around these anvils, rather than being heated and beaten into their final form. The smith cut the sheets of tin plate, which were generally eleven by fifteen inches or less, with a large pair of shears, often marking the sheets by scratching around tin templates before cutting. Pieces were joined together with solder, which was smoothed by soldering irons heated in a small charcoal stove or brazier which sat on the smith's workbench. Other tools were used to crease, roll, or crimp edges, to punch holes in such products as lanterns, graters, and colanders, or to create raised designs on teapots and other hollowware.

In the first two decades of the nineteenth century, American inventors revolutionized the tinsmithing trade by introducing several specialized, geared machines, which eliminated much of the skilled and time-consuming handwork. Tinware became more uniformly shaped, and many new practitioners entered the trade. Although many older craftsmen objected to the new devices, the new technology caught on rapidly. By the 1850s, some tin shops, particularly in Connecticut, had expanded into small factories, using the machinery to mass produce lines of virtually identical items. Connecticut wares were marketed far and wide by itinerant tin peddlers. These now legendary entrepreneurs traveled by wagon and bartered tinware for such things as rags, old pewter, feathers, wood ashes, tallow, furs, and animal skins, all of which could be recycled for profit. Some of this material, in turn, could be traded to the tin merchant in exchange for more inventory to take out on the road.

While factory products reached an increasingly wider market and inevitably competed with many types of handwork, handmade tin remained important in some rural communities throughout the nineteenth century. However, by the early years of the twentieth century, virtually all tinware was factory made and the tinsmith, like many other handcraftsmen, had become an anachronism.

◄ SPILL HOLDER

Artist unknown. Possibly 1840–1860. Probably Pennsylvania. Tinplate. Abby Aldrich Rockefeller Folk Art Center, Williamsburg, Virginia. Gift of Mr. and Mrs. William P. Earls, Sr.

Spills were slender strips of wood or twisted paper used to light candles, lamps, or pipes. This tin holder, decorated with a punched heart and star, would have been hung near a hearth, where the spills could be lit from coals in the fire.

▲ STRAINER

*Unknown Shaker artist. c. 1850.
Probably Sabbathday Lake or Alfred,
Maine. Tin plate. 2 3/4 x 8 1/4 x
4 1/2 in. The United Society of
Shakers, Sabbathday Lake, Maine.*

The two large handles on this Shaker
strainer allowed it to be rested over the
top of a stoneware jug while pouring liquid. The bottom is slightly convex for
improved drainage.

◄ TENTH ANNIVERSARY
TEAPOT

*Artist unknown. 1866. Region
unknown. Tin. Height: 9 1/2 in.,
width: 10 in. Abby Aldrich Rockefeller
Folk Art Center, Williamsburg,
Virginia.*

This teapot was made as a gift to cele-
brate a tenth, or tin, wedding anniversary. Most tenth anniversary tinware
was intended to be humorous; gag gifts
such as tin hats, combs, canes, fans, and
slippers were common. This teapot,
however, offers a touching and utterly
serious scene of devotion, and probably
represents a gesture of continuity and
renewal from husband to wife. The pot
also differs from most tenth anniversary
tinware because it is functional.

The couple standing under the canopy
on the lid were cut from sheet tin. The
eared and spurred tin handle is painted
black, and the lid is hinged. The date
1856 is impressed on one side of the
concave shoulder; 1866 is on the other.

▼ FANCY BASKET

Artist unknown. c. 1860–1880. Northeastern United States. Tin-plated iron. 8 x 6 x 9 1/2 in.
The Shelburne Museum, Shelburne, Vermont.

This small and decorative open work basket may have been used to hold sewing accessories.
The tiny tin bow at the base of the handle reflects the special care that went into its creation.

G L O S S A R Y

Albany slip: A dark brown slip formed by mixing water with a fine-grained brown clay first found near Albany, New York. Often used to glaze stoneware pottery.

Alkaline glaze: A glaze popular among southern stoneware potters made by mixing lime, wood ash, and clay.

Amish: Of or pertaining to strict Mennonite religious sects founded by the seventeenth-century Swiss bishop Jacob Ammann.

Anvil: A heavy iron block on which metals are hammered and bent into shapes.

Appliqué quilt: A quilt decorated with pieces of fabric sewn directly to a ground.

Bandbox: A wooden or pasteboard box covered with wallpaper and used to hold hats, apparel, or personal accessories.

Barn-frame loom: A large homemade loom made from hand-hewn framing timbers.

Bayeta: A machine-woven red wool flannel prized by early Navajo weavers. The cloth was woven in England and Spain and imported to the United States; Navajo weavers unraveled it to reuse the richly colored bayeta yarns.

Bed rug: A heavy needlework rug used as a bedcovering in early America.

Bickern or **Bickhorn:** A small, thin, pointed anvil used by metal smiths, especially tinsmiths.

Black pottery: Pueblo Indian vessels colored black by smothering the kiln during firing, thus driving sooty smoke into the walls of the pottery.

Blowhorn: A small anvil with a curved cowl at one end, primarily used by tinsmiths for bending tin plate.

Braided: The weaving together of strips or strands of fabric, rawhide, or horsehair.

Brazier: A small, portable container for live coals used as a forge by a tinsmith.

Burl: Scablike tree growths often used to fashion bowls and other woodenware.

Caliper: An instrument used to measure diameters, usually consisting of adjustable paired legs.

Cantled: A term describing the upward curve of the rear portion of a saddle.

Charger: A large plate; a platter.

Chief's blanket: A heavy and densely woven striped textile made by Navajo weavers between 1800 and 1885.

Chisel: A wedgelike tool with a cutting edge at the end of its blade; used to shape wood.

Coiling: Layering strips of clay or fiber to form a vessel or basket.

Crazy quilt: A quilt made of many different sized pieces and types of fabric, often arranged in random patterns and embellished with embroidery.

Crochet: Needlework made by using a hooked needle to draw thread or yarn into intertwined loops.

Dado plane: A woodworker's plane used to cut a groove across the grain.

Degikup: A small-mouthed circular ceremonial bowl or basket.

Double blocks: Enclosed rotating grooved pulleys around which rope can be passed for hauling or hoisting.

Double cloth: A coverlet made of two layers of cloth woven simultaneously, one above the other, with their colors reversed.

Drafts: Pencil drawings of weaving patterns.

Fid: A large, pointed pick, made of whalebone or hardwood and used to separate strands of rope for splicing.

Finery: A refinery where cast pig iron is refined into malleable wrought iron for use by blacksmiths.

Finial: A small ornamental knob or protrusion at the top of an object.

Flax hetchel: A tool consisting of wrought iron spikes set at right angles to a wooden base and used to separate the long and short fibers of flax.

Flux: Material such as lime or charcoal which combines with impurities in ore during the smelting process to produce disposable waste slag.

Folk art: Paintings, sculpture, and other works made by nonacademically trained artists.

Forge: A fireplace or furnace in which metal is heated before being shaped by a smith.

Fraktur: Decorative calligraphic drawings and paintings made by Pennsylvania German scribes, generally recording births, weddings, and other rites of passage.

Fret: A ridge of metal or other material set across a stringed instrument's fingerboard to guide placement of fingers in stopping strings.

Fuller: A half-round hammer used by a blacksmith to groove and spread iron.

Glaze: A hard, glasslike coating covering a piece of pottery.

Greenware: Unfired pottery.

Hardie hole: A hole in the rear of an anvil where a hardie, an inverted chisel used to cut bars of iron, can be inserted.

Harness: In weaving, a frame on a loom through which warp threads are drawn.

Hooked: A type of rug made by pulling strips of fabric up through a woven foundation.

Jacquard loom: A complex loom named after French inventor J.M. Jacquard (1757–1834) which made possible the weaving of intricate geometric and figural patterns.

Jagging wheel: Pie crimper consisting of a fluted wheel for cutting pastry and a handle.

Kiln: A furnace in which pottery is fired to dry and harden wet clay and to melt glazes.

Knitted: A type of textile made by joining loops of yarn.

Lariat: A long, noosed rope used to catch cattle or horses.

Lathe: A foot-, water-, or electric-powered machine that shapes pieces of wood by rotating them against a cutting blade.

Lightship baskets: Tightly woven rattan baskets made aboard the Nantucket, Massachusetts, lightship *New South Shoal* between 1856 and 1892.

Mandrel: Cone-shaped iron form around which heated metal can be shaped into rings.

Milk paint: Paint made by mixing linseed oil and pigment with cow's milk.

Mortise: A hole or slot made to receive a tenon.

Olla: Pueblo Indian basket or ceramic food storage container.

Overshot: The most common coverlet weave, made with long passes of supplementary weft over the foundation.

Pieced quilt: A quilt made by sewing many small pieces of fabric together to form a top. The pieces are usually arranged in repeating blocks of geometric patterns.

Plain quilt: A quilt with a top made of a single piece of fabric.

Plow plane: A sophisticated tool made to cut panel grooves in drawer sides, door frames, and chest frames.

Pommel: The forward horn of a saddle.

Pony beads: Large glass beads popular among early nineteenth-century Native Americans for decorative weavings.

Pritchel hole: A hole in an anvil measuring one-half inch in diameter into which a metal rod can be inserted, and around which hot iron can be bent.

Quirt: Mexican term for a whip, often made of braided rawhide and used by cattle herders or horse herders.

Redware: Popular name for somewhat porous earthenware pottery fired between 1650 and 1940 degrees Fahrenheit.

Riata or **reata:** Mexican term for a braided rope, usually used by herders for roping calves.

Ribbed: In basketry, a term describing a basket that is formed by weaving around vertical framing elements.

Rig: A group of decoys used in the field by a hunter.

Rush light: A candlelike device made from the porous pith of a meadow rush and soaked in lard or tallow before burning.

Schrank: A large, standing wardrobe or closet made by early Pennsylvania German cabinetmakers.

Scorp: A handled metal scoop used to hollow out a bowl.

Seed beads: Tiny glass beads popular among Native Americans for decorative weavings.

Serape: Spanish/Mexican term for a longer-than-wide woven cloak adapted by Navajo weavers.

Sgraffito: Pottery decoration created by scratching through a slip layer to reveal a contrasting clay surface; most common on Pennsylvania German redware.

Shaker: Of or pertaining to a strict Millennial religious sect that espouses celibacy, communal ownership of proper-

Glossary/
Index

•

America's
Traditional
Crafts

•

307

ty, and a simple way of life.

Shirred: A type of rug made by sewing strips of cloth or yarn to a foundation.

Silica: Silicon dioxide, the glass-forming element in glazes that, when fired, fuses; silica occurs naturally as quartz, sand, and flint.

Slag: Waste material formed during the process of smelting iron ore; slag is made of flux and impurities in the ore.

Slip: A liquid mixture of clay and water used to bind or decorate clay surfaces.

Solder: To fuse or join metal parts by applying a melted alloy.

Spindle: A carved or turned vertical rod rising from the seat of a Windsor chair and forming an element of its back.

Spline: To force a thin strip of wood into a precut groove.

Splint: A strip of plant fiber, most commonly ash or oak, used in basketry.

Spokeshave: A cutting tool with a blade set between two handles and used to cut and shape rounded edges.

Stake: A small, metal smith's anvil with a wedge-shaped bottom that often was driven into the butt of a log and placed on the floor of the shop.

Stile: A vertical framing member in a piece of paneled furniture, into which the panel is inserted.

Stoneware: Dense, nonporous pottery

fired between 2200 and 2370 degrees Fahrenheit.

Stretcher: A horizontal member in a chair or table that braces the legs.

Summer and winter weave: An overshot coverlet weave that produces a densely woven reversible textile with a light side and a dark side.

Sun plane: A curved plane used by coopers to shape the top of a barrel.

Swage: A grooved tool used by a blacksmith to form metal into rods and other shapes.

Swallowtail: The distinctively-shaped pointed joint on a Shaker box, named for its resemblance to the forked wingtips of a swallow or swallowtailed butterfly.

Tap: A blacksmith's tool used to cut threads to receive a screw on the inside of a hole.

Template: A paper, metal, or wooden pattern.

Tenon: A projection formed at the end of a piece of wood to fit into an equal-sized mortise.

Tied: In quilting, a method of securing layers of the quilt together with yarn or floss.

Till: A small, lidded box built into the interior of a lift-top chest.

Tilts: Moveable wooden or metal feet

placed into the bottoms of chair legs, allowing the chair to be balanced at different angles.

Tobacco spit: Popular name for running drips of dark alkaline glaze on southern stoneware pottery.

Traveler: A tool used to measure the circumference of a wheel.

Treen ware: Bowls and other tablewares made from wood.

Turned: Wood worked on a lathe.

Upset: To thicken a piece of white-hot iron with carefully placed hammer blows.

Vaquero: Mexican term for cattle herder.

Vitrification: The process by which soft clay fuses into hard, nonporous, glasslike pottery.

Warp: Threads placed vertically in a loom that form the lengthwise threads in a woven textile.

Weft: Threads woven horizontally across the warp to form a woven textile.

Weld: To join two pieces of metal into one by heating and hammering them together on the anvil.

Witches' hat: Popular name for mandrel. *See* mandrel.

I N D E X

Page numbers in italic denote illustrations.